CURTAIN OF LIES

CURTAIN OF LIES

The Battle over Truth in Stalinist Eastern Europe

Melissa Feinberg

Oxford University Press is a department of the University of Oxford. It furthers
the University's objective of excellence in research, scholarship, and education
by publishing worldwide. Oxford is a registered trade mark of Oxford University
Press in the UK and certain other countries.

Published in the United States of America by Oxford University Press
198 Madison Avenue, New York, NY 10016, United States of America.

© Oxford University Press 2017

All rights reserved. No part of this publication may be reproduced, stored in
a retrieval system, or transmitted, in any form or by any means, without the
prior permission in writing of Oxford University Press, or as expressly permitted
by law, by license, or under terms agreed with the appropriate reproduction
rights organization. Inquiries concerning reproduction outside the scope of the
above should be sent to the Rights Department, Oxford University Press, at the
address above.

You must not circulate this work in any other form
and you must impose this same condition on any acquirer.

CIP data is on file at the Library of Congress
ISBN 978-0-19-064461-1

9 8 7 6 5 4 3 2 1

Printed by Sheridan Books, Inc., United States of America

CONTENTS

Acknowledgments	vii
Introduction: Two Camps, Two Truths	ix
1. Telling Lies, Making Truth	1
2. The Fight for Peace	31
3. Battling the Big Lie	60
4. That Funny Feeling Creeping Up Your Back	88
5. Soporific Bombs and American Flying Discs	117
6. The Power of the Powerless	143
Conclusion	175
Notes	179
Selected Bibliography	217
Index	227

ACKNOWLEDGMENTS

This book began in the aftermath of 9/11, when I found myself in an archive in Prague reading about a show trial. I knew about show trials as perversions of justice based on false charges and false confessions, but it was only when I started reading more about them that I realized they were also part of a larger attempt to mobilize a population through fear, a topic that had a new resonance for me at that moment. It was a long time before I realized exactly where the inspiration I had then would take me. It is a pleasure to finally be able to thank the many people who helped me along the way. I started thinking about this project when I was at the University of North Carolina at Charlotte, but most of it was completed at Rutgers University, New Brunswick. In both places, I have been fortunate to work among colleagues who constantly inspire me to be a better historian. This book is much better because of your influence. I am also grateful to UNCC and the School of Arts and Sciences at Rutgers University for the financial support that made the research for this book possible.

It was only when I realized that what began as a book about fear was really a book about the political uses of truth that this volume finally started to take shape. For that, I owe a great debt to the members of the Kennebunkport Circle—David Frey, Eagle Glassheim, Paul Hanebrink, and Cynthia Paces—who read a very early draft and helped me see how much work I had to do. A fellowship at the Imre Kertész Kolleg in Jena gave me the time to do much of that work. I am grateful to the Kolleg staff and to all the other fellows for providing me with such a stimulating working environment. A number of people graciously made very useful comments on one or more chapters of the manuscript, including Barbara Cooper, Melanie Feinberg, David Foglesong, Jochen Hellbeck, Lutz Niethammer, Joachim von Puttkamer, Mate Tokić, the participants in the Philadelphia Area Modern Germany Workshop, organized by Paul Steege (who read several chapters despite the fact they had no Germans in them), the participants in the Iron Curtain Crossings Workshop at Ohio State University, organized by Malgorzata Fidelis and Theodora Dragostinova, the participants in the

Ethical Subjects Seminar at the Rutgers Center for Historical Analysis, organized by Seth Koven and Judith Surkis, and the two anonymous readers for Oxford University Press. I owe a tremendous thanks to Bonnie Smith, who heroically read the entire manuscript at a very late stage and provided me with invaluable feedback and even more invaluable encouragement. At Oxford University Press, Nancy Toff and Elda Granata were wonderful to work with. I am also grateful to Dáša Frančíková for her help in obtaining several of the images used in this book. Thanks also to Courtney Doucette for her excellent work on the index.

A very preliminary sketch of chapter 1 was previously published as "Die Durchsetzung einer neuen Welt. Politische Prozesse in Osteuropa, 1948–1954," in *Angst im Kalten Krieg*, ed. Bernd Greiner, Christian Th. Müller, and Dierk Walter (Hamburg: Hamburger Edition, 2009), 190–219. The last section of that chapter was published in "Fantastic Truths, Compelling Lies: Radio Free Europe and the Response to the Slánský Trial in Czechoslovakia," *Contemporary European History* 22, no. 1 (2013): 107–125. An early version of chapter 5 was published as "Soporific Bombs and American Flying Discs: War Fantasies in East-Central Europe, 1948–1956," *Zeitschrift für Ostmitteleuropa-Forschung* 62, no. 3 (2013): 450–471. I thank the publishers for permission to use that material again here. Thanks also to John Connelly for organizing the publication of the article in *ZfO*.

This book would likely never have existed without Paul Hanebrink. He commented on every chapter many times, tirelessly listened to me try to puzzle out its themes, comforted me when I despaired, gave me insight, and even allowed me to raise the temperature in our shared office in Jena above what he would have ideally preferred. I have been lucky in many things, but I am luckiest of all to have him in my life.

INTRODUCTION: TWO CAMPS, TWO TRUTHS

On March 12, 1947, President Harry S. Truman stood before a joint session of the US Congress to announce a fundamental change in American foreign policy. The forces of Communism, Truman declared, were threatening the very existence of the United States. The world had become irrevocably divided into two opposing camps, each representing a distinctive way of life. One way—the American way—was characterized by freedom and individual liberty. It emphasized free thought, free speech, and democratically elected governments. The other way of life—the Communist way—was its direct opposite. Truman equated Communism with totalitarianism, a word used to describe both Nazi Germany and the Soviet Union under the rule of Joseph Stalin.[1] Totalitarian regimes were dictatorships ruled by fear and terror. There was no freedom under such regimes. Government-controlled media restricted the open flow of knowledge and spewed false propaganda. In Truman's view, no nation, if given a free choice via free elections, would willingly accept Communism. The Soviets, he warned, were denying many nations the opportunity to choose freedom. They had already forced the Poles, Bulgarians, and Romanians to accept Communist governments, and they threatened to do the same in Greece and Turkey. If they succeeded in those countries, they would set their sights farther afield, gathering more and more of the world into their sphere of influence. To save its own way of life, the United States must halt this relentless spread of totalitarianism, using its economic and military might to assist other nations in keeping their freedom.[2]

Communists saw the world quite differently. Six months after the proclamation of the Truman Doctrine, in September 1947, representatives of nine European Communist parties met in the Polish mountain town of Szklarska Poręba, where they would agree to create the Communist Information Agency, or Cominform. At the meeting, a leading Soviet Communist, Andrei Zhdanov, issued a stern rejoinder to Truman. Zhdanov agreed that the world was rapidly being divided into two competing ideological camps, each with its own distinct way of life. For Zhdanov, however, it was the Americans who were the aggressors, coercing other nations into declaring their allegiance to the United States. Zhdanov charged that American capitalists were bent on a course of imperialist expansion that they masked with strategic lies. American officials offered economic "assistance" to other countries, as with the Marshall Plan, only to bring those countries into economic bondage: Americans "saved" a country from starvation only to force it into submission. American capitalists used similar tactics with their own working class. These plutocrats kept the masses under control by flooding the public sphere with malicious anti-Soviet propaganda. Their lies convinced the American people to support virulent anti-Communism, even though this only deepened their own exploitation.[3]

Truman and Zhdanov portrayed the Cold War the way we usually imagine it—as a global struggle between two ideological enemies that had nothing in common. This picture, however, is misleading. The two sides in the Cold War may not have shared much in the way of ideology, but they quickly developed a common political vocabulary based on the parameters of their shared conflict. Their rivalry created a distinct political culture that encompassed both camps. *Curtain of Lies* examines this shared political culture by analyzing the ways both sides relied on the tropes of truth and lies to justify their political vision. Like Truman and Zhdanov, actors on both sides of the Iron Curtain placed truth at the center of politics, making the Cold War a moral contest that pitted right against wrong. In this context, truth was an absolute that could be possessed by only one side. The ideas of one's adversaries could only be lies; anything they said was slander or propaganda, cleverly designed to fool the ignorant or the desperate. Both sides emphasized the need to expose the other side's lies and reveal the truth about its real nature. Getting that truth to the masses became a major policy objective.

Eastern Europe played an important role in the creation of this common Cold War political culture. As the site of Europe's first lasting Communist regimes outside the Soviet Union, Eastern Europe exemplified the dual moral economy of Cold War politics. For each side, the state of affairs in Eastern Europe provided crucial evidence to support its version of the truth and reveal its enemy's lies. In their speeches, both Truman and Zhdanov made pronouncements about what they saw as the true state of affairs in Eastern Europe. Truman called it a land of conquered slaves, whereas for Zhdanov the region had "finally broken with imperialism and set forth on the path of democratic development."[4] From the Soviet perspective, Eastern Europe would show the world how Communist policies could improve people's lives and illustrate the dangers of Western imperialist sabotage. From the American perspective, conditions in Eastern Europe served as a cautionary tale illustrating the ways Communist regimes brought poverty and oppression. Sustaining these visions required papering over the more complex realities of actual conditions in the region, which were not as clear-cut as either side wanted them to be. Each was more concerned with finding evidence to promote its ideological vision than with the nuances of actual experience. There was little room for contradiction in the drive to reveal the essential truth about one's ideological enemy.

Truman and Zhdanov made their pronouncements about Eastern Europe as representatives of the world's ruling superpowers. East Europeans, however, were not merely the objects of superpower concern. They played key roles in producing the competing truths about their region. East Europeans participated in and helped to shape Cold War political culture in a variety of ways and on both sides of the Cold War divide. People from the region were the primary source of political propaganda both from and about Eastern Europe. Inside the Soviet Bloc, East European government officials, journalists, and Communist party activists tried to build enthusiasm for socialism at home and abroad, while also demonizing the capitalist West. At the same time, in the United States, anti-Communist East European émigrés helped to formulate American beliefs about what Communism had done to their homelands. One of the peculiarities about Eastern Europe is that the domestic audience for this propaganda was also partly responsible for its content. East Europeans who illegally fled to the West were interviewed by researchers eager to learn about life behind the Iron Curtain. These refugee stories about life under Communism provided an evidentiary foundation for what became established knowledge about the Soviet Bloc in the West, knowledge that would shape American perceptions and policies.

Truman and Zhdanov both emphasized that the socialist and capitalist societies were completely different worlds—as indeed they were. Socialism and capitalism inspired distinct political and economic systems based on different sets of values. My goal is not to compare these two systems or erase their differences by claiming that they were somehow equivalent. Yet, in the early years of the Cold War, these two very different societies nonetheless shared a common political logic based on absolutes. There was, both sides agreed, one, pure truth that had to be defended, with little room for nuance or alternative points of view.

On either side of the East–West divide, government officials and their populations used the concept of "truth" (or "lies") to indicate their conviction in their own rightness and to give their view of the world the weight of a fact or a moral absolute. Although they spoke in terms of truth and lies, factual accuracy was usually not their primary concern; "truth" was determined more by ideology than by any kind of objective corroboration of fact. Some of their contentions may have been accurate; many were not. Therefore, in these pages, the words "truth" and "lies" generally indicate an ideological judgment on the part of the speaker, not my evaluation of that speaker's veracity. Rather than indicate that by putting both words in scare quotes throughout the text, I have used the quotation marks only when particular emphasis on the subjective nature of the term seemed necessary.

Eastern Europe under Stalinism

I define "Eastern Europe" as Bulgaria, Czechoslovakia, Hungary, Poland, and Romania. These countries, often referred to as the "People's Democracies," all had Communist governments after the Second World War and were economically and militarily allied with the Soviet Union. Yugoslavia, though Communist, split off from the Soviet alliance in 1948 and is not included for that reason. After 1949, the German Democratic Republic was an independent Communist state allied with the Soviet Union; Albania was also a Soviet ally until 1960. I have not included these countries, because the interview collections that form the primary source base for the second half of this book did not include any East German or Albanian respondents. Since the end of the Cold War, there has been a proliferation of terms used in English to refer to the former Soviet satellites. Many have rejected "Eastern Europe" as inaccurate or even pejorative.[5] Though I understand those concerns, I have used this term because it is the most readily understood phrase in English for denoting the geographical space I cover, particularly when dealing with the period of the Cold War.[6]

Rather than take a comparative approach, I consider the countries of Eastern Europe together as a region and examine the political culture that united them. It is undeniable that each country had its own experience of Communist rule; indeed, much of the recent research on Communism in Eastern Europe has been devoted to illustrating these differences. Although it has been important to understand this diversity, there were nonetheless common features that tied the Soviet Bloc together, particularly in the years before 1956. Some of these unifying elements emanated from the Soviet Union, which called upon Eastern Europe's Communist governments to establish and defend a set of general truths and encouraged them to use a similar language and a similar set of practices in doing so. At the Soviets' instigation, East European governments held show trials and participated in the international peace movement. In both of these cases, Eastern Europe's Communist regimes promulgated the same messages in largely the same ways and worked to mobilize their populations in support of these messages using similar techniques. The Soviet Bloc was, therefore, not merely an economic and military alliance. It was a region united by common political themes and tactics, which entailed a certain measure of common experience on the part of its inhabitants.

This regional identity was not merely the creation of the Soviet Union or a common Communist ideology. The United States and its allies also played a role in making the Soviet Bloc something more than a set of political alliances. Just as the region's Communist governments insisted that their countries were part of a united socialist movement, the American media also emphasized their sameness, by presenting the countries of Eastern Europe as united in their status as Soviet victims. These parallel views of Eastern Europe as a cohesive region did not make the countries of the Soviet Bloc the same, but they did form part of a common culture that their citizens shared.

The battle over truth took place during the Stalinist period in Eastern Europe, an era conventionally dated 1948–1956. This standard periodization does not work equally well for all countries or topics of investigation—in his study of postwar Hungary, for example, the historian Mark Pittaway argued that understanding the relationship of workers to the socialist state requires seeing the era divided into eight specific periods, beginning in 1944 and ending in 1958.[7] The ways in which governments and individuals talked about the truth and their interpretation of it did not change much during this period, however. Unlike specific policies in particular places, these political discourses stayed relatively consistent, at least up until the beginning of de-Stalinization.

The year 1948 marked the beginning of Communist rule across the entire region. By February, Eastern Europe's Communist parties had all begun to establish one-party rule in their countries.[8] As they consolidated their power at home, these new dictatorships began facing enormous pressure from the Soviet Union to adopt Soviet models of political, economic, and cultural development. Previous plans for a more gradual or nationally distinct road to socialism were abandoned to Soviet demands for conformity, and all the countries of the Soviet Bloc began to implement policies similar to those the Soviet Union had followed under the rule of Joseph Stalin. They quickly adopted a common core of economic policies, including centralized planning, the nationalization of industry, and the collectivization of agriculture. This economic transformation was to be matched by a social revolution. Communist governments enacted policies to remove the bourgeoisie from influence. They declared women equal to men and encouraged them to become workers as well as mothers. Rapid industrialization began to move peasants away from the land and into the working class. The implementation of this social revolution was not always as smooth as the rhetoric extolling it implied, but it did provide an ideological foundation for many policies in this period and beyond.[9]

Under Stalinism, there was little tolerance for dissent. Just as Eastern Europe's Communist parties became newly subordinate to Soviet dictates, they subjected their own cadres to more control from the top. Each country had a leader who gathered power into his own hands; these men were often referred to as the "little Stalins." People who publicly voiced opposition to Communist policies were intimidated into silence, imprisoned, or forced into emigration.[10] Security forces grew rapidly. Those identified as enemies of the regime were persecuted, fired from their jobs, deported from their places of residence, arrested, or sent to labor camps. Hundreds of thousands of people across the region faced this kind of repression. Violence also became a way of silencing opposition within the Communist parties themselves. Purges of party rolls cost hundreds of thousands of people their jobs or even their freedom.[11]

Despite this terror, some East Europeans embraced the establishment of Communist regimes, believing that they would bring happiness and prosperity to the masses. Some kept this faith, but others quickly became disillusioned with Communist policies. Workers, for example, often welcomed Communist governments initially, but grew discouraged by Stalinist policies that prioritized greater productivity over living standards. Beginning in 1948, regimes around the region began to implement ever-increasing quota systems that pushed workers to continually work harder and faster, without any corresponding increase in their wages.[12] Central planners funneled resources into production rather than consumption, causing constant shortages of basic goods, even as the prices of those goods increased. Most peasants, meanwhile, had never approved of plans for the collectivization of agriculture and resisted attempts to force them into cooperatives.[13]

Understandably, much of the historical research on Eastern Europe during this period has been preoccupied with the idea of agency. Some historians take an approach informed by the concept of totalitarianism; in their work, they emphasize the power of Communist dictatorships and the terror they wielded.[14] According to this perspective, ordinary citizens had little agency. They lived with their heads down and rationally tried to avoid coming into contact with the regime that ruled them. Other historians, however, have shown the limits of this approach by detailing in careful and nuanced ways how ordinary people resisted, negotiated with, and even influenced these regimes. These histories do not deny that Communist regimes exerted great power over their populations, but they emphasize how peasants and workers acted to assert their own needs, rejecting the state's attempts to define their lives. They were not always successful, but their actions nonetheless had a significant impact on the states that ruled them.[15]

My own research takes a different approach. Rather than concentrating on whether individuals did or did not have agency, I want to move beyond the dichotomy of totalitarian terror and resistance and examine how Cold War political culture shaped and limited the ways individuals could conceive of their own experience. There is no question that, in the early Cold War, East Europeans lived under dictatorships that restricted their freedom. Some supported these regimes; others resisted them. Some did a bit of both. But none of their actions took place in a vacuum. All occurred within the transnational political culture of the Cold War, and this culture was what gave these actions their meaning, defining them (whether at the time or in retrospect) as authentic or coerced, or as collaboration or resistance. Many people believed that individual experience was the objective bedrock of truth. What they did not recognize was that the meaning they gave to their thoughts and actions was itself an artifact of the Cold War world in which they lived.

Just as Stalinism in Eastern Europe did not have one unambiguous starting point, it did not have one clear end. Stalin died on March 5, 1953, but the system that he authored did not immediately disappear and the effects of de-Stalinization were felt unevenly around the Soviet Bloc. Still, in general, economic conditions began to improve and terror lessened in the years after 1953. Stalin's rule was openly repudiated by his successor as the leader of the Soviet Union, Nikita Khrushchev, in the so-called secret speech of February 25, 1956. This sparked more vigorous change in the region, particularly in Poland and Hungary, where reform efforts followed popular protests. In Poland, the result of the Polish October (named for events in October 1956) was the ascension of the popular Władysław Gomulka to power and greater autonomy in domestic policy. In Hungary, mass protests to bring the Communist Imre Nagy back to power spiraled into a revolution against Hungary's Soviet alliance that was quelled only with the intervention of Soviet troops on November 4.

The events of 1956 were an emotional watershed for many East Europeans. The failed Hungarian revolution showed anti-Communists both within and outside the region that the Soviets were willing to fight to keep their hegemony and that the West would not come to liberate them, even after revolution had broken out. Although Cold War tensions remained high, a new emphasis on peaceful coexistence suggested that Communist governments in Eastern Europe were there to stay. At the same time, the gradual liberalization of the Stalinist system signaled to many that they could build lives worth living within the confines of state socialism. The combined realization that Eastern Europe's Communist regimes would not be easily swept away, but might also evolve and be made more livable, began to change the political culture across the region, marking an end to the environment of extreme fear and antagonism that had characterized the Stalinist era.

Uncovering the Hidden Truth: Fear and Cold War Political Culture

If truth was at the center of a common Cold War political culture, fear was its necessary complement.[16] At the close of his speech in Szklarska Poręba, Andrei

Zhdanov warned that the American imperialists wanted to intimidate through fear. They fomented war to frighten other countries into acquiescing to their own subjugation. This was not an empty threat; the imperialists would not blanch at taking innocent lives. To defeat them, Communists would need to wield truth as a weapon, using it to attack the warmongers and their allies. It was not enough merely to refute American lies: Communists would have to find—and neutralize—those who spread them. The Americans, warned Zhdanov, had hidden agents inside Communist countries. All good Communists needed to monitor their own populations and denounce the traitors among them.[17] Zhdanov's call to eliminate the enemies within illustrated the reciprocal relationship between fear and truth within the political culture of the Cold War. The fight for truth admitted no bystanders; it demanded that everyone be declared either friend or foe.

East European governments duly complied with Zhdanov's demand for all Communists to join together in the fight against Western imperialism. As the region's Communist regimes gradually consolidated their rule, they sought to use fear as a means of uniting and purifying their populations. A variety of propaganda campaigns in Eastern Europe sounded similar themes. The citizens of the People's Democracies were bombarded with images of the perfidy of the warmongering West and its threats of atomic destruction. After the outbreak of the Korean War, newspapers were filled with stories about American war crimes, including massacres of civilians and the use of biological weapons. At the same time, Eastern Europe's Communist leaders insisted that legions of Western sympathizers, spies, and traitors lurked unseen in their countries, working feverishly to undermine the socialist camp from within. They exhorted their citizens to be wary of each other, noting behaviors or comments that would enable them to detect and denounce these traitors.

Fear served multiple political purposes in Eastern Europe. As a component of both propaganda and policy, it was meant to inspire and energize. Fear-filled propaganda was tied to plans to mobilize the masses in support of Communist policies, both domestically and internationally. To show their rejection of Western warmongering, East Europeans marched in parades for peace, took part in political meetings, signed petitions condemning traitors, wrote letters demanding increased vigilance on the part of their coworkers, gave money to peace loans, signed up to receive Communist newspapers, and agreed to work on volunteer brigades. In most cases, we cannot know if those who marched against capitalist imperialism did so because they were truly afraid of a new war, because they were afraid that not participating would mark them as an enemy, or simply because they had nothing better to do that day. What we can say is that they acted, filling the parade grounds with the spectacle of a united people. Their actions had a life and a meaning that extended beyond their own beliefs and motivations, helping to create a political culture based on participation, driven largely by fear.

Like Zhdanov, Truman pointed to fear as a crucial element in East European politics. But whereas Zhdanov and his fellow Communists turned to fear as a means of mobilizing the masses, Truman posited paralyzing fear as the true reality of everyday life under Communist rule. Most American politicians and commentators in this era described Eastern Europe in totalitarian terms. They referred to East Europeans as captive slaves, powerless to resist their brutal Communist rulers. They were terrified into submission by armies of secret police agents, who carefully monitored the population at all times. Rather than inspiring them to action, fear rendered them victims, incapable of meaningful interventions in their own lives.

Because they are diametrically opposed, it is easy to see these two perspectives on fear in Eastern Europe—one originating in the East and the other in the West—as operating in completely separate worlds. Instead, they were the product of a complicated network of transmission from East to West and back again. Eastern Europe's Communist governments actively limited contact between their citizens and the West. Despite their efforts, the Iron Curtain was not as completely impenetrable as its name suggested.[18] Ideas and information moved across it, in letters, with travelers, and via the radio waves. Western radio stations like Radio Free Europe (RFE), Voice of America (VOA), and the British Broadcasting Corporation (BBC) broadcast programs to Eastern Europe in the local languages. East European émigrés were heavily involved in researching, writing, and delivering many of these broadcasts. Although their governments tried to jam the signals or decry the broadcasts as malicious slander, many Bulgarians, Czechoslovaks, Hungarians, Poles, and Romanians avidly listened to these stations and discussed them with others.[19] Through these radio transmissions, those who had left Eastern Europe taught their compatriots at home how to interpret the societies in which they still lived.[20]

Through 1956, illegal migrants from Eastern Europe continued to flee to the West. These new émigrés also became sources of information about life under Communism. Journalists and policymakers turned to these migrants—whom they usually called refugees—as sources, interviewing them about their views and experiences. Refugees were asked about everything from the price of goods in the stores to their opinions of various government policies and their personal relationships. Because these researchers, like most Western observers at the time, believed that fear was an essential element of everyday life in Eastern Europe, they often asked refugees about their fears. Researchers were especially interested in three kinds of fear: the fear of spies and informers, the fear of war, and the fear of scarcity. The stories interviewees told in response to their questions illustrate the ways in which the two seemingly disparate Eastern and Western perspectives on fear formed part of a common Cold War political language.

Refugee Experience and the Creation of Knowledge about Totalitarianism

In late 1951, a young Pole named Norbert Rak fled his homeland. Rak had a diploma from a technical high school in the Baltic town of Szczecin and had worked as a technical assistant on the installation of hydraulic systems. He claimed he had come to the attention of the Office of State Security (Urząd Bezpieczeństwa, or UB) after helping to organize a protest march against Soviet soldiers stationed in Szczecin. Fearing that he would be imprisoned, he swam across the Oder into East Germany and snuck onto a train to Berlin, where he made his way to the British sector and turned himself in to the German authorities. He hoped to immigrate to Canada. On December 4, 1951, Voice of America interviewed Rak in a refugee camp in West Berlin.[21]

During his interview, Rak was asked a variety of questions about his life and home and his views of the world, particularly his use of news media, his knowledge of current events, and his impressions of the United States. Rak, who as a high school graduate was more educated than many of those who fled Poland in the early 1950s, described himself as a savvy media consumer. He regularly read two daily Polish newspapers (he had been compelled to purchase one of them by union officials) and often bought several illustrated weeklies. Although he did not own his own radio, he occasionally listened to domestic radio broadcasts. Rak claimed many Poles regarded their local press and radio as mere propaganda, but his own perspective was more nuanced. He noted that the Polish papers did have a similar and distinctive point of view. For example, he said, "They write that in Russia there's a Socialist paradise, while in America there's only hunger, poverty, unemployment and revolution of the workers."[22] The Polish press also tended to choose subjects like "the six-year plan, reaching (output) quotas, work competition, stunts of shock workers and such things." While he found it tended to be predictable and repetitive, Rak observed there was actually "a bit of truth" in the Polish press. But finding it required sifting through the propaganda to isolate the facts nestled within. Most people were too tired for that, and so they concentrated on the sports news and entertaining features from the illustrated weeklies, which Rak claimed were mostly free of propaganda.[23]

Rak supplemented his diet of Polish newspapers with Western radio broadcasts. Because he did not have his own radio, he listened with friends who did. Most people he knew listened to these broadcasts somehow. For Rak, foreign radio also had its biases. No news source ever told "the whole truth."[24] Something was always left out or deemphasized for political reasons. But Rak considered Western radio broadcasts to have a much larger percentage of truth than local Polish media. Though foreign radio programs contained anti-Communist propaganda, this was, he said, propaganda based on "real facts." Rak liked the BBC best, because he thought it was more objective than the other radio stations. But some Poles, he said, liked to listen to VOA precisely because it was more "propagandistic." The hard-hitting diatribes against the Polish Communist government they heard on these broadcasts gave them hope.[25]

Rak himself used the concept of truth in complicated and contradictory ways. At times, he used the word to refer to pieces of objectively provable knowledge, as when Communist papers contained "a bit of truth," and he judged news organizations on their ability to provide this knowledge. He actively compared the Polish press with what he heard on foreign radio broadcasts in order to make informed judgments about what was true and what was not. He also evaluated foreign broadcasts for their accuracy, noting when VOA had gotten a story wrong or when the BBC's reporting of events in his hometown of Szczecin seemed accurate given his own experience.[26] But at other moments, Rak was less concerned with objectivity than with how information might be mobilized in the service of larger political or ideological truths. At one point in his interview, he advised VOA to counter Communist propaganda "by stating facts . . . so as to prove they [VOA] are right." He particularly thought VOA should use facts to refute Communist claims about racial discrimination in the United States, which he believed must be lies, presumably because they did not fit into his received notions of what the world's defender of freedom was really like.[27] Similarly, Rak claimed that any Communists who listened to foreign broadcasts could not be "true" Communists. If "true Communists" did listen to VOA, he said, they would not be able to believe anything they heard. Regardless of the facts, their beliefs would lead them to a different truth.

Rak's comments illustrate the ways in which some East Europeans used, adapted, manipulated, and shaped political discourses from both sides of the Iron Curtain in order to make sense of their own experience. Rak, like most of his fellow interviewees, was quite familiar with both Polish media and Western broadcasts directed toward Eastern Europe. His concern with ferreting out the facts and his identification of truth with ideological rightness were reflected in both sources. Their mutual influence was also apparent in the way he characterized both Polish and foreign news as at least partly propaganda. For him, both news services had the same goals, and imparting knowledge of world events to the reader or listener was not first among them. In his interview, Rak talked about propaganda not as an evil, but as a tool. It was something that could be used on him, but also by him. Rak, who like almost all refugees presented himself as an anti-Communist, requested facts to use as weapons in the battle for hearts and minds that characterized the Cold War. Far from being a passive consumer of political messages, he was an active participant in the production of the truth, both for himself and for others.

Interviews like that with Norbert Rak, collected by Voice of America and Radio Free Europe during the years between 1950 and 1956, are a unique resource for historians.[28] As historical sources, these interviews have definite limitations. Refugees did not represent a statistically typical sample of the population. A majority of the respondents were, like Rak, unmarried young men, often of limited education and from border regions. They were interviewed in a particular ideological climate—that of the refugee camp—and by interviewers who had a strong anti-Communist orientation. Refugees were sometimes offered money for their thoughts and may have believed that their answers would influence their attempts to obtain immigration visas, although this was not the case. Yet, despite these limitations, most of which were recognized even at the time, refugee interviews are historically important. Radio stations broadcasting to Eastern Europe, along with intelligence officials and others, interviewed refugees from the region in the early 1950s precisely because they had knowledge about the countries they had fled that was simply not otherwise available. Today's historians have access to archival sources from the region that were not available to early Cold War era researchers. But these archival sources have their own problems. Secret police reports on the mood of the population purportedly documented the speech of individuals who did not know they were being monitored.[29] Refugee interviews are different; they reflect interviewees' attempts to process or make sense of their experience in light of the interviewer's questions. They therefore allow us to consider not merely what might have happened in these people's lives, but the meaning they gave to their experience in retrospect.

Interviews like Norbert Rak's can be read in a variety of ways. Traditional approaches to such materials concentrate on the question of the interviewee's own intent. At the time the interviews were produced, evaluators and researchers who used them tended to focus on whether or not a respondent was telling the truth about his or her life. They wanted to ascertain whether the events recounted in an interview had occurred as the respondent reported them.[30] Some historians have evaluated and used these sources in this way, critically questioning their accuracy and then using the reports they judged to have a basis in fact as a source of information about everyday life in a totalitarian system.[31] Other historians have insisted that, no matter how critically they are examined, such sources have little to say about everyday experience in Eastern Europe. They argue that interview respondents were canny operators who told their Western interlocutors only the stories they wanted to hear. Refugee interviews, therefore, contain no useful facts about life in Eastern Europe, even on the level of individual experience. Such interviews are useful, they say, only for studying the organizations that commissioned them.[32]

My approach is different. I do not consider refugee interviews simply as records of individual experience.[33] Although I do not ignore questions about the accuracy of a person's account, this is not my primary concern. Instead, I show how refugee stories were shaped by, and in turn helped create, a Cold War political culture that revolved around the poles of fear and truth. The narratives that interviewees constructed about their lives took on a meaning independent of their factual accuracy, both for the respondents themselves and for the Western analysts who evaluated their reports.[34] Researchers for both VOA and RFE evaluated refugee interviews as possible sources of knowledge about Communist societies. Yet they have just as much to tell us about how Western convictions about life under Communism were created and sustained. Western analysts tended to interpret refugee stories in ways that upheld their existing beliefs. In my own analysis of these sources, I look for contradictions or nuances in refugees' narratives of their experience that seem to have been ignored at the time. There is little evidence that these earlier interpretations were willfully misleading. Instead, the polarizing ideological climate of the Cold War colored the ways in which a particular story could be either told or read. In the same vein, contradictions within an interview do not necessarily indicate a respondent's intent to deceive. Rather, the contradictions illuminate the ways in which individuals might discount even the facts of their own experience in order to find a deeper truth about Communist society.

When analyzing interviews with East European émigrés, I examine how particular incidents might reflect a respondent's emotions or anxieties about his or her experience; regardless of whether or not the incident occurred precisely as the interviewee related it, telling the story became a way for the respondent to express those feelings. Fear became a language refugees could use to understand and communicate meaning about their experience. Refugees often made comments about how fear of the police or Communist oppression paralyzed them. Norbert Rak, for example, claimed that "no one" would say anything about politics in public, "because doing so gets you directly to jail."[35] Because Western analysts expected that fear would be the defining element in a totalitarian society, they tended to give stories about fear the weight of truth without interrogating them too closely. Like Norbert Rak, who looked to the radio to provide facts that would confirm his preexisting ideas and corroborate what he believed to be the truth, refugee stories provided Western analysts with knowledge that bolstered their preconceptions about Eastern Europe's Communist regimes. Yet, the language of fear refugees used to describe their experience did not simply arise from that experience itself. Its vocabulary was shaped in dialogue with the competing political discourses of fear that surrounded them, including the very Western radio broadcasts that their interviews were meant to inform. Refugees did not need to consciously craft their stories to fit the expectations of Western researchers; Western radio broadcasts had already helped to shape the way they interpreted the world.

Norbert Rak's interviewers spoke to him because they wanted to find out about the lives and perspectives of East Europeans trapped behind the Iron Curtain. While they thought they were looking for facts about a place they could not visit, they were really in pursuit of a larger truth: the confirmation of totalitarian evil. The knowledge that was created from these refugee interviews was shaped by this desire; in turn, it created the basis for many future Western analyses of Communist Eastern Europe. While knowledge is always dependent on the culture in which it is made, this is perhaps most eloquently illustrated by the first years of the Cold War, when the contest over truth occupied the center of global politics.

1 TELLING LIES, MAKING TRUTH

On September 16, 1949, László Rajk and seven other men were put on trial for espionage, sedition, and the violent overthrow of the Hungarian government. The accused pleaded guilty to all charges. Their complicity taken as a given, the defendants were nonetheless compelled to stand in front of the court and narrate the story of their crimes. Rajk, who before his arrest was a member of the Politburo and the foreign minister of Hungary, confessed that he had been a police spy and foreign agent for decades. He said his betrayal had begun in 1931, when he was arrested on suspicion of illegal Communist activity. To save himself, he agreed to serve as an informer and agent provocateur for the Hungarian police. Ever since that moment, he had worked against the party, his time as an informer easily bleeding into espionage. His career as a spy began, he claimed, during his involvement in the Spanish Civil War, where he fought against Franco. Initially recruited by the French, Rajk later spied for the Gestapo, the Americans, and Tito's Yugoslavia. While serving as minister of the interior from 1946 to 1948, he created a network of spies and traitors to facilitate the takeover of Hungary by Titoist forces, personally passing sensitive documents to Yugoslav agents. By his own admission, his ultimate goal was to destroy the Hungarian People's Democracy and lead Hungary back into the imperialist camp.[1]

In his closing arguments, the prosecutor, Gyula Alapi, described Rajk and his co-conspirators as "crawling, sneaking snakes" who operated by "hiding in the dark and penetrating into the leading Party of our People's Democracy and into the state machinery of our Republic."[2] What made the defendants so detestable and so dangerous was not simply their opposition to the Communist regime, but their duplicity. Rajk and his co-defendants were liars who hid their true identities and cloaked themselves in the guise of Communist virtue. They cleverly convinced the world they were loyal Communists, but their hearts were dark and twisted. The trial unmasked the traitors and allowed Hungarians to see the "pure truth."[3] The ultimate significance of the trial, Alapi asserted, was that it revealed the hidden reality behind their lies.

To many Western listeners, Alapi's statement could only have been made ironically. The trial of László Rajk was what is referred to as a show trial. Rajk and his co-defendants were not actually spies and traitors; their testimony was fabricated in advance and memorized for proper delivery in court. Schooled by literature like Arthur Koestler's 1940 novel, *Darkness at Noon*, which was based on the Moscow trials of the late 1930s, the American press quickly judged the Rajk trial accordingly.[4] As Selden Chapin, a former American minister to Budapest who was mentioned in the trial as a player in the conspiracy, told the *New York Times*, "Anyone familiar with Communist methods . . . whereby people can be forced to testify against their own convictions and against what they know to be the truth" could see that Rajk's testimony was false. Such perversions of justice, he said, were "now standard practice behind the curtain."[5] For Chapin, as for many Western readers of Koestler, if the East European show trials had any meaning, it was to demonstrate how Stalinist terror and brutality could destroy an individual, leading a person to willingly trade truth for lies.[6] Most historical research on show trials in Eastern Europe has proceeded from this perspective: it has focused on proving the innocence of the accused and showing how the trials were fabricated by members of the local security police and their Soviet advisers, who reported directly to Stalin in Moscow.[7]

The real significance of show trials, however, is not whether they held to Western standards of criminal procedure and scientific evidence. Some historians of the Soviet Union have argued that show trials were more than just a politically convenient way of eliminating potential opposition. In the Soviet Union of the 1930s—as in postwar Eastern Europe—only a small minority of those arrested for political offenses appeared in public trials. Nonetheless, state security officers tirelessly interrogated everyone they arrested, regardless of the fact that the confessions they so painstakingly extracted would never be made public. The historian Igal Halfin has argued that we should not be preoccupied with whether these interrogations revealed facts or were obtained under duress, but should concentrate instead on their ideological function. Halfin treats interrogations as a form of political discourse and considers how they helped to create the realm of imaginative possibility in which Soviet citizens acted. Interrogations, he suggests, were like laboratories where the meaning of ideology was contested and made. Interrogators believed that criminality was found in a person's character, not in a person's actions. The purpose of interrogations was not to reveal evidence about actual events in accordance with Western standards, but to expose the evil in an oppositionist's soul.[8]

According to Halfin, interrogation records provide a window into the dialectical relationship between ideology and individuals. Unlike an interrogation, a show trial was a public event that reached the masses. The transcripts of show trials were nonetheless also a form of political speech that served to delineate the boundaries of the imaginative landscape in Eastern Europe. Once the proceedings had begun, the most important interaction was not between the state and the defendants, but between the state and the audience, the people who listened to the trial on the radio or read about it in the newspaper. Like the trial of László Rajk, all show trials revolved around convoluted and fantastic conspiracy stories that, at least to Western audiences, seemed too incredible to be real. But verisimilitude was not the point of these narratives. Their task was to communicate to their audiences larger truths about the Cold War world and the place of Eastern Europe within it. Show trials taught their audiences about the nature of socialism's enemies and sought to push them into active battle to support the socialist camp. These common enemies would become a crucial element of the glue that bound the countries of the Soviet Bloc together, uniting them in a common fight against the West.

Show trials made the tropes of Communist propaganda real. When show trial defendants confessed, they rendered abstract ideas about socialism's enemies into flesh and blood. Their lies were transformed into more fundamental truths about the deviousness of the imperialist West and the threat it posed to the countries of Eastern Europe. These truths had to be accepted by show trial audiences; ordinary citizens were not allowed to remain silent observers. Publicity campaigns that accompanied the trials urged the masses to actively condemn the accused and to be vigilant in rooting out more traitors. Most people complied. One question that is often raised is whether they did these things because they sincerely believed in a defendant's guilt or merely because they were afraid of what would happen to them if they did not. This question assumes, however, that belief is an either-or proposition. Instead, it was possible for people to accept some aspects of a particular trial and reject others. It is also the case that accepting a trial's lessons did not necessarily hinge on the question of belief. It was, perhaps, less important for people to be certain that the events related in a show trial had happened exactly as they were described in court than for them to understand the trial's lessons about the Cold War world and their place within it.

Unmasking the Enemy

Although political trials or forced public confessions have occurred in myriad times and places and under a wide variety of circumstances, "show trial" is a term particularly associated with Stalinist terror. Show trials occurred in the context of the mass arrests of perceived enemies of the party that occurred under Stalinism; the trials themselves generally presaged more arrests and the search for more enemies. The term was first associated with the Moscow trials of Communist leaders that took place during the Great Purges in the Soviet Union from 1936 to 1939. It then came to describe a series of similar trials that took place across Eastern Europe from 1948 to 1954.

Show trials were so named because they resembled theatrical productions more than judicial proceedings. They were conducted according to a prepared script; officials in the local security services and their Soviet advisers composed the testimony of defendants and witnesses and arranged the verdict in advance. Soviet advisers played crucial roles in the construction of show trials throughout the region. Soviet officials pushed Eastern Europe's Communist parties to search their own ranks for traitors and helped interrogate those identified as possible spies.[9] Particularly in trials of Communist luminaries like Rajk, Soviet advisers took the lead in fashioning trial scenarios and choosing the defendants.[10] For their source material, they used protocols from the interrogations of prisoners, bending real events to fit a narrative of treasonous activity. Participants were compelled to memorize their lines and were supposed to deliver them verbatim in court. Though witnesses were called to the stand, the real evidentiary basis of all show trials was the confession. All defendants were required to plead guilty and admit to the crimes outlined in the script, even though they were fictions. The participants were carefully chosen to fit whatever scenario trial planners had devised. Out of the hundreds of thousands of East Europeans arrested for political reasons during the years of Stalinist terror, only a select few wound up on stage in a show trial.[11]

In Eastern Europe, show trials occurred at the moment Communist regimes were consolidating their power and liquidating political opposition to their rule. The first defendants in show trials in the region were not Communists but members of the anti-Communist opposition, including politicians, members of the clergy, representatives of prewar elites, and sometimes foreigners. But the biggest show trials were those in which major Communist figures stood in the dock. The trial of László Rajk was the first show trial of a leading Communist official in Eastern Europe. After his trial, other Communist parties in the region were urged to find their own Rajk. The trials of Traïcho Kostov in Bulgaria (1949) and Rudolf Slánský in Czechoslovakia (1952) were on a scale similar to that of the Rajk trial. In Poland and Romania, preparations were begun for trials of equally prominent figures (Władysław Gomułka and Lucrețiu Pătrășcanu), but they were never realized. Although there was no Polish or Romanian Rajk, staged public trials of some sort did take place in all of the People's Democracies.[12]

Across the bloc, all show trials had similar features, both in the construction of their narratives and in the method of their publicity. No matter who was on trial, the cases presented similar scenarios and expanded on similar themes. Individual cases often had a domestic political purpose, such as destroying the leadership of local anti-Communist opposition or getting rid of a troublesome faction within the Communist party itself. Nevertheless, as propaganda instruments, show trials had a consistent set of messages no matter their country of origin. The heavy participation of Soviet advisers in the fabrication of the trials ensured that this was the case. It is therefore possible to analyze them together as a unitary phenomenon common to the entire region.

All show trials had one central theme: the socialist camp was under siege, menaced by hidden and dangerous enemies who plotted to destroy it from the inside. Trials revealed elaborate networks of spies who had managed to operate unseen, often for decades, until they were finally caught and neutralized. The scariest thing about these spies was their ability to cloak their true identities and motives. Socialism's enemies wore masks that enabled them to hide in plain sight.[13] The more unlikely a group of defendants seemed, the more their confessions emphasized that socialism's enemies could be found anywhere. It was impossible to know who might be a traitor in disguise. Anyone's colleague, neighbor, friend, or relative could turn out to be living a lie. It was the task of all citizens—but especially Communist party activists—to unmask these enemies before they could do their evil work.

The largest and most heavily publicized show trials revealed villains in the most unlikely place of all: at the heart of the Communist party itself. Men and women who had spent decades in the inner circles of the party were suddenly unmasked as traitors. Leaders like Hungary's László Rajk, Bulgaria's Traïcho Kostov, and the Czechoslovak Rudolf Slánský had spent their entire lives as ostensibly loyal servants of the party. All had suffered for their commitment: Rajk had fought in the Spanish Civil War and spent time in French internment camps, Kostov spent eighteen years in prison for his beliefs, and Slánský had participated in the Slovak National Uprising and watched his friend Jan Šverma die in the process. In the years after 1945, each became one of his country's most prominent leaders. But in their trials, their entire past was revealed to be no more than a facade.

Slánský's case illustrates how show trials rewrote the life stories of their defendants. Slánský had been a member of the Czechoslovak Communist Party (Komunistická strana Československa, or KSČ) since the age of twenty. By 1948, he was the general secretary of the party and second in power only to the KSČ leader, Klement Gottwald. Only months before his arrest, he was publicly feted on the occasion of his fiftieth birthday and given the Order of Socialism.[14] Yet, he claimed in his testimony, his dedication to the party had never been anything but a lie. He reiterated again and again that he had "never been a real Communist." The seeds of his betrayal lay in his "bourgeois" origins, as the son of a "wealthy rural shopkeeper." As a child of the petit bourgeoisie (and, it was understood, as a Jew), he could never truly be part of the workers' movement. He had, he claimed, always acted as an opportunist, had accepted Trotskyite deviations, and became a foreign agent in 1930. Even his role in the Slovak National Uprising was alleged to be a lie, as Slánský now admitted he was responsible for his friend Šverma's death. He was not discovered, he claimed, "because I masked myself, I covered my hostile activities and outwardly behaved like an adherent of the Bolshevik movement."[15] The trial removed the mask to reveal the true face of this villain. The supposedly solid past was only a clever illusion, like a magician's trick. It was the trial that represented reality, as grotesque as it seemed. As *Rudé právo* (Red right), the official newspaper of the KSČ, claimed, "The mask has been stripped from Rudolf Slánský once and for all, and the face that emerges from beneath it is that of a cannibal."[16]

As they exposed hidden spies, show trials taught the public to recognize socialism's enemies in all of their many guises. Different trials highlighted particular groups that would now have to be considered dangerous. The Slánský trial cast Zionism and the new state of Israel as a threat to socialism, suggesting that any of Czechoslovakia's Jewish residents might be foreign agents. Eleven of the defendants, including Slánský himself, were of Jewish background, and this heritage was made integral to their supposed crimes. The indictment described the three defendants with no Jewish roots as "Czech" or "Slovak," while the other eleven were listed as "of Jewish origin," implying that their primary loyalty was to their Jewish identity.[17] Slánský and many of the other defendants claimed to have worked closely in connection with Zionist networks and to have promoted Zionists (meaning Jews) to positions of power and influence in order to extend their web. Slánský even testified that he had protected Zionist organizations in Czechoslovakia by organizing a campaign against antisemitism. Through Slánský's testimony, attacking antisemitism was itself turned into a traitorous act.[18]

The Slánský trial was the only major trial to target Zionism as an enemy of socialism. But the defendants in many trials were exposed as Titoists. Josip Broz Tito was the head of the Yugoslav Communist Party. Tito asserted his party's independence from the Soviet Union, resulting in Yugoslavia's expulsion from the Cominform in 1948. Show trials showed the rest of Eastern Europe that Tito was their enemy. Trial narratives painted Tito as an instrument of Western imperialism whose goal was to lead other Communists back into the imperialist fold. Tito allegedly sponsored countless spies and saboteurs throughout the Soviet Bloc. At the Rajk trial, Gyula Alapi drew a straight line "from Dulles to Rankovich [Yugoslavia's minister of the interior and head of military intelligence] and Tito." Alapi acknowledged Western criticism of the trial, which charged that the trial was not "objective" and that Rajk was being used as a scapegoat for Tito. There was some truth in this, Alapi said, but for Alapi the "truth" rested on Rajk and Tito's mutual guilt. "It is true and right," he declared in his closing remarks, "that the Hungarian People's Court . . . should also pass sentence, in a political and moral sense, on the traitors of Yugoslavia . . . We are exposing their duplicity, their perfidy, their intrigues against democracy and socialism."[19] Just as the trial proved that Rajk was a spy, it proved that Tito was a traitor to socialism at large and had been for years. It also made it abundantly clear that any supporter of Tito, or anyone who asserted national priorities over Soviet wishes, would be defined as an enemy of socialism.

But Tito was himself only a pawn of socialism's real enemy: Western capitalist imperialism. The ultimate goal of all traitors was to bring their country back into the imperialist fold. Thus, the goal of Slánský's "Trotskyite, Titoist, Zionist, bourgeois nationalist" conspiracy was for "Czechoslovakia to become again a land dependent on imperialists, where the Czechoslovak people were once again subjugated by imperialist exploitation, ruled over by industrialists, bankers and estate owners."[20] In the Rajk trial, Gyula Alapi declared in his closing remarks that Rajk and his associates were, in the end, merely "puppets" of "their foreign masters, their imperialist instigators of Belgrade and Washington."[21] The same was true in the trial of Vasile Ciobanu in Romania. Ciobanu was an airline pilot who had supposedly been a spy for the Turkish government. His defense attorney argued for mercy on the grounds that, although his client was guilty, he was simply a "pliant tool" for "the true authors and odious instigators to these crimes, the Anglo-American imperialists."[22] Traïcho Kostov's trial in Bulgaria ended with an eerily similar refrain, as the prosecutor declared that "the conspiracy was directed, inspired and assisted by foreign powers . . . this conspiracy is only one of the large links in the whole chain of the conspirative and hostile policy of the Anglo-American imperialist circles against the people's democratic regime in our country."[23] According to all of these trials, the West could only represent the enemy.

The trial of Claude Henry Turner in Poland spotlighted the evil intentions of Western diplomats and military personnel. Turner had been the air attaché to the British Embassy in Poland, where he became involved with a young Polish woman, Barbara Bobrowská. After a failed attempt to get her out of the country, he was arrested, along with two British sailors who had helped with the escape attempt. Although Turner was not formally charged with espionage (only with arranging Bobrowská's flight), his trial became a way of illuminating the danger of foreign spies in Poland. At the trial, after giving testimony about his role in the Bobrowská affair, Turner was suddenly asked by the prosecutor about his intelligence activities. He calmly agreed to tell the court all about them. While his story was long and detailed, several themes emerged. In his testimony, Turner emphasized the connections between American, British, French, and Canadian intelligence services. As he described it, there was a network of foreign agents working together to gain sensitive information about the Polish, Soviet, and East German air forces and defenses. Turner claimed that foreign intelligence operatives like him had no trouble ferreting out Poland's secrets. In part, they were assisted by Poles who had been in the Polish air force in London during the war and opposed the Communist regime. But they were also simply able to amass information as they traveled freely around the country. Even ordinary people on the street could unwittingly serve the interests of Western spies, Turner told the prosecutor. Ominously, he said, "I wish to stress that even [the man in the street] can often materially assist the experts trained in the gathering of intelligence."[24]

The message of Turner's testimony was clear. The trial, claimed the prosecutor in his closing statement, had "torn down the curtain" and revealed "in all their monstrosity, the treacherous work of the imperialist hirelings who are now plotting against Poland and against peace."[25] Poles had been living in a false reality, unaware of the dangers that lurked all around them. But in truth, imperialist spies could be anywhere. Now that the real world had been exposed, Poles (and by extension all residents of the socialist camp) could see that they needed to remain vigilant at all times. Turner's admission that all the Western powers worked together and his claim that they wanted to know about air capacities and industrial installations around the Soviet Bloc as a whole gave the affair even more urgency. An article published about the trial in the Polish newspaper *Trybuna ludu* (People's tribune) underscored this point. The author, Jerzy Rawicz, claimed that Soviet citizens were so patriotic and vigilant that the only way foreign agents could obtain information about planes in Moscow was "to look at them in the sky on Aviation Day." Turner's testimony showed the dangers of "slack" Polish attitudes when it came to consorting with Westerners. "Some snobbish members of the intelligentsia are still credulous enough to be tempted to go with Anglo-Saxons to a restaurant, play tennis with them, and talk when drinking cocktails," he wrote. "In this way, they are serving the enemy."[26] Rawicz gave a clear warning to anyone who might wish to deny the new division of the world into East and West. No one could ignore the battle lines of the Cold War, his article implied. Ignorance was no excuse for abetting the enemy.

It was these common enemies—from Tito to Western imperialism—that knit together the countries of the Soviet Bloc. Each faced similar threats and needed similar tactics to defeat them. Trial narratives explicitly referred to trials in other countries as a way of showing how the nations of the socialist camp were waging a common battle against spies and traitors. In the trial of Traïcho Kostov,

Visual propaganda reinforced the need to watch carefully for potential spies and saboteurs. This 1952 Czechoslovak poster warns, "Don't talk about what you're doing. You don't know who's listening." *Poster by Kra-Ma-Vot, All-Trade Union Archive of the Bohemian-Moravian Confederation of Trade Unions, poster collection*

the prosecutor, Vladimir Dimchev, noted in his closing remarks that British and American intelligence agents had found willing agents in Tito, Rajk, and Kostov and his co-defendants. This success in three countries proved, he said, that "much vigilance and caution are needed not to allow the enemy to grow roots in the party, the Fatherland Front, and in the State apparatus."[27] Josef Urválek, the prosecutor in the Slánský trial, explicitly linked Rudolf Slánský with the already executed Rajk and Kostov and with two potential traitors, Gomułka in Poland and Pătrășcanu in Romania (both had been arrested, but neither charged or tried).[28] This equation of each villain with all those who had gone before implied that all the enemies of socialism, no matter where they operated and no matter the specifics of their actions, were merely different faces of the same enemy, linked via common tactics and a common hatred of socialism, the Soviet Union, and its allies. In uncovering these traitors, the People's Democracies were all fighting the same fight.

In this way, the show trials educated East Europeans about the new reality of the bipolar Cold War world. Trial scenarios made it clear that the gap between East and West was vast and impassable. In trial narratives, the West was represented only by its spies and imperialist ambitions; almost all of the individuals from non–Soviet Bloc nations who showed up in trial scenarios were pursuing nefarious ends. In many cases, Westerners appeared only as characters in the testimony of others. They were the shadowy agents or spymasters who recruited the weak for espionage and were the handlers to whom the accused passed their information.

In both the Rajk and Slánský trials this role was taken by the same man, the American Noel Field. Field was a Communist sympathizer who had briefly been a Soviet agent in the 1930s, when he worked in the US State Department. During the war, he was the head of a relief agency in France and Switzerland and assisted quite a few Communist refugees, with the help of his former State Department colleague, Allen Dulles, at that time a Swiss-based official for the Office of Strategic Services. Afraid his work with Soviet intelligence would be revealed if he returned to the United States, Field and his wife, Herta, hoped to gain residence in Czechoslovakia with the assistance of some of the Czech Communists they had helped during the war. But in the new atmosphere of the Cold War, Field's American citizenship and connections with Dulles made him suspicious. He was arrested in Prague in 1949 and handed over to the Hungarian security service. They interrogated him repeatedly and kept him in prison until 1954. Field never faced a trial, but his name appeared in the Rajk and Slánský cases as the coordinator of a vast network of agents. Communists who had been helped by Field in Switzerland (including several of the defendants in both the Rajk and Slánský trials) found their contact with him had been "unmasked" as espionage.[29]

Show trial narratives depended on the idea that the world had been sundered into two diametrically opposed camps: "the front of peace, democracy and socialism, headed by the great Soviet Union, and the front of the imperialist aggressors and warmongers."[30] The camp metaphor was used by prosecutors, witnesses, and even third parties. In the Turner trial, the witness Alexander Majewski claimed that the British squadron leader Dobree Bell, who was no longer in Poland but alleged to be the mastermind behind a spy network, had told him that "at the moment there existed two camps in the world, that in his opinion that current international situation was due to the existence of two camps."[31] The socialist camp, as described by the Hungarian prosecutor, Gyula Alapi, was simply trying to build a peaceful future of well-tilled fields, humming industries, and model schools. It did not invite attack. The imperialists, however, yearned to destroy it. This was just their nature; nothing could change their desire. Diplomacy, trade, or cultural exchange between the sides was useless. The imperialists would just use any attempt at dialogue to search for weaknesses in their quest to break the socialist camp. There was only one way to see the global situation: as two separate worlds. In Alapi's words, "The world of construction and peace faces the world of ruin, war and devastation."[32]

Not only did show trials reflect this view of the world, they helped to create and instantiate it. This could happen in quite concrete ways. In the world the trials described, all embassies, legations, consulates, and cultural centers from outside the Soviet Bloc were filled with suspicious characters working to undermine socialist regimes. The trials literally helped to make this the case. East Europeans who worked for Westerners were among those most likely to be unmasked as spies. The Pole Irene Findeisen, arrested to appear as a witness in the Turner trial (in these trials witnesses were generally also prisoners), fell under suspicion because she worked in the US Embassy. In a rare moment of seeming ironic candor during a trial, Findeisen remarked that she "had learned during the two and a half years of my confinement that spies are more and more frequently discovered among the diplomats."[33] The lesson she had to learn in prison was to be absorbed by the rest of the population via courtroom dramatics. The trial taught its listeners to question the loyalty of Poles who had any contacts with either the West or Westerners, including men who had been in the Polish exile air force in London during the war.

This dynamic was a thread that ran through trial transcripts. The briefest contact with the West could turn into a suspicious act. In his capacity as secretary of the Central Committee for the Bulgarian Communist Party, Traïcho Kostov was invited to lunch at the home of the Allied representative in Sofia, British General Oxley. However, because of a miscommunication, he showed up on the wrong day. He was asked to stay and eat anyway, and this meal, which was not attended by any other Bulgarians, was transformed in his trial into the beginning of his career as a British spy.[34] The lunch had actually occurred, although it had not involved espionage. But what "really" happened was immaterial. The meeting had a meaning that went beyond the content of the events themselves. As the trial made clear, in this new Cold War, there were no innocuous meetings between East and West. As Kostov discovered, arguing that lunch was just lunch was not a viable defense. The party had redefined such encounters as treason. Those who heard the trial proceedings could abide by this message—or they could ignore it, but they would do so at their own risk.

Out for Blood

In show trial narratives, the West was socialism's irreconcilable enemy, bent on its destruction. But given that the forces of socialism meant to resist this implacable onslaught, this could mean only one thing: war. The specter of a new world war was a central image in trial stories. At the beginning of the Cold War, it was not hard to imagine that the conflict between the United States and the Soviet Union would break out into violence. Bellicose rhetoric was a staple on both sides of the Iron Curtain. The trials themselves were a part of this wider discourse. They helped to make the possibility of war imaginable by detailing the perfidy of imperialist spies and warmongers and insisting on the West's desire for war as the means to world domination.

War was the ultimate goal of all the spies and saboteurs who found themselves on trial, and the nightmare of armed conflict was constantly held up as the price of failing to uncover the conspirators. In the trials of Rajk, Kostov, and Slánský, each of the accused confessed to planning some kind of armed insurrection. The Rajk and Kostov trials both took place in 1949, in the immediate aftermath of the Yugoslav–Soviet split. In each trial, the stated goal of the conspiracy was to kill the country's current leader (Rákosi in Hungary, Dmitrov in Bulgaria), take power via a coup, slowly turn the people against the USSR, and make the country a satellite of Yugoslavia. In the end, Hungary and Bulgaria would become pawns of the power behind Tito: American imperialism. Although this was presented primarily as a regional scenario, with agents supposedly working across the Balkans to bring Titoists to power, the fear of a larger conflict lurked in the background. In his final speech to the court, the Hungarian prosecutor, Gyula Alapi, declared, "The American and British intelligence services purchased Tito and his clique even during the war against Hitler, to prevent the national and social liberation of the peoples of South Eastern Europe, to isolate the Soviet Union, and prepare for the third world war."[35] Unless they were stopped, the warmongering American imperialists would unleash their fury on the hapless inhabitants of the People's Democracies.

One way of illustrating the bloodthirsty and rapacious violence of the imperialist camp was to link it with Hitler and fascism. To equate Western governments with fascism was to tie them to fascist policies of imperial expansion, armed conflict, racism, and brutal occupation regimes. Trial narratives often asserted that the Americans and British had made common cause with the forces of fascism, even though they had so recently been at war. The fact that the two were engaged in rebuilding Western Germany amid rumors about West German rearmament put teeth to such accusations (the Federal Republic of Germany would formally join NATO in 1955). One of the witnesses in the Turner trial, Alexander Majewski, claimed that British officers floated the possibility with him of an armed Federal Republic invading Poland; he told them Poles would fight the Germans tooth and nail.[36] In the case of Hungary, the West was linked to Hungary's own fascist groups. In the Rajk trial, the indictment charged that once war had broken out and Yugoslavia had moved to take over Hungary, their units would be supplemented by "gendarmes, arrow-cross men and Horthyists in Hungarian uniform—all collected in the British and American occupation zones."[37] The implication was that even though the Hungarian Communists had rid their homeland of its native fascists, the Americans would bring them back.

The alliance between Western imperialism and fascism was often made tangible in the defendants' own stories. Several of the accused in the Slánský trial confessed to having worked with the Nazis during the war. Their connection with Nazi brutality and violence vividly illustrated the utter lack of morality that characterized the imperialist cause. Josef Frank, one of the three defendants not of Jewish background, had been imprisoned in the Buchenwald concentration camp during the war. During the trial, he confessed that he had been given a privileged position as a clerk in the camp and used it to assist his Nazi jailers. Of his own volition, he put Russian nationals on the lists of prisoners selected for transport to work camps, all but ensuring their deaths. He also testified that he helped the Nazis keep order in the camp by beating prisoners who did not follow camp rules.[38] His fellow defendant Karel Švab similarly confessed to helping the Nazis while a prisoner in Sachsenhausen. Švab claimed he had beaten his fellow prisoners and stolen their food. He learned, he said, from the Nazis how to torture others, and he admitted he had denounced another prisoner for stealing a piece of bread and targeted Russian and Ukrainian prisoners for physical abuse.[39] Bedřich Reicin had escaped Nazi camps by spending the war in the Soviet Union. But he was nonetheless unmasked as a confidante of the Gestapo, which he claimed had turned him after an arrest in April 1939. His flight to Moscow, he said, was arranged by the Germans, who sent him there as their agent. After the war, as head of Czechoslovak military intelligence, he continued his treason, now for his new British and American bosses.[40] In all of these cases, the accused went almost automatically from assisting the worst elements of the Nazi regime (concentration camp guards, the Gestapo) to working for their Anglo-American masters. For these men, there was simply no difference between the Nazis and the Americans; spying for one was the exactly the same as spying for the other.[41]

Although trial narratives alluded to the Second World War and its villains as a way of inviting their audiences to envision a return of the violence many of them had already experienced, it was also clear that the next war would be different. After the detonation of atomic bombs over Hiroshima and Nagasaki by the United States in 1945, Europeans had to imagine the consequences of atomic warfare. A "third world war" could easily be, as the Czechoslovak prosecutor, Josef Urválek, declared, "the most barbaric and destructive war in history."[42] After August 1949, both sides in the Cold War had atomic capability (by 1953 both had developed far more destructive thermonuclear bombs), but in trial transcripts it was only Americans and their allies who flirted with the possibility of using such weapons. Mention of atomic weapons served to further demonize the West and emphasize its bellicosity. This was evident in the Romanian trial of Vasile Ciobanu. One of the co-defendants was Nicolae Popescu, the driver for the Papal Nuncio in Bucharest, Patrick O'Hara. Popescu confessed to spying for his employer, who asked him to "carry on intense pro-American propaganda in talks with friends and acquaintances, to praise the destructive power of atomic weapons, etc." Popescu also confessed to ferreting out information about troop movements and military strength to pass on to the Nunciature, which sent it to the Americans.[43]

There was a similar effort to link Americans with the glorification of atomic destruction in the Turner trial in Poland. Irene Findeisen, the former clerk in the US Embassy who served as a witness in the trial, claimed she had attended parties hosted by the American air attaché in Poland, Jessic. At one of these parties, she said, he showed the film *The Atomic Bomb at Bikini*.[44] Findeisen's interest in the film was one of the elements used to cast aspersions on her character. Combined with her background as a member of the landowning class, her employment at the US Embassy, and her friendship with Poles who had fought with the British during the war, this was evidence of her ill will toward the workers' state. In his closing arguments, the prosecutor returned to this aspect of Findeisen's testimony. What was the goal of class enemies like Findeisen, he asked? Nothing but the "restitution of their former wealth by means of a new war of conflagration unleashed by imperialism." And how was this revealed? "Let your memory revert to the film to which Jessic invited Mrs. Findeisen," he told the judges. "Blinded by class hatred with illusory visions of the atom bomb conjured up before their eyes by imperialism, they tumbled into the slime of treason."[45] According to the trial script, Findeisen and others like her thought nothing of using the immense destructive power of atomic weapons to fulfill their selfish goals of ending socialist rule in Poland.

The fear of nuclear war was the emotional high point in the trial of the Czechoslovak opposition politician Milada Horáková in 1950.[46] This was the largest trial of non-Communist opposition figures in Czechoslovakia. Horáková and her co-conspirators were charged with spying for Czechoslovak exiles and attempting to bring about a war that would destroy the socialist state and restore "bourgeois democracy." According to the official narrative, as part of the conspiracy, Horáková and her associates had worked to create a network of supporters within Czechoslovakia to act as a fifth column when war broke out. In the published testimony of the trial, Horáková admitted that her bosses in London would be willing to allow the dismemberment of Czechoslovakia ("a new Munich" in the words of the prosecutor) if this was the price of an alliance with the West. Knowing that Czechoslovaks would resist another partition of their country, "we counted upon war," she said, as the means for realizing their plans. The prosecutor then remarked that any new war would probably be a nuclear war and asked if this was what she had in mind. Horáková demurred, claiming she did not know how the war would be waged. The prosecutor then asked if she had reckoned with the fact that in a war bombs would probably fall upon Prague, the city where her sixteen-year-old daughter lived. Horáková answered that yes, she had.[47]

This exchange was at the center of the Czechoslovak press coverage of the trial. In newspapers and magazines, and on the radio, commentators stressed Horáková's willingness to start a war in which Prague might be laid waste. One article noted that "the trial of the traitors who cold-bloodedly participated in the preparations for war against their own people, is a great lesson showing that there is no neutral territory between the camp of the defenders of peace and the camp of the warmongers."[48] Many claimed that by advocating war Horáková had betrayed not only her country, but her femininity, giving up any hope for mercy on the grounds of womanhood.[49] For Jan Drda, the chair of the Czechoslovak Writers Union, the essence of the Horáková trial was the "calm . . . with which Horáková considered the question of whether she had counted on war and if she had taken into account that our women and children could be murdered." Writing in *Rudé právo*, Drda questioned Horáková's humanity and wondered if it was possible to call such a creature a woman.[50]

Other articles compared her to various Nazi war criminals. This was particularly ironic given that Horáková had been imprisoned and nearly executed by the Nazi regime for her work with the Czech resistance during the war. One such piece, published in the newspaper *Svobodné slovo* (Free word) by a parliamentary representative, Josef Šafařík, asked if there was any difference between Horáková and Ilse Koch, wife of the SS officer in charge of the concentration camps at Buchenwald and Majdanek, who was widely reputed to have made objects out of the skin of murdered prisoners (Šafařík mentioned a toiletries set and book bindings, but most rumors involve lampshades). Horáková was as much of a sadist as Koch, Šafařík insinuated, because she wanted to bring about a change of regime even "at the price of a new global catastrophe."[51] In a similar vein, the Communist writer Jarmila Glazarová said it was unfathomable that Horáková so "cold-bloodedly" and "with earth-shaking bestiality" relied on war to realize her plans when "every normal person knew that the first hammer the Americans would swing at us would be American-equipped SS-men."[52] The press coverage, along with the trial, created a set of self-evident facts about the anti-Communist opposition in Czechoslovakia. They were traitors and sadists who could care less about killing innocent people to achieve their ends; their true models were not democrats, but Nazis. Given this insistent refrain, it was perhaps not surprising that Horáková and three of her co-defendants were sentenced to death and executed a few days after the trial.

Beware the Saboteur

According to Communist officials, socialism was the only path to the good life. Although many East Europeans disagreed with this assessment, such views had no place in the public arena. According to trial narratives, as in all of the popular media, socialism was the road to a glorious future. But this prosperous world of tomorrow was threatened by people who plotted to undermine the socialist economy while it was still in its fragile infancy. These traitors hoped that by wrecking socialism's economic achievements they could turn the people against their government and help to bring about the restoration of capitalist exploitation. One role of the show trials was to make these saboteurs and their ingenious plots come alive.

Economic sabotage was the central focus of many trials. A typical example was the Vogeler trial in Hungary, which concerned a case of purported economic sabotage at the Standard Electric plant (a subsidiary of International Telephone and Telegraph).[53] The Vogeler trial featured an unlikely assortment of conspirators, including Robert Vogeler, an American businessman; his British colleague, Edgar Sanders; several of the Hungarian managers from the Standard Electric plant; a Communist official from the Ministry of Industry, who was revealed to be a British agent and a Trotskyite; a Catholic priest from the landed gentry; and a barmaid at the Hotel Astoria, who had also belonged to the prewar landowning elite (she was occasionally referred to as "Baroness" by the prosecutor).[54] At the trial, the managing director of the Standard Electric plant, Imre Geiger, confessed that he had been ordered by his American superiors to sabotage all of its production. As a member of the bourgeoisie, he claimed to be motivated by his hatred of socialism. His activities supposedly resulted in a laundry list of problems that reads exactly like later analyses of the issues endemic to the centrally planned economy.[55] Under Geiger's direction (and with the complicity of many of his subordinates), the Standard Electric plant hoarded raw materials that could have been productively used elsewhere, produced shoddy goods, and then falsely reported its output. To assist the West in the event of a war, telephone exchanges and transmitters for the Soviet Union, Romania, and Bulgaria were constructed with inferior materials or bad parts, whereas orders for Turkey and Yugoslavia were completed correctly and on time.[56] Geiger also testified that he had "deliberately reduced the productivity of labor" by causing work stoppages and delays. He claimed to have deliberately mismanaged the ordering of parts and tools so that essential machinery was kept out of commission for long stretches, leaving the workers idle and causing essential equipment for the Hungarian post office to be delivered two years late.[57] Geiger's sabotage was considered so ruinous that he was sentenced to death and executed for his crimes.

The plot was very similar in a Romanian trial that spotlighted industrial sabotage, most prominently at the Reşiţa works, formerly owned by the industrialist Max Auschnitt. Auschnitt had fled the country and was being tried in absentia. Auschnitt and his co-defendants had supposedly been given the idea for sabotage by the Americans, who they hoped would help them restore the prewar regime. According to Reşiţa's general manager, Alexandru Popp (who had not been as lucky as his boss and was in the dock), "Sabotage was calculated in every detail, in a diabolical spirit." The conspirators confessed to mismanaging the planning process so that necessary raw materials were never in the right place at the right time, leaving workers with nothing to do. They failed to assign the personnel to unload transport trains, leaving them unattended for weeks while their contents were needed elsewhere, and kept machinery in ill repair, so that it was ready for the trash heap after only half a year's use. The foundry was such a mess it could not function properly, and explosive projectiles were mistakenly thrown in with metal being smelted, blowing up the furnaces. The result was "delayed production, chaos and disorder" that rippled through Romanian industries dependent on Reşiţa for raw materials or finished goods. The sabotage even supposedly extended into the workers' food supply. Factory catering offices first paid exorbitant prices for the food to subvert government price controls. Then they neglected to distribute it to the workers until it had spoiled. The defendants delayed the workers' pay, increasing their dissatisfaction with the regime.[58]

This idea that failures in the new planned economy were due to sabotage and not the regime's own mistakes appeared in the trials of Communist figures as well, especially the trial of Traïcho Kostov. Ironically, since Kostov had first displeased Stalin by arguing that Bulgaria needed better terms in a trade pact with the Soviet Union, Kostov was charged with trying to engineer Bulgaria's economic ruin. Unlike other accused Communist leaders, Kostov suddenly recanted his planned testimony on the day of his trial and declared his innocence. Unprepared for such an eventuality, prosecutors speedily declared that his earlier sworn depositions could stand in for live testimony and simply read them out in court.[59] In the prepared depositions, Kostov had confessed to placing an extensive network of agents in positions where they could have a devastating effect on the economy; among these were the former minister of finance (Ivan Stefanov), the minister of electrification (Manol Sakelarov), and a top economic adviser (Nikola Nachev Pavlov).

With the help of these men, Kostov claimed to have strangled Bulgarian industry. He allowed capitalist business owners to keep their enterprises or to strip them of assets before they were confiscated, stopped construction on several dams and power plants, and wasted extensive resources building a completely unnecessary tunnel at the Topolitsa dam. He also claimed that he and Nachev had dreamed up harsh policies on grain and wool requisition from peasant proprietors specifically to cause discontent with the socialist regime. According to Nachev's testimony, this "stifled the initiative of peasant producers, in consequence of which a cruel quota system was created . . . as a result of which the food supply of the large working centers was impeded and dissatisfaction was created in the towns as well as in the villages."[60] In a similar vein, in his own testimony, Stefanov claimed to have ruined the state-owned tobacco industry and wrecked Bulgaria's financial system. He also took responsibility for instituting personal income tax policies designed to cause discontent among the working people.[61]

These tales of sabotage were meant to explain the economic failures of the early state-socialist period and to justify the need for workers to pull Saturday shifts or adopt the quota system, with its ever-increasing norms (both widely despised throughout the region).[62] With vigilance and hard work, the saboteurs would be caught, new industries would be built, and prosperity would come to the working class. But there was a tension in the way that trial narratives told this story. On the one hand, the fact that the conspirators had been caught emphasized the power of the state and its citizens, who had foiled the nefarious plans of the imperialists. But the scope and deviousness of the plots, and the fact that the accused had sometimes supposedly carried out their sabotage for years and caused significant economic damage, might also make it seem as if the socialist camp was powerless in the face of imperialist deception. Although the particular group of conspirators on trial had been caught, who was to say how many others lurked in the shadows? Indeed, the fact that prosecutors often implied there were other saboteurs just waiting for their opportunity to strike could breed feelings of powerlessness rather than strength and vigilance.

True Confessions

It has long been established that the fantastic conspiracies uncovered by these political trials were fabrications. But for the trials to perform their political and pedagogical function, these fantasies had to be accepted as the truth. The first step in creating this acceptance was to convince the accused to confess their guilt. Their public confessions were symbols of submission, acknowledging the power of the party to mandate what was real and what was true. The path to confession typically involved a complicated process of psychological pressure and physical torture. Local interrogators and their Soviet advisers presumed a prisoner's guilt and worked to redefine his or her past actions to fit that presumption. Gradually, the prisoners were convinced to accept this reworking of their past and agreed to play their parts in the public trial. In most cases, they said their lines faithfully. With their confessions, the accused turned the stories told at the trials into reality.

During the trials, guilt was something that interrogators "established" by redefining previously unremarkable moments in prisoners' lives as evidence of their guilt. Interrogators pressed them to admit that their previous actions were crimes. Béla Szász was an official in the Hungarian Ministry of Foreign Affairs before he was arrested in conjunction with the Rajk trial. Szász had spent the war in Argentina, and this contributed to the suspicion against him. During his interrogations, his ÁVH (Államvédelmi Hatóság, or Hungarian state security) interrogator, László Farkas, worked hard to convince him that his wartime conversations with British or American citizens in Buenos Aires were "essentially" espionage. Farkas's logic went as follows: it was possible that some of the people Szász worked with were agents of some kind, whether or not Szász knew it. The fact that these people *could* have been spies was, said Farkas, "essentially" the same as if they actually were spies. Szász admitted that he openly discussed the affairs of the Hungarian movement in exile with them. Hence, Szász willingly gave information to spies, and therefore he was "essentially" a spy and a traitor himself. Whether or not he had intended to commit espionage or had actually revealed any classified information was insignificant. For Farkas, these were simply details that could be filled in later. The real proof of his criminality was the mere fact of his contact with Westerners, who could, essentially, all be spies. This was the real truth of the West, and Szász needed to bow to that truth.[63]

Czechoslovak interrogators put things in a similar fashion. Artur London had also spent the war abroad, first working with the French Resistance and then as a prisoner in a German concentration camp. After his return to Prague, he served as deputy minister of foreign affairs until he was arrested in 1951. He would eventually be one of the three defendants in the Slánský trial to walk away with his life. London's interrogators told him that it didn't matter if he did not know that Noel Field, who had helped him receive treatment for tuberculosis after the war, was a spy. Nor did it matter that his conversations with him were innocuous. Field was a spy and London had known him. Because he had contact with a spy, London was "objectively" guilty of espionage. The "subjective" aspect of London's guilt was not immaterial for his interrogators, but they thought it could be filled in more easily later, once he had admitted to the objective outlines of his treason.[64]

Detainees were initially kept in isolation; when out of their cells, they were blindfolded so that their only human contact was with guards or interrogators. They were interrogated for hours or even days at a time, often at night, without food or rest. The interrogations usually consisted of minute probing into the contents of their lives. Interrogators would insist that ordinary events, like having lunch with foreign acquaintances or carrying out the government's policies, were really criminal acts: what had been trivial actions were transformed into contacts with American intelligence agents or economic sabotage. If prisoners refused to sign protocols to this effect, the interrogations would continue, on and on over the same question, with the interrogators insisting that their interpretation of events was correct. When not being interrogated, recalcitrant detainees were deprived of sleep at night and forced to stand or walk incessantly in their cells for sixteen hours a day until their feet had swollen like balloons. They were kept in tiny cold cells with no blankets, warm clothes, reading material, or cigarettes and given only enough food to survive. Those who tried to disobey orders to stand or walk were taken to dank cellars or even smaller bare cells without beds where the floor was so cold it was preferable to walk rather than sit on it.[65] Some were savagely beaten. In Hungarian prisons, striking the soles of the feet, the hands, and the back directly above the kidneys with a rubber truncheon was a preferred way to cause pain while leaving no marks.[66] Most did eventually confess.

For many observers outside the region, these confessions represented a betrayal or annihilation of the self. Arthur Koestler's influential novel *Darkness at Noon* provided a blueprint for how Western anti-Communists would interpret confessions.[67] In the novel, the main character, Rubashov, is eventually persuaded, by a combination of sleep deprivation and argument, to abnegate his true self and confess for the good of the party. In the aftermath of his confession, Rubashov becomes even more convinced that it is really the individual—and not the collective—that is sacred, but he nonetheless sacrifices himself for socialism.[68] Educated by Koestler, the American media portrayed show trial confessions in Eastern Europe as the inevitable result of totalitarian ideology, which reduced individuals to automatons blindly serving a collective.

In the case of László Rajk, newspaper coverage emphasized how "avidly," "eagerly," and "fluently" Rajk confessed to espionage and treason, "piling confession on confession," even as the Western diplomats and officials he accused of being his co-conspirators steadfastly denied their involvement.[69] The only way of explaining such behavior was that Rajk had lost every shred of his individuality, becoming no more than a vessel to be filled with whatever the party wanted. According to a *New York Times* editorial, the Rajk trial was "peculiarly horrifying" because it showed "the breakdown of the mind and free will of human beings to whom were given the right when born at least to be themselves and not automata." The editorial implied that this was the inevitable fate of all those who lived under Communism, noting "such is life behind the Iron Curtain in this twisted century," and urged Americans to study how Communists broke down individuals so that they could defend themselves against these tactics.[70]

Another *New York Times* editorial published during the trial of Milada Horáková about six months later elaborated on this theme, suggesting that the goal of Communism was to transform individuals into chastened "stooges" blindly executing the will of Moscow. The Czechoslovak Communists, it alleged, hoped to transform the originally "Western European" Czechs into "Eastern Europeans of the Stalinist type."[71] In similar fashion, John MacCormac, reporting on the Slánský trial for the *New York Times*, set up a clear dichotomy between the "Western" and the "Communist" mind. "Western minds" could simply not comprehend how Communists like Slánský could willingly sacrifice their very souls for the party.[72]

In the case of Eastern Europe, the tendency of most historians has been to read the experiences of those who faced interrogations during the Stalinist period in this way.[73] Some Soviet historians, however, have challenged this interpretation. They argue that the liberal notion of the self as articulated by Koestler or in the *New York Times* editorials simply does not fit the experience of many Soviet Communists during the purges of the 1930s. In Koestler's novel, Rubashov goes through an extended process of introspection in prison that leads to his ultimate betrayal of what he has finally realized is his true self. In contrast, the historian Jochen Hellbeck has argued that we should not necessarily see the confessions of Soviet Communists as capitulations. In his analysis of the prison writings of Nikolai Bukharin, the executed Soviet theoretician who helped inspire the character of Rubashov, Hellbeck claims that Bukharin did not confess because his personality was destroyed or erased, either by torture or by his own submission to party discipline.[74] Instead, his confession was part of a personal attempt to reconcile his subjective self with the objective force of history.[75] According to Hellbeck, Bukharin saw himself, even in prison, as engaged in a process of revolutionary self-transformation that was not meant to annihilate his personality, but to place it in tandem with the forward motion of history. Bukharin's experience cannot be considered universal, even for the 1930s Soviet Union, and postwar Eastern Europe cannot be equated with the USSR, despite the presence of Soviet advisers and interrogators in the region. We should admit the possibility, however, that an East European defendant's experience of confession might not match the Western view of it.[76]

American media coverage of East European show trials tended to take it for granted that the listening audience would hear defendants' confessions only as lies.[77] But just as we cannot be sure that the experience of confession adhered to paradigms developed outside the region, we cannot rule out the possibility that confessions made in the courtroom had the ring of truth for some domestic audiences. As some remembered it later, the sight or sound of the accused admitting their guilt made even the fantastic stories they told seem plausible. It was hard to imagine how anyone would willingly confess to crimes he or she had not committed. Even some relatives of the accused claimed they began to believe in the guilt of their loved ones when they heard their voices in the courtroom confessing to treason.[78] But even if a listener did not accept that a defendant had actually committed the acts to which he or she confessed, the reality of the confession itself had meaning. The public act of confession was the physical sign of the party's power to shape the world in which it operated and to create the truth it desired. Whether or not that truth was believable was secondary to the fact that it was obeyed.

With Us or Against Us

It was a tiny minority of the imprisoned who were given a public role in a show trial. Trial audiences, however, also had a part to play. Passive listening was not enough; state and party officials asked ordinary Eastern Europeans to indicate their acceptance of the proceedings by condemning the traitors and their imperialist masters. They would repeat the lessons of the trials in their own words and indicate their own emotional response to what they had seen. This participation could take a variety of forms. While a trial was in progress, local audiences attended meetings and demonstrations where they expressed their disgust for and hatred of the conspirators. They accepted extra work shifts to make up for the traitors' sabotage. And they signed resolutions declaring the intensity of their hatred and demanding the strictest punishments for the accused. More than ten thousand resolutions poured into the prosecutor's office in Prague during the Slánský trial demanding death for the defendants.[79] In Hungary during the Rajk trial, people attended "blitz meetings" at their workplaces dedicated to attacking the conspirators and expressing disgust at their crimes. Thousands acted like the telephone factory worker who declared at a workplace meeting that Rajk and his gang should receive the "burning hatred of all mothers."[80]

The propaganda campaign around the trial of Milada Horáková was a typical example of how bystanders were urged to become participants in the drama of a trial. As the largest trial of the anti-Communist opposition in Czechoslovakia, the Horáková trial was intended to show the impossibility of further political opposition to the Communist regime. A vociferous public reaction against the accused was one way of sending this message. During the trial, the KSČ organized an extensive campaign to inform and involve the masses in the case. The goal, in the words of the Ostrava district KSČ office, was to "increase vigilance and watchfulness and to awaken a pogrom-like (*pogromistickou*) mood towards the all of the enemies of the Republic and their sponsors, the Anglo-American warmongers."[81] To create this mood, which would have people screaming for the blood of the traitors, walls were covered with newspaper articles and posters. There was saturation radio coverage, with broadcasts aired in workplaces, pubs, train stations, schools, and other public spaces. Thousands of protest meetings were organized by local KSČ cadres in villages, factories, and other locations to "reveal the disgusting face of the traitors."[82] Their participants sent more than 6,300 group resolutions condemning the accused and demanding they receive the death penalty. The resolutions also often promised that their signatories would make up for the sabotage of the accused by accepting higher work norms (daily production targets).[83] Some people were so incensed by the trial's sensational revelations of evil that they wrote personal letters to the prosecutors, judges, or officials like the president of Czechoslovakia, Klement Gottwald, to demand the execution of the traitors.[84]

The thousands of resolutions sent to the prosecutors were not simply copies of the same text put out for public approval. They reflected the media coverage of the trial and sometimes used stock phrases from that coverage, but still retained their own voices. In their joint resolution, the female workers of the Tanvald cotton-spinning factory declared that they could not actually consider the three women on trial to be women, "because they could not have carried out the kinds of things they have done if they loved their children even a little." Because the accused did "not belong to today's human society," the cotton spinners said, they should be punished severely.[85] The members of the district committee of the Sokol gymnastics association in the town of České Budějovice also had their own take on the trial's lessons. Like many others, they demanded the strictest punishment for the accused, but added that they promised to "raise the political standard . . . and the physical fitness of the entire Sokol membership and to ensure the highest vigilance and defense capability."[86]

Resolutions from state and party offices tended to more closely follow the language of the newspapers, as in a resolution from the National Committee (city government) of Pardubice, which carefully listed all of the accused and demanded their deaths. But while they followed the lines of the press coverage, they did not simply duplicate its phrases. The resolution concluded, "We residents of Pardubice don't want to live through the terrible air raids of the Second World War again and we demand that the State Court consider the great guilt of the wreckers and issue a just, but strict, verdict."[87] The Administrative Committee of the Czechoslovak Astronomy Society had a different take on the proceedings. Its resolution asserted that the accused had forfeited their membership in the nation, writing that "their true homeland (*vlast*) was the capitalist world, their true friends were the imperialists who wanted to sell out our people and surrender them again to all the nightmares of crisis, unemployment and war. Such people do not deserve compassion!" Strikingly, this letter was signed by Luisa Landová-Štychová, a KSČ parliamentary deputy from the 1920s and prominent feminist activist, who had likely worked with Horáková on feminist causes during the interwar period.[88]

Signing a resolution does not necessarily indicate a belief in its contents. But, whatever they thought about the trial, most Czechoslovaks publicly accepted its narrative and joined in the call to punish the traitors. By participating in these rituals and displaying the requisite anger and hatred, they enacted their roles as good Communist citizens.[89] Viktor Heller, former officer of the national Sokol organization and employee of the state insurance company in Prague, remembered a meeting that had been convened at his workplace to condemn the traitors. A resolution demanding death for the "viper Horáková" was read out, and the man leading the meeting called on all those who agreed to raise their hands. A sea of hands went up into the air. The meeting leader then, Heller said, sarcastically asked if anyone was "perhaps" against the resolution. Heller slowly raised his hand. He was the only one to do so. The meeting leader, he remembered, looked at him with horror and then pointed right at him and exclaimed, "One traitorous voice!" This incident shows the potential consequences of noncompliance, but it also perhaps demonstrates even more eloquently how rare such public manifestations of support for Horáková and her co-defendants were. In Heller's recollection, all the other employees appeared shocked when he raised his hand at the wrong time; they looked, he said, "with alarm" in the direction of the meeting leader's outstretched finger.[90] Whatever they may have thought about Horáková's guilt, they publicly accepted the regime's right to construct the truth about her by joining its condemnation of the traitors.

The imperative to accept a trial's truth was also apparent in the ways that the wives and families of the accused were often treated by others, even when no one was watching. Heda Margolius Kovaly, wife of one of the defendants in the Slánský trial, had already experienced what it was like to be shunned by her neighbors when she returned to Prague in 1945 after escaping from one of the Auschwitz death marches. After her husband, Rudolf, was arrested in 1951, Kovaly became a self-described leper all over again. Friends crossed the street to avoid speaking to her, she lost her job at a publishing house, and most of her belongings were confiscated. During the trial itself, Kovaly was lying in a hospital bed suffering from numerous ailments caused by stress, malnutrition, cold, and overwork. Along with her fellow patients, she saw the transcripts of the trial as they appeared in the newspaper and heard the radio broadcasts of her husband's confession, feeling all the while that the hospital, and the country as a whole, were "simmering with hatred." The hospital staff, like employees at workplaces throughout Czechoslovakia, gathered to condemn the traitors and demand their death. They also demanded that the traitor's wife be immediately expelled from their institution. Despite her serious condition, Kovaly was released and forced to make her own way home.[91]

All of the women married to defendants in the Slánský trial had similar experiences, and several of them spent time in prison themselves. Lise London, wife of Artur London, was forced out of her job as director of the French division at Czech Radio after her husband's arrest. The official who informed her she would have to leave expressed his sympathy and even gave her a large sum of money so that she could feed her children and elderly parents while she looked for another job. Tellingly, however, he told her to make sure no one found out; even her husband's memoir, written in France more than a decade later, does not mention him by name. Through the intervention of a sympathetic manager, London managed to find work at a factory that repaired car and airplane engines, but after the trial (it was played on the loudspeakers at her workplace) the factory committee demanded she be fired, along with another worker known to be her friend and the manager who had hired her.[92] Josefa Slánská, wife of Rudolf Slánský, was interned for the duration of her husband's imprisonment and not allowed to return to Prague until years after his execution. Even then, many people refused to renew their acquaintance with her. They had reason: in her absence, some of her acquaintances had been punished for their association with her. The doctor who had delivered her daughter four years before the trial, also a friend, lost her job and was expelled from the party.[93]

Many individuals were required to show their loyalty personally by denouncing colleagues who had been arrested. When the Czechoslovak party chief, Klement Gottwald, informed the presidium of the Central Committee that Rudolf Slánský had been imprisoned, no one dared to defend their colleague. Men who had known Slánský for years, and whom he considered to be friends, accepted the idea of his guilt and opined that they had known there was something wrong about him.[94] In prison, detainees were often shown copies of the denunciations of their friends and co-workers during their interrogations in the hope that this would convince them to confess.[95] For those called in to give potentially damaging evidence against others, the choice was clear. Those who refused to accept the guilt of people the regime had labeled traitors immediately came under suspicion themselves.

George Paloczi-Horvath was an idealistic Communist writer and journalist when he was arrested as part of the massive search for spies that occurred in Hungary in the wake of the Rajk trial. After he was released in 1954, he received a letter from an old acquaintance who wanted him to know that when called to party headquarters he had "told them all the slanders they wanted to hear about you." As the man explained, he did not know what would happen to his crippled wife if he went to jail, so he did what was asked of him.[96] The vast majority of those in show trial audiences did not face such a personal and wrenching choice. But they were similarly expected to accept trial narratives as the truth and act accordingly. Some may have been suspicious of the way each defendant's testimony merged seamlessly into the next or surprised that all had confessed despite the lack of any real evidence against them, but they did not voice such doubts and signed resolutions condemning the traitors instead. This was how, regardless of their inaccuracy, show trials came to embody a truth all their own.

The Boundaries of Belief

The resolutions sent to prosecutors during the Horáková trial are full of hate and fear. They excoriate the accused as heinous traitors and feverishly promise to help ferret out any other spies that might be lurking in the shadows. The very existence of these documents shows that the trial was successful. When called upon to accept the trial as the truth, most people responded affirmatively, acknowledging the state's ability to set the boundaries of knowledge. But did they really believe these fantastic stories? It is generally difficult for historians to determine with any certainty whether or not people believed things that contradict their public statements, especially on a mass scale. Given the lack of evidence, such conclusions themselves often come down to a matter of faith. In the case of show trials, it is certainly possible to find anecdotal evidence that supports both sides. Memoirs from former Communists tend to include examples of people who believed everything, whereas memoirs from anti-Communists deny that anyone could have believed such a show.[97]

Instead of considering belief as an either-or proposition, it may be more productive to think of it as falling on a spectrum and consider reactions to a trial as representing a range of responses.[98] A close examination of the reaction to one particular show trial, that of Rudolf Slánský, reveals that the trial was often compelling to listeners, for a wide variety of reasons. It held people's attention and awakened a variety of emotional reactions. These responses often did not hinge on the question of belief. Many simply began from the presumption of guilt and proceeded from there. While each trial had its own local dynamics and the response to the Slánský trial cannot be generalized to every case, this example is also illustrative of the range of responses to show trials.

The Czechoslovak security services (Státní bezpečnosti, or StB) were tasked with reporting on the response to the trial among the population at large. To determine this, they compiled reports from agents and informers, often listing the comments of individuals by name. The response to the trial was also investigated by the KSČ. Information bulletins prepared for top party leaders included data from StB informants combined with reactions recorded in letters sent by party members to the Central Committee. Reports from local party instructors to their superiors also discussed reactions to the trial. These kinds of sources do not necessarily tell us what individuals believed in their innermost hearts. But they do tell us what they said, either at party meetings or within the earshot of an StB informer, and they can also tell us what people did in response to what they were hearing about the trial.

According to StB reports, some portions of the population were openly skeptical about the trial. They said it was a sham, with the accused, as if drugged, simply reading out testimony that had been written for them in advance.[99] The StB claimed "reactionaries" made most of these comments, but they recorded similar reactions by some workers and KSČ members. One example noted that "some employees of the district court in Karlovo náměstí [Charles Square]" were whispering that the accused must have been given injections of some kind. Anyone else on trial, they said, "shows uncertainty, stammers, denies [things], etc., whereas these criminals speak as if they were at a podium."[100] Another report from the Prague regional StB office mentioned the Hotel Paris. The "bourgeois" clientele who came into the hotel during the trial supposedly said, "People, listen, this court is a complete charade, the accused are answering as if they are reciting for the class. It isn't possible that they are confessing so voluntarily."[101]

However, the same sources make it clear that many people proceeded from the assumption that the trial's allegations were valid. Both StB reports and documents from regional and national party officials emphasize the large number of people who claimed to take the testimony at face value, whether or not this reflected their "real" beliefs. Internally, party officials reported that, as of December 12, 1952 (shortly after the end of the trial), 8,520 workplace resolutions and individual letters had poured into the Central Committee demanding the deaths of the traitors.[102] Many also spontaneously wrote letters to party officials about the need to search for more traitors; some were anonymous, others were signed. Some of these letters denounced specific people their authors suspected of being traitors. One man, for example, was convinced that a party of Slovak Jews he had seen at a spa in 1951 must have been involved with Slánský. Another denounced a Jewish KSČ official for denying him membership. Others claimed people they knew had collaborated with the Germans during the war.[103]

People may have denounced others as spies or written warnings about more traitors for a wide variety of reasons: they may have been afraid of more plots and conspiracies to overthrow the regime, they may have thought this would divert suspicion from themselves, they may have hoped to settle a personal grudge, or they may have simply wanted to seem like good citizens and conform to regime expectations. No matter the reason behind them, these kinds of responses all preceded from an acceptance of the trial's basic premise: the accused were guilty. Whether or not these individuals believed that was the case, their letters took guilt as a given and offered information or made demands based on assumption.

Although many of the reactions people had to the trial indicated they accepted the premise that there were spies on the loose, this did not mean, however, that their reactions were welcomed by the Czechoslovak Communist regime. Some openly used the trial as a way of expressing resentment and indignation toward the KSČ. Many workers and KSČ members were recorded by the StB or party instructors saying they were angry and appalled that such a massive conspiracy had existed within the party for so long. Taking the trial as reflecting actual events, they wondered how the party's top brass, including party chief and state president Klement Gottwald, could not have known what was going on right under their noses. They had to be either incompetent or traitors themselves. How could the workers trust the leadership if this was the case?[104]

Reports from workplace KSČ meetings in Prague are riddled with confusion, anger, and resentment at top officials. Party members in the district of Prague 4 demanded a complete reorganization of the Central Committee and suggested that Gottwald himself perform self-criticism.[105] Functionaries at the enterprise Auto-Praga railed against the luxurious lifestyles of upper-level party officials and declared that Central Committee members should be open to criticism, despite doctrines of democratic centralism.[106] Others were furious that Central Committee members had allowed enormous economic sabotage to go on right under their noses while the workers had been working themselves to the bone to make their quotas.[107] These are just a few of the many recorded instances of indignation, disgust, and disillusionment in the wake of the trial. Such reactions took Slánský's guilt as a given and accepted the need to protect the country from its enemies.[108] They also show that some people who accepted the trial's basic premise did not simply parrot the prosecutors or the newspapers, but invested the case with their own meaning. Trial planners might have hoped the testimony would ultimately inspire more faith in the KSČ leadership, but they could not control the emotional responses of listeners. When they heard about the extensive damage to their country that the fiendish Slánský band had supposedly caused, many felt that the trial had made their leaders look weak rather than heroic. The trial made them angry because it revealed the powerlessness of all Czechoslovaks in this new Cold War environment. KSČ leaders were presumably powerless to stop the sabotage, and the workers also felt disempowered, because they had no control over the results of their labor.

The Slánský trial stood out from other show trials for its overt antisemitism. For many Czechoslovaks, this proved to be the most resonant aspect of the trial; antisemitic comments fill the reports on the public response to the Slánský case.[109] The idea of a dangerous conspiracy of highly placed spies in the pay of foreign powers that existed secretly for decades and supposedly posed a serious threat to the survival of the nation dovetailed with widely held attitudes about Jews as potentially dangerous aliens. For example, one StB report quoted a retired KSČ member from the Liberec region, who said, "A person's reason stops when listening to the main proceedings, but with Slánský anything is possible, because he's a Jew. I spent some years in Slovakia where I had the chance to recognize the behavior of Jews who wormed their way into the party and distorted the correct political line."[110] For this man, the incredible charges raised in the trial became much more plausible if one considered that the culprits were Jews, who were by nature devious and untrustworthy.

His comments were echoed by many others, who said the trial confirmed what they already knew about Jews. In a telling example, the regional Prague StB office reported that Roman Catholic priests said that while it could not be true that Slánský and his band worked for the Americans, it was possible that they had been Israeli agents who wanted to take over the Czechoslovak Republic and "create a Jewish order here, as it was said they had in the Soviet Union, where Jews rule."[111] The charge that Slánský worked for the Americans did not fit the priests' preconceptions, but they could readily envision Jews as traitors to the Czechoslovak nation, just as they imagined that Jews dominated Communist parties and had the real power in Communist governments.

Antisemitic comments were recorded throughout the population, regardless of class or political affiliation. The StB noted that, in its perusal of domestic mail, a majority of the 6,776 letters it opened from November 20 through November 24, 1952, contained anti-Jewish sentiments.[112] Both StB agents and KSČ party instructors frequently included overheard antisemitic remarks in their reports, some of them quite violent.[113] Some local party cells passed resolutions demanding that all Jews be expelled from the party, their property confiscated, and their jobs taken away.[114] Some StB reports claimed that those outside the KSČ were more vicious in their antisemitism, tending to look approvingly back to Hitler's genocidal policies.[115] There is no compelling evidence to back up this assertion, which may simply have come from the authors' own tendency to see "reactionaries" as Nazi sympathizers. What is clear, however, is that a substantial number of both KSČ members and their non-Communist compatriots found the idea of Jewish spies and traitors compelling, and this could have enabled them to find the whole trial scenario more plausible.[116] A report about the response to the trial in a savings bank on Wenceslas Square in Prague noted that both KSČ members and other employees did not trust Jews because "it is a world Jewish conspiracy, they want to get into the Communist parties of all countries." The report then clarified that this distrust of Jews was not racist, but stemmed from fears of class enemies.[117]

Though Czechoslovaks may not have been afraid of foreign spies and saboteurs, many publicly accepted the idea of their existence. They urged each other to unmask the traitors and wrote letters denouncing those they claimed might be spies. In the Slánský trial, the perception of danger was compounded by the Jewish roots of many of the defendants. Jews, believed to be alien to the nation, were likely spies and traitors.

Lessons from the Courtroom

Those who have studied show trials have been concerned mostly with how they were staged and what compelled their participants to lie. Yet the historical importance of show trials goes beyond what happened in the courtrooms. When defendants confessed to crimes they had not committed, their testimonies revealed larger truths about the nature of the Cold War and the relationship between East and West. Show trials taught their audiences that any pretense of amity from the West was only a mask: the forces of capitalist-imperialism were their enemy. Whether or not they believed what the defendants said was true, East European audiences were pushed to incorporate this new knowledge about the West into their own lives, joining the hunt for more spies and saboteurs and condemning those who had already been captured. In this way, show trials—regardless of their factual accuracy—shaped reality in early Cold War Eastern Europe.

Show trials compelled emotion as well as action. They aimed to awaken fears of Western imperialism by telling tales of devious and daring traitors who thought nothing about unleashing atomic bombs to achieve their nefarious ends. But this fear was supposed to energize, not paralyze, the population. After all, the defendants in these trials, however clever they might have been, had been caught. Their confessions were supposed to show the power of Communist regimes, inspiring vigilance and renewed vigor. The reaction to the Slánský trial, however, revealed an unexpected and troubling trend. Rather than seeing this trial as evidence of Communist strength, some workers wondered how their leaders could have allowed the traitors to do so much damage before they were captured. They felt angry and betrayed, upset that their hard work to build socialism had been rendered void by events that seemed completely outside their control. The trial had aroused their emotions, but not in the ways its architects had anticipated.

2 THE FIGHT FOR PEACE

At the November 1949 meeting of the Cominform in Hungary, a Soviet Central Committee member, Mikhail Suslov, gave a speech denouncing the United States and its allies as imperialist warmongers. The Americans, he said, aspired to achieve hegemony over the entire world and were willing to use war to this end. They had already devised the Marshall Plan to colonize Western Europe. Soon, they hoped to re-arm the fascist nations of Germany and Japan and use their populations as cannon fodder in a war to serve the "covetous aims of a handful of billionaires."[1] They hid their evil intentions, Suslov declared, behind a sophisticated wall of propaganda, "doping the masses by the frenzied preaching of race fanaticism and hate propaganda, and by fostering atomic psychosis and war hysteria. Every medium and psychological influence—the press, literature, radio, cinema, the church—has been brought into action."[2] By these means, the United States tried to convince the world's masses that the Soviet Union and its allies were their real enemies. They hoped to get the people of the world to agree to their own exploitation by convincing them that the only way to avoid destruction at Communist hands was to accept American rule and American values.

The socialist camp, declared Suslov, must fight back against this imperialist assault by embracing the cause of peace. Communist parties all over the world would launch a "peace offensive" to reveal the true character of the warmongering West. The battle for peace that Suslov proposed proved to be an elastic concept that could encompass a wide variety of policies and campaigns in individual countries. But at its heart it was a battle over definitions. For Communist peace activists, the West was defined by its imperialist greed, its close ties to fascism, its pernicious racism, and its terrible war crimes. The peace offensive's first task was to spread this view of the West. Although it would also dispute Western images of Communism and illustrate the ways that socialism supported peace and global well-being, the peace movement concentrated on demonizing the West as the force that threatened the world with another world war. In speeches, publications, and demonstrations, East European peace organizations tried to awaken feelings of anger, fear, and revulsion toward the imperialist camp.

Like the show trials, the peace campaign was meant to be a vehicle for mass mobilization against the evils of the West. But unlike them, the peace campaign was part of a movement that extended beyond the Soviet Bloc. This global peace movement was centered around the World Peace Council (WPC), which had its origins in the World Congress of Intellectuals held in Wrocław, Poland, in 1948. With national committees and local organizations in more than seventy countries by 1950, the WPC was the largest peace organization in the world.[3] It was not formally tied to the Cominform or any Communist party, but it was nevertheless widely considered in the West to be a Communist front organization.[4] Many historians, including the leading historian of the nuclear disarmament movement, Lawrence S. Wittner, have also treated it this way.[5] The same is true of the Women's International Democratic Federation (WIDF), a global federation of nationally based women's groups that was also very active in the peace campaigns of the 1950s. Many in the West refused to recognize that participants in these organizations could be authentically devoted to peace (or, in the case of WIDF, feminism). Recently, some historians have challenged these views as the relics of Western Cold War biases that rejected any form of leftist activism as mere Soviet propaganda.[6]

Although individual participants had a variety of motives for working with these organizations, the WPC and WIDF nonetheless served as international stages on which Soviet Communists and their East European allies could present their version of the truth to global and domestic audiences.[7] After the November 1949 meeting of the Cominform launched the "peace offensive," the WPC and WIDF became the most prominent vehicles for Communist peace activism. Before 1956, the Soviet Union and its East European allies tended to form a united front within both organizations, speaking the same language and making the same ideological claims. Thus, some of the participants at international WPC conferences may have presented different views, but the WPC also provided a home for Communist peace activists from around the world who used the same vocabulary (despite speaking different languages) and relied on a consistent set of beliefs and assumptions. The content of WPC speeches, resolutions, and other publications reached East European audiences through local media coverage of WPC events, as well as through the activities of local peace campaigns, which took their ideological direction and inspiration from the council.[8] Through the WPC, Communists from Eastern Europe were able to define a set of truths that outlined how they expected their citizens to interpret the world and their place within it.[9] The point of these truths was not factual accuracy, but the elaboration of a more essential series of ideas that, in the minds of their creators, superseded any individual fact.

Like the show trials, the peace campaign highlighted the complicated relationship between truth and fear in the Soviet Bloc. Both presented their audiences with a unitary way of seeing and being in the world, one that depended on fear in multiple ways. The Manichaean worldview that leaders on both sides of the Iron Curtain accepted as the reality of the Cold War offered the masses few alternatives to fear. On the one hand, by presenting the socialist camp as beset by enemies who plotted its destruction and had atomic weapons at their disposal, the peace campaign encouraged East Europeans to see the world as a fearful place. A world in which murderous Western leaders thought nothing of slaughtering innocents in pursuit of their own enrichment was a scary world. But to refuse this picture also meant courting danger. By positing their ideas as a series of essential truths, Communist peace activists required their listeners to accept them or be labeled enemies. As the show trials made clear, enemies of the state would be dealt with harshly.

Inside the countries of the Soviet Bloc, peace activities were aligned with a variety of government and Communist party institutions and organizations. The rhetoric of the peace campaign was ubiquitous; it was represented in posters on factory walls, in newspaper articles, on radio programs, and in the speeches of officials on all levels, from the workplace to the highest reaches of government.[10] Existing organizations, particularly women's organizations, were tasked with working for peace and making sure that the population was vigorous in its support of the peace campaign. As in the case of the show trials, participation in the peace campaign can be hard to categorize. It is difficult to know whether individuals found the messages of the campaign emotionally resonant and compelling. But it is clear that a substantial majority of people did indeed participate in peace activities, signing petitions and attending peace demonstrations. Whether or not they agreed with its ideological foundation, in public, most East Europeans accepted their role in the fight for peace.

Hyenas and Jackals

In August 1948, the World Congress of Intellectuals was held in Wrocław, Poland.[11] Organized by a joint Polish–French committee, the congress was ostensibly held to address the rapidly growing gulf between East and West. Invitations were issued to 500 scholars, writers, and artists from around the world, with all expenses to be paid by the Polish government.[12] About 450 of the invitees accepted: most were left-leaning; many were Communists or sympathetic to the Communist cause, but not all fit that description.[13] Before the conference, organizers emphasized that the congress was intended to build bridges between scholars in the name of peace. In a letter written to the organizing committee in July, Albert Einstein (who did not attend) praised their efforts: "I have noted with great interest that the congress is to discuss the promotion of a true and genuine peace." Einstein urged the committee to maintain its goal of dialogue and nonpartisanship, writing, "We must have the courage to discuss problems of great actuality without losing ourselves in the petty political controversies of everyday life."[14]

Contrary to Einstein's hopes, the Wrocław World Congress would do more to accentuate and deepen Cold War divisions than to bridge them.[15] Disagreements arose even before the congress began. In an article published a week before the opening session, the *New York Times* reporter Sydney Gruson wrote that the advance press for the congress in Poland suggested that "officially at least it is hoped to make the gathering another sounding board for support of the Soviet Union's policies against the United States and Britain." Gruson quoted the official invitation, which described organizers as people dedicated to achieving peace "despite the incitement to a new war."[16] In response, the Polish organizing committee refused to grant Gruson the credentials to attend the event. The chair, Major Jerzy Borejzsa, said it was clear from his article that Gruson had already decided how the congress would unfold and therefore he did not need to be there. He might as well compose his dispatches about it remotely from Warsaw (he did).[17]

The congress opened on August 25, 1948. After a few brief welcoming remarks, Alexander Fadeyev, a novelist and the head of the Soviet Writers Union, took the rostrum to give the first formal speech. Fadeyev proceeded to deliver a blistering attack on the United States as the greatest enemy to peace.[18] After the Second World War, Fadeyev declared, the world had become inextricably divided into two opposing camps: a socialist camp of peace, progress, democracy, and antifascism and a camp of militarist, reactionary, capitalist imperialists led by the United States. In the mode of Hitler's Germany, American "monopolists" were driving the world toward war, hoping to destroy progressive socialist forces and consolidate their power.

Given that the venue was a gathering of intellectuals and scholars, Fadeyev concentrated his remarks on American efforts to shape the cultural sphere. In the United States and allied countries, he charged, progressive thinkers were bribed, intimidated, and persecuted under the "threat of cold terror" and faced possible jail time for expressing "dangerous" ideas. More insidiously, the Americans had mastered the use of popular culture as a weapon of propaganda. American films, radio programs, and magazines were banal but sophisticated ideological instruments. Under the rubric of entertainment, they glamorized violence, valorized greed, normalized racism, and demonized progressive, socialist ideals. These dubious cultural forms helped shape an environment in which capitalism and imperialist aggression were unthinkingly accepted, insidiously persuading the exploited to consent to their own domination. With American might, these degenerate films and magazines flooded global markets, gutting local cultural production.

At the emotional high point of his speech, Fadeyev excoriated well-regarded literary figures like Eugene O'Neill and John Dos Passos, calling them "the literary agents of reaction." He continued, "If jackals could learn to operate a typewriter and hyenas to push a fountain pen they would no doubt produce something strongly resembling the writings of the Henry Millers, the Eliots, the Malraux and sundry Sartres." This reactionary culture, said Fadeyev, was no more than "poisonous gas" that promoted militarism and racism using the dubious aesthetic techniques of "pornography, mysticism, and the brutalization of man."

Fadeyev's speech was greeted with great applause by most of the delegates, but it shocked some of those from the West. As the *New Statesman* editor, Kingsley Martin, who was part of the British delegation, noted later, even those who did not agree with the politics of T. S. Eliot or Jean-Paul Sartre "felt hot under the collar" when they were compared to typing hyenas and fountain pen–wielding jackals.[19] Most of the proceedings continued in the same tone, with delegates rising to give prepared speeches that criticized the United States and its allies, while praising the Soviet Union and its followers.[20] A few of the Western delegates, including Julian Huxley (a British biologist and the director-general of UNESCO), Bryn J. Hovde (the head of the New School for Social Research in New York), and the British historian A. J. P. Taylor, spoke more critically from the rostrum.[21] Their interventions were coldly received by the rest of the delegates.

Hovde later remarked that when he tried to posit democracy as a precondition for peace, it seemed as if he were "throwing flat stones on an icy lake."[22] Taylor's speech was considered even more incendiary. Taylor took aim at Fadeyev's broadsides, declaring that Fadeyev had himself turned the congress into "a piece of warmongering" with his hate-filled remarks.[23] Intellectuals, said Taylor, should resist the use of wild epithets like "fascist" and "imperialist" to describe policies they did not agree with. At home in Oxford, Taylor claimed, he spoke out against those who would liken the Soviets to the Nazis; now here in Wrocław he urged the Soviets to give their opponents the same courtesy. Instead of hatred and name-calling, he encouraged tolerance, cooperation, and "the pursuit of truth."[24]

The endpoint of the congress was to be a resolution about the need for peace. The wrangling over this resolution exemplified the difficulty inherent in the congress's goals: to unite scholars and intellectuals from around the world against war. The Soviet delegation, supported by many of the attendees, wanted a firm denunciation of Anglo-American imperialism. But, as Kingsley Martin remembered it, though many of the American and British delegates were happy to criticize their countries' foreign policy, they were not willing to sign "a Communist manifesto."[25] After a lot of negotiation, a resolution emerged that many of the Western participants called meaningless in its vagueness. It declared that "a handful of self-interested men in America and Europe" who had inherited "fascist ideas of racial superiority" and "fascist methods of solving all problems by force of arms" were pushing the world toward a war that the masses around the globe did not want.[26] Martin suggested that the Soviets and their allies did not contest the phrase "men in America and Europe," although it could be interpreted to include the leaders of the Soviet Union as well as the United States, because in their political vernacular, bands of evil people plotting war were always Americans or their henchmen. The resolution would still resonate with domestic audiences as they intended.[27]

Despite the changes, some of the British delegates did not like the one-sided tone of the resolution. They wrote their own statement saying that it should be the goal of intellectuals to bridge conflicts between the world's ideological camps and that the congress was a "wasted opportunity" because it promoted one side at the expense of cooperation. But, to their dismay, one of their own number leaked their document to the American press. Outraged that they had been used as pawns to score political points for the Western side, many of these delegates then also signed the congress resolution as a protest.[28] In the end, a large majority of the assembled delegates did sign it.

For A. J. P. Taylor, who did not sign the resolution, the problem with the congress was that there was no real opportunity for dialogue. From his perspective, the Soviets and their allies were "monopolists of truth," who were so convinced of their own rightness that they had no interest in hearing another point of view.[29] His colleague, Olaf Stapleton, shared this belief. Stapleton appreciated that the congress had allowed scholars from so many countries to meet and was glad to have had the opportunity to make so many new personal contacts. But, he said, although the Russians he met were pleasant and willing to listen, in the end they were "generally convinced that their truth was the whole truth."[30]

Feliks Topolski, a Polish painter who had become a British citizen, concurred that in the end the congress seemed less about compromise than about asserting the primacy of one's own beliefs. Watching the speeches, he thought, "Since its supposed aim of a search for compromise is clearly lost, it [the congress] becomes a poignant demonstration of Communist strength, a cry of faith-declaring, the loudest yet challenge, a denouncement of the enemy. One watches the waverers cease to waver and start to glow with conviction." For Topolski, this was true of partisans on both sides of the Cold War divide. But, he said, at the congress it was hard to even remember there was another side, since even the opposition in Wrocław came from the Left.[31] Topolski recognized the appeal of simplifying complicated differences into a story of good and evil, but resisted falling into that pattern himself. As he wrote in the conclusion of his account of the congress, "Each of us . . . had his own idea of the truth . . . we were all following our various believed courses."[32] Unlike most of the congress delegates, Topolski was willing to see truth as a subjective and constructed category rather than as an indicator of objective rightness that foreclosed opposition.

The media coverage of the congress tended to reinforce the Manichaean view of the world that Topolski tried to reject. In the Anglo-American press, the congress, to the extent that it was mentioned at all, was generally taken as a sign of Soviet aggression.[33] Fadeyev's comments about American culture being trashy filth made it into several major American papers, along with his charge that respected Western writers were no better than typing hyenas and jackals.[34] In the *New York Times*, the coverage emphasized conflict. Headlines declared that speakers had "scored" off each other, as if they were engaged in a game that would have a winner.[35] The *Washington Post* used similar language, noting that intellectuals (the constituency of the congress) were "naïve," "innocent," and "absent-minded fellows" who often lacked the "savvy" to know "what the score is and how many are out." Sitting inside their ivory towers, they were so insulated from the hard realities of the world that some of them mistakenly thought that fences could be mended with the Soviets over a "few more friendly chats with the generous spirits on either side." The congress, opined the writer, had shown some of them how badly they had misjudged the Soviet side.[36]

Continuing this theme of essential differences between East and West, the *New York Times* article covering the last day of the congress began by reporting the number of Americans and Brits who had refused to sign the final resolution. In fact, far more American attendees had voted for the resolution than against it, but the article omitted this entirely. By mentioning only those who refused to sign, the article changed what could have been a story about global cooperation into one of American resistance to Soviet hypocrisy. The reporter emphasized the conflict even more by noting that the Soviet writer Ilya Ehrenburg had referred to the Americans and Britons who did not sign the resolution as "imbeciles" and "idiots" and stating that 35,000 Polish workers and students had marched in support of the congress, chanting "Down with Wall Street imperialism."[37]

In Eastern Europe, the Czech-language press told a rather different story. In the Czechoslovak Communist Party daily, *Rudé právo* (Red right), there was little mention of conflict at the congress, although the paper devoted significantly more space to the event than the American papers. In the American press, Alexander Fadeyev's speech was highlighted as a vicious assault on the West; in contrast, *Rudé právo* mentioned Fadeyev's remarks about "degenerate" Western popular culture only briefly, allotting more space to his positive assessment of culture in socialist societies.[38] An article giving highlights of the second day of speeches did mention A. J. P. Taylor's riposte to Fadeyev, but referred to it only as a cynical "defense of imperialism" that was easily refuted by the stirring addresses of delegates from colonial nations.[39] Rather than conflict, *Rudé právo*'s coverage emphasized the ideological unity manifested in Wrocław. Articles stressed how the vast majority of delegates, even those from the West, agreed that Anglo-American imperialism was the greatest threat to world peace.[40] In marked contrast to the *New York Times*, *Rudé právo* noted that all but four of the forty-five national delegations unanimously accepted the final congress resolution and emphasized that even a clear majority of American participants had signed it, more than three times the number of those who voted against it.[41]

In a front-page analysis that ran on September 2 under a bold red headline, Jiří Hronek declared that the congress had irrefutably established "two truths" about the world. The first was drawn directly from the congress resolution itself, or at least its Czech-language version: a "group of exploiters from America and Europe," inspired by fascist ideas and methods, threatened the world with another war.[42] Hronek stressed how this fact was given weight during the congress by the accumulated speeches of the delegates from around the world who illuminated the wrongs of Western imperialism. The second truth, according to Hronek, was that the Soviet Union was the great defender of peace, along with its allies in the People's Democracies and among progressive people all over the world. The congress had shown, Hronek declared, that "progressive thought has no borders." Yet while this progressive community might transcend national or regional boundaries, it was, at least according to Hronek, bound together by a common worldview. To be a part of the progressive community meant agreeing that the Soviet government was on the side of peace and justice, while the American government represented the heritage of fascism and war. Given the status of truth, the two lessons of Wrocław were not up for debate.[43]

In his article, Hronek quoted Alexander Fadeyev, who said at the close of the conference, "The Congress is over, but our work is just beginning."[44] Along with passing the final resolution, the congress delegates elected an organizing committee to continue working on the peace cause and designated delegates to start national peace committees in their home countries. Within Eastern Europe, these national peace committees became the domestic focal point of the peace offensive and the link between domestic activism and the international movement.[45] On the international level, the organizing committee formed at Wrocław became the nucleus of what was first called the Partisans for Peace, renamed the World Peace Council (WPC) in 1950. Soon, the WPC, under the direction of its president, the French physicist Frédéric Joliot-Curie, would become the largest peace organization in the world, with affiliates in more than seventy countries. In the 1950s, the WPC sponsored large annual global congresses of peace activists and spearheaded a massive international campaign to ban atomic weapons.[46]

In addition to creating the institutional basis for the international peace offensive, the Wrocław World Congress laid out its fundamental discursive strategy. Alexander Fadeyev devoted the first half of his speech to elucidating the nature of the danger American popular culture posed for the world: by normalizing violence and extolling individual greed, it created the popular basis for Western imperialism. In the second half, he considered the superior virtues of cultural production under socialism. He ended with a call to mobilize progressive forces around the world to defend true culture in the face of reaction.[47] In similar fashion, in his November 1949 speech to the Cominform declaring that Communist parties around the world must dedicate themselves to peace, Mikhail Suslov began by dramatically describing the evil plots of the Western warmongers to consolidate their power around the world. After drawing this picture of the enemy and debunking its propaganda as lies, Suslov moved on to describe the strengths of the socialist peace camp and to propose how Communists and workers should begin to fight for peace.[48] This threefold approach was typical of the Soviet-led peace movement during the period before 1956. Peace activists from across the region strove to define and illuminate the face of the imperialist enemy, making clear why no progressive person should support the imperialist camp. They then contrasted this picture of evil with the glories of socialist society, explaining how socialism would lead the world to peace and happiness instead of destruction, exploitation, and war. Finally, they tried to inspire people in the Soviet Bloc and around the world to work for the cause of peace.

Tearing Down the Curtain of Lies

At the December 1952 Congress of the Peoples for Peace, organized by the WPC in Vienna, the Polish delegate Viktor Klosiewicz, president of the Polish Central Council of Trade Unions, warned against insidious forces that wanted to "bamboozle the people who are seeking the real causes of conflict." Ordinary men and women, he claimed, only wanted to live in peace. But their greedy capitalist rulers manipulated them with clever propaganda designed to frighten them into a "mass war psychosis." Scared and ignorant of the real conditions around the world, these people "did not know how to penetrate the dense curtain of lies and deceit being woven around them." For Klosiewicz, the task of the WPC was clear. "The eyes of these people must be opened," he declared. The delegates gathered in Vienna were there to "look truth in the eyes sincerely" and to bring this truth to the masses of the world.[49] Klosiewicz's speech revealed the dual task of the peace movement for its Communist backers. Within the Soviet Bloc, the peace campaign represented official knowledge. Like show trials, its speeches and resolutions conveyed non-negotiable truths about the world that East European populations needed to accept. Outside the bloc, the peace campaign represented an alternative form of knowledge. It provided a critique of how Western governments, particularly the American government, portrayed their policies and ideals. The speeches of Soviet and East European delegates at WPC events were constructed to work along these parallel tracks.

Revealing the true nature of Western governments and their capitalist backers was crucial for both audiences. Soviet and East European peace activists used the international stage of the WPC to dismantle the "dense curtain of lies" that the West told about itself. At WPC meetings and conferences between 1950 and 1953, they articulated a consistent set of messages about what they claimed was the true West.[50] Though the examples here are taken from a few representative WPC events, the themes of these speeches were constantly reiterated in media coverage and local events throughout the Soviet Bloc (some would even say they were repeated ad nauseam).[51] A few examples can therefore give a reasonably complete picture of the common themes that linked the language of the peace campaign throughout the region.[52]

First among these themes was that the West was at the mercy of a relatively small coterie of wealthy capitalists concentrated in the United States. These men hoped to turn the world into their empire, controlling all of its natural resources and markets. In their drive for global dominance, they exploited those they claimed were their allies. They took their resources, exploited their labor, and hoped to use them as pawns in wars fought to further American interests. Those who loved peace and national independence should not trust the United States, but fear it. This fundamental characterization of American policy was at the core of the final resolution of the 1948 Wrocław World Congress and Mikhail Suslov's 1949 address to the Cominform announcing the peace offensive. According to Suslov, the Marshall Plan was "an economic, political and military instrument" for American imperialists to "bring the economy of Western Europe under their control . . . convert it into a colonial adjunct of the United States of America." It could then serve as "a base and vantage ground in the preparation of a new war."[53] For the Americans, allies were only useful tools in their campaign to crush the democratic socialist camp and colonial independence movements in Asia and Africa. The truth of the United States was that it cared nothing about its friends; it merely used them to further its own imperialist interests.

The Soviet writer and peace campaigner Ilya Ehrenburg forcefully expounded on the topic of American imperialist selfishness and greed in his speech at the 1952 WPC congress in Vienna. According to Ehrenburg, the United States required its allies to effectively relinquish their national sovereignty. Even Europe's colonial powers now found themselves colonized by the Americans, whose arrogant ambassadors went around "behaving like viceroys." The Americans demanded, claimed Ehrenburg, that "Englishmen must live more frugally and carry themselves more modestly ... French and Italians must turn their ancient cities, precious to all humanity, into bases for foreign armies ... [and] the republics of Latin America must punctually deliver to their North American neighbor not only raw materials but also cannon fodder."[54] Ehrenburg's analysis was echoed by others at the same conference, including the Polish writer Jaroslav Iwaszkiewicz, who described the stranglehold American corporations like Standard Oil, Anaconda Copper, and United Fruit held over the developing world. These corporations, explained Iwaszkiewicz, sapped the independence of America's supposed allies, leaving them with no choice but to agree with their own exploitation.[55]

As Ehrenburg described it in Vienna, the United States was able to force its will on Western Europe and Latin America because it convinced these countries that only their subjugation to American power would protect them from Soviet aggression. Ehrenburg claimed this was ridiculous. The Soviet Union was dedicated to peace and harbored no designs on these regions. Instead, it was the United States that pushed the world toward war with its relentless greed. Ehrenburg was a fixture at WPC congresses, and he liked to punctuate his speeches with quotes ostensibly from American politicians and military personnel that showed their bloodthirsty disregard for human life. In an address at a 1950 WPC congress in Warsaw, he inserted a stream of such examples. One was a remark by Congressman John R. Walsh (D-Indiana): "The time is rapidly approaching when irate America will deluge Russia with atom bombs ... It won't just be a one-bomb attack, it will be a deluge. We have at least 250 bombs and one hundred ways of reaching Russia."[56] The effect of this kind of talk, declared Ehrenburg, was to help create a culture that normalized killing.

To emphasize this point, later in the same speech he cited Ellwood Nance, president of the University of Tampa, who allegedly said, "I believe we should have total preparedness based on the laws of the jungle, that everyone should learn every art and science of killing. I would not ask mercy for hospitals, churches, educational institutions or special groups."[57] In Ehrenburg's speech, Nance represented the epitome of American culture: he was a university president who advocated educating young people to be more efficient murderers. His words gave dramatic weight to Ehrenburg's argument that American leaders knowingly fostered a culture of violence they hoped would psychologically prepare their citizens to fight another war.

After the Korean War began on June 25, 1950, American conduct in Korea became a constant topic among Soviet and East European peace activists.[58] As they portrayed it, the war provided a graphic illustration of the effects of American imperialism. At the 1950 WPC congress in Warsaw, held only a few months after war had broken out, Alexander Fadeyev declared that American aggression had started the Korean War. Korea had posed no threat to the United States, and Koreans wanted only to live in freedom after finally being released from Japanese imperialism. But US leaders "refused to listen to positively every proposal for a peaceful settlement of the Korean question, no matter where these proposals came from and why." Instead, they turned to violence and within months had "reduced [the country] to a heap of ruins, to cinders and ashes." As a result, Korea "is drenched with the blood of little children," Fadeyev charged.[59]

Fadeyev's claim that the Korean War revealed the cruel and murderous nature of American imperialism became a constant feature of the Communist peace movement during the early 1950s. Communist peace activists often used examples of American atrocities in Korea in their speeches, resolutions, or articles to delegitimize American claims of supporting democratic and peaceful solutions to global problems. In 1951, the Women's International Democratic Federation, which was intensely involved in Communist-led peace campaigns both within and outside the Soviet Bloc, sent a fact-finding mission to Korea to investigate the situation there (the delegates visited sites in the north and were chaperoned by Korean Communist hosts). Its resulting report was a searing indictment of American actions. It cataloged numerous atrocities committed by American and English troops, including torture, forced prostitution, mass murder of innocent civilians, and the use of incendiary bombs in civilian areas. One woman, Chai Chun-Ok, showed the WIDF Commission "a gigantic pair of tongs which she said had been used for squeezing the prisoners' feet and similar tortures." She claimed that the Americans had shot seven of her children in a mass execution in a cave and exclaimed to the commission, "The Americans are wild beasts. They came into our town and killed everyone here."[60]

One group of delegates was shown bodies in a mass grave in Southern Pyongyang province; they wore peasant clothing and had their hands tied behind their backs. Asked if South Koreans had committed these murders, the people replied, "In this district there were only Americans. They did it." They also told the commission that when the Americans occupied the district, they burned food stocks, destroyed rice fields, and took tens of thousands of bags of grain with them when they left, as part of a conscious strategy of civilian starvation.[61] Summarizing their findings, WIDF committee members declared, "These mass tortures and mass murders surpass the crimes committed by Hitler Nazis in temporarily occupied Europe."[62] They concluded that the primary responsibility for the terrible devastation in Korea lay with the US government and urged women and mothers around the world to unite in demanding that foreign troops be withdrawn from the entire Korean peninsula.[63]

For Communist peace campaigners, images of slaughtered innocents, flattened cities, and mass graves in Korea represented the truth of American "liberation." The rhetoric of liberation had been entwined with American foreign policy toward the Soviet Union even before the Cold War, but it became more prominent with Dwight D. Eisenhower's presidential campaign in 1952.[64] East European peace activists drew on reports of American atrocities in Korea to ridicule the idea that their countries needed to be saved from tyranny and oppression by the United States. In a December 1952 speech to the WPC in Vienna—given in the wake of Eisenhower's successful campaign and its embrace of liberation as a cornerstone of American foreign policy—Traian Savulescu, president of the Romanian Academy of Sciences, disputed the idea that American military intervention meant liberation. What the Americans would really bring, he said, was what they had brought to Korea: "life under bombardment, life—if one can call it such, in which houses, monuments and hospitals are destroyed by bombs, mothers with children in their arms burned by napalm, peaceful men killed by epidemics caused by germs dropped from aircraft."[65] "'Liberation' by force," said Savulescu, was really a brutal imperial conquest trying to disguise itself as a "civilizing mission."[66]

With its brutality and its lust for conquest, the United States mimicked the fascist regimes it had recently defeated. It was a truism for Soviet and East European peace campaigners that the United States was the new face of fascist brutality and fascist aggression. Left unchecked, the Americans would bring the same misery to the world as Hitler with his campaigns of conquest, occupation, and murder. Beginning with the resolution of the Wrocław World Congress, Communist peace propaganda frequently linked American leaders with fascism and Nazism. In his 1950 speech in Warsaw, Alexander Fadeyev remarked that American actions in Korea merely reproduced "all the horrors of the fascist atrocities that came up at the Nuremburg trial."[67] His comrade Ilya Ehrenburg said the same in his Warsaw speech, likening the way American culture promoted violent aggression to way in which "the idea of conquest, the racial and national arrogance, the ferocity and amorality were instilled into the German Volk by Nazi leaders, the Nazi press and the Nazi schools."[68] Their compatriot, the Soviet playwright Alexander Korneichuk, echoed these sentiments in 1952 at the WPC Vienna congress. According to Korneichuk, the Americans had "nursed Hitler" and hoped he would destroy the Soviet army. Now, after Hitler's demise, they had taken up his crusade against Communism. Like Hitler, the Americans sought to impose their brutal rule over all of Europe. "Do they not," dramatically demanded Korneichuk, "insist on their [Europeans'] complete purification from the terrible sin of National Independence and Sovereignty, demanding of them lengthy fasting and labours beyond their power so as to defend the old men of Wall Street who dream of creating an ideal world with atom bombs, napalm and cholera?"[69] All three men insisted that an American empire would merely recreate the Nazi empire, down to its relentless exploitation and racial hierarchy.

Bringing out the persistence of racism and segregation in the United States was another way in which Communist peace campaigners hoped to reveal the true nature of their capitalist enemy. In a speech given at an extraordinary session of the WPC in Berlin on July 4, 1942, Ilya Ehrenburg skillfully skewered American hypocrisy for claiming to speak in the name of freedom and democracy around the world while ignoring racist attitudes at home. Though the speech was given in Berlin, Ehrenburg addressed an imaginary audience of ordinary Americans (the speech was later published in English as a pamphlet by the Chicago Council of American–Soviet Friendship). In the speech, Ehrenburg told the American masses that peace depended on them. Their leaders, he said, were trying to force "the American way of life" on the world by force of arms, arguing that Soviet aggression had made this necessary. This was nonsense, Ehrenburg claimed. The Soviet people liked some things about America and disliked others, but they recognized that each of the world's peoples had the right to define their own way of life. As Ehrenburg explained, "To us Soviet people there is much in America itself we find distasteful; for example, we frankly wish Americans disliked evil deeds and not black skins; that they respected the dollar a bit less and men a bit more. However, that's the Americans' own business."[70] Racism, Ehrenburg argued, was a key component of the American way of life. If Americans suggested to their allies around the world that racist thinking was peripheral to their culture, they were lying. Nonwhite peoples should not expect otherwise.

According to Communist peace propaganda, when the United States offered liberation, it really meant imperialist domination. To those it conquered, the American way of life was one of violence, racism, war, and destruction. The real face of American policy was revealed by the war in Korea, where Americans proved themselves to be heartless murderers, no better than the Nazis. Not only should the United States be condemned, Communist peace activists suggested, it should be feared. If left unchecked, the United States would drag the whole world into a war that could potentially be even more destructive than the war in Korea. It would be the task of the world's progressive people to make sure that this could not happen. In his 1952 speech in Vienna, Alexander Korneichuk said to the assembled WPC delegates, "But we must tell the truth to those Americans who want to found their well-being on war, on the sorrow and death of others. Against this way of life, we, the peoples of the world, will not only protest, but will carry on a struggle, unsparing of our strength."[71] Standing outside this struggle, and rejecting this truth, would not be an option to the citizens of the People's Democracies.

Peace as Socialist Civilization

In his July 1952 speech to the WPC in Berlin, Ilya Ehrenburg told his imaginary audience of ordinary Americans that they had been deceived. Their leaders had claimed they wanted peace, when they really prepared for war. Those same leaders had lied about the Soviet Union and its intentions, using fear of Soviet tyranny to promote their own agenda. But it was simply not true. Despite what the American media or American politicians claimed, Ehrenburg said, "the Soviet Union wants Peace with any America . . . It wants Peace with the American workers and with the American capitalists; it wants Peace not only with its friends, but with its enemies. It wants Peace not because it is fainthearted or weak, but because its heart is large."[72] While they might not have found a large audience in the United States, Ehrenburg's words encapsulated the dual challenge of Communist peace propaganda. On the one hand, Soviet and East European peace campaigners wanted to convince their audiences at home and abroad of the perfidy of the warmongering West. On the other, they needed to illuminate the true nature of their own peace camp. As Ehrenburg noted, Western governments and Western media claimed that the Soviet Union and its Communist allies wanted to spread oppression, penury, and tyranny all over the world. Communist governments used the peace campaign to counter this Western propaganda and argue instead for the positive virtues of socialism.

Insisting on the benign nature of the Soviet Union was fundamental to this effort. In his 1952 Berlin speech, Ehrenburg argued that the Soviet Union "has never encroached upon, nor will every encroach upon, the American way of life. Let every people live according to its lights; let every people find the path to Peace."[73] Although he was not above insinuating that Soviet values and policies were superior to Western ones, Ehrenburg claimed the Soviet Union had no interest in forcing other peoples to follow its path or adhere to its ideals. He fiercely denied that the Soviets wanted to acquire their own empire or dominate any people against their will. That was only American slander. Soviet delegates to WPC events often devoted time in their speeches to similar denials. Ehrenburg's colleague Alexander Korneichuk was vehement on this point in his address at the 1952 WPC congress in Vienna. Korneichuk emphatically declared, "The Soviet people never intended, and do not intend, to impose their ideology upon anyone. As to the Soviet army that is said to threaten other countries, this falsehood, too, is contradicted by the facts."[74] Korneichuk charged that the American governments spread these pernicious "slanders" about the Soviet Union only to justify its massive construction of foreign military bases and increased military presence around the world.

In a similar vein, Russian Orthodox Metropolitan Nikolai proclaimed at the 1950 Warsaw congress, "That every people has the right to self-determination and to decide its destiny freely and independently in accordance with its own discretion is with us a self-evident truth, ingrained in the concept of justice and morality of every Soviet citizen." "Indeed," he continued, "how can the Christian conscience reconcile itself to the oppression of colonial peoples or race discrimination against Negroes?"[75] Like his compatriots, Nikolai portrayed the Soviet Union as misused and misunderstood by the West. It did not desire to dominate others; it did not have the stomach to impose its beliefs on the unwilling. The rostrum of the WPC, "a rostrum without like in history," was a tool to share this knowledge with the world.[76] Some East European delegates to WPC events similarly used this stage to defend the Soviet Union against its Western detractors. The USSR was not their imperial overlord, they declared, but their friend and protector. Professor Todor Dimitrov Pavlov, president of the Bulgarian Academy of Sciences, told the WPC audience in Vienna that the Soviets had liberated Bulgaria—twice. Now they "were selflessly helping her in all fields of economic, scientific and cultural life." The Soviet Union was strengthening Bulgarian independence and helping the country realize its freedom.[77]

Communist peace rhetoric relied intensively on the play of opposites to create meaning. The meaning of the peace camp was revealed in its contrast to the brutality of the war camp. The West made claim to civilization and virtue, but in truth it valued only violence and personal gain. The essence of the war camp was its willingness to slaughter civilians, to burn down their homes, and to raze their farms; the war camp refused to obey even the laws of war. The peace camp, however, utterly rejected such violence and condemned civilian suffering. This was the fundamental rationale for the WPC's campaign to ban all atomic weapons, a campaign that Western governments ridiculed. Soviet and East European peace activists emphasized that their dedication to peace sprang from their personal experience with the horrors of war, an experience, some noted, that most Americans had been spared.[78] This knowledge of suffering knit together the peace camp and formed the basis of its visceral rejection of war. When the Polish trade union activist Viktor Klosiewicz told the audience in Vienna in 1952, "The struggle for Peace is the struggle for life," the reality of having seen death lurked behind his words.[79] His statement highlighted what activists claimed as the stakes of the peace campaign. As Ilya Ehrenburg dramatically asked in 1950, "Must Warsaw be visited with thugs and incendiaries again? Must Paris again hear the iron tread of the invader? Must London again listen to the war in the sky and hide away its children underground?"[80]

WPC delegates from Eastern Europe answered that question with a resounding no! Being in the socialist camp, they claimed, was what enabled them to move beyond the horrors of war and build new societies dedicated to peace. The Hungarian historian Erzsébet Andics told the assembled WPC delegates in Warsaw how the experience of the Second World War had taught her country to love peace and trust socialism. "In the few years since the liberation of Hungary by the Soviet Union," Andics said, "we have not only succeeded in repairing the ravages of war, but have built new power stations, new bridges and libraries and even new cities."[81] As Andics described it, socialism represented a "conversion" from the war camp (Hungary had fought with the Axis powers) to the peace camp. Having rejected war and imperialism, Hungary was finally able to rise above its past of poverty and oppression and realize a new prosperity that reached the masses. Quite simply, Hungarian liberty and Hungarian happiness could be realized only within the peace camp. Knowing this, Hungarians were dedicated to resisting the American warmongers, even militarily if necessary. As Andics described it, working for peace did not require pacifism. It was less important to avoid all violence than to protect the socialist peace camp, which had made Hungary's progress (and all progress) possible.[82]

A Czechoslovak delegate to Warsaw, Anežka Hodinová-Spurná, also equated promoting peace with building socialism. Like Andics, Hodinová-Spurná contrasted the experience of war and, in her case, Nazi occupation with the new life Czechoslovaks had achieved with peace and the socialist policies of the people's democratic regime. As she put it, "We emerged from the darkness of tyrannical occupation into the light of unparalleled progress and peaceful construction."[83] It was only at this moment, she asserted, that Czechoslovakia became a truly happy place. Hodinová-Spurná's definition of happiness made little distinction between peace and socialism. As states of being, they were essentially the same thing. Under this joint influence, Czechoslovaks had been able to build themselves a new earthly paradise. Living standards had risen, and new opportunities for work and education were available to all. Czechoslovaks knew that war would threaten all they had accomplished. Most of all, they wanted to work quietly at home, "to build in peace and create a better life." This work would, Hodinová-Spurná declared, itself promote the greater cause of peace by building a strong socialist society. But Czechoslovaks would also fight on behalf of the peace camp, to protest American actions in Korea, to condemn the remilitarization of West Germany, and to "win over ever larger numbers of peace lovers, and to weld and cement their unity."[84]

Traian Savulescu, a Romanian, also used the WPC stage to brag about the prosperity that being part of the peace camp had brought to his country. In a 1952 speech he noted how much progress had been made in the four years since the socialist regime had taken full control. Romania had recently embarked on a large-scale industrialization drive. Several new power plants had already been built, and

Cold War artists often identified peace with mothers and happy children, making them symbols of a better future. This 1949 Hungarian poster urges viewers to vote for the National Front in the name of peace. *Poster by György Pál, Hungarian National Museum*

"a great iron and steel combine, an aluminum combine, a ball bearing factory, and huge hydro and thermo-electric stations" were in the works. Industrial production had passed agriculture as a share of GDP for the first time in the country's history, and foreign trade had increased. With its new industrial capacity, Romania was no longer dependent on foreign nations to supply equipment to develop its oil fields. Bucharest was undergoing a significant modernization project that would offer residents "living conditions at a high level of civilization." These achievements had occurred despite the machinations of the imperialists, who had closed their markets to Romanian goods in a cheap effort to stifle its socialist regime. Romania, however, would never take such a course. As a peace-loving nation, Romania based its trade policy on "equality of rights, on mutual respect of independence and national sovereignty and on mutual advantages."[85] With this speech, Savulescu captured the essence of the Communist peace camp. "Peace" as Soviet and East European peace workers generally used the term did not mean merely the absence of war, but also the presence of socialist policy and socialist values. Peace was a centrally planned economy, state-centered industrialization, modernization, and new "civilized" living standards, coupled with an egalitarian value system that rejected colonialism and racial discrimination.

Put this way, "peace" embodied everything that united the socialist camp. And this was another function of the peace movement: to show that the Communist nations of Eastern Europe were part of a larger socialist world.[86] As the Bulgarian Todor Dimitrov Pavlov remarked at the WPC's Vienna congress, the point of the peace movement was to "find that which we have in common, what brings us together and not what separates us, what unites us in our great struggle."[87] Before they became part of a Soviet sphere of influence, there was little that bound the countries of Poland, Czechoslovakia, Hungary, Bulgaria, and Romania together. In the nineteenth century, their territory had belonged to four different empires (the German, Russian, Habsburg, and Ottoman). After independence, they had not all been allies. It was only with the imposition of Communist regimes in these countries that they became linked, economically, politically, and culturally. Peace activism, as Pavlov noted, provided a vocabulary of unity and a unifying cause that could tie Communist nations, and their individual citizens, together. Pavlov asked, "Who among us does not passionately love life, civilization, work, the arts, his people, family, parents and his own self? Who among us has not dreamed or does not dream of that supreme happiness, of supreme justice, of more beauty in human life?" Pavlov listed "civilization" as one of several values, but civilization was really the concept that linked them all. Peace was the foundation of a socialist civilization, a civilization devoted to individual flourishing, not global exploitation.

In his speech in Vienna, Todor Dimitrov Pavlov emphasized that it was not enough to intellectually or emotionally support the peace movement; peace could be maintained only with the engagement of the masses around the world. His fellow delegate in Vienna, Václav Rohlena from Czechoslovakia, intimated the same when he told the congress, "All the people of Czechoslovakia realize their duty to world Peace. They know that they must contribute to strengthening Peace and its security."[88] Peace, claimed Rohlena, could not exist without effort. The machinations of the capitalist-imperialists constantly threatened to undermine it. To foil their efforts would require more than goodwill, more than vigilance. It would require battle.

We Want Peace!

Inside Eastern Europe, the rhetoric of the international peace campaign was ubiquitous during the early 1950s; residents encountered it constantly: in the newspaper, on the radio, or on posters that graced workplace walls.[89] But the battle for peace would not only be fought with words and slogans. The peace campaign quickly became a vehicle for mass mobilization across the Soviet Bloc. In his 1949 speech to the Cominform inaugurating the peace offensive, Mikhail Suslov gave the region's Communist parties the challenge of involving as many people in the peace movement as possible. Activists, he said, should try to bring "ever larger sections of the population into the movement . . . making it the universal and irresistible movement of the day."[90] Communists were exhorted to involve all sectors of society in the peace campaign by working with a wide variety of mass organizations, including unions, women's groups, youth organizations, sports clubs, educational societies, and religious communities. Suslov recommended "diverse forms and methods" to involve ordinary people in the fight for peace, including "mass demonstrations, outdoor and indoor meetings, petitions and protests, popular referendums, formation of peace committees in town and country."[91] Like show trials, the peace campaign could not simply be ignored. Whatever they might have thought of the peace movement's messages, East Europeans would be compelled to take part in its activities and publicly register their acceptance of its agenda.

The push to get all the citizens of the Soviet Bloc to participate in their countries' peace movements was reflected in domestic campaigns in support of the Stockholm Appeal. At its meeting in Stockholm in March 1950, the coordinating committee of the WPC released a petition demanding a complete ban on atomic weapons. The WPC sponsored a global effort to obtain signatures for this petition, which became known as the Stockholm Appeal. In Eastern Europe, Communist peace activists were tasked with getting their country's entire adult population to sign it. To direct this effort, the Stockholm campaign spurred the creation of local peace committees in towns, villages, schools, and workplaces across the region. At the start of the campaign that March, Bulgaria claimed to have established 500 peace committees in factories and 1,400 in villages. The numbers increased with each passing month. The Romanian national peace committee reported having 13,548 local branches (with 182,000 members) in April 1950 and 17,000 by May. In June, Hungary declared 9,000 local peace committees had been established.[92] By the time the campaign ended in October 1950, Poland announced it had created 88,000 local peace committees, with an active membership totaling 730,000. According to official statistics, these Polish groups had helped to organize 80,000 lectures, rallies, and meetings across the country.[93]

During the roughly eight months the campaign lasted, organizers made it hard to avoid signing the Stockholm Appeal. As one tactic, the peace movement utilized May Day festivals to reach the public. In Romania, peace workers reported selling 6 million "In Defense of Peace" badges during May Day celebrations.[94] At the festivities in the Polish city of Katowice, youth representatives enthusiastically shouted, "Peace, Stalin, Bierut," for hours. The decorations at the demonstration highlighted the division of the world into two camps, with images of Stalin and working class heroes on one side and caricatures of evil warmongers on the other.[95] In Czechoslovakia, May Day parades throughout the era similarly featured floats that personified the peace and war camps. The peace camp floats typically carried figures of Stalin, Czechoslovak President Gottwald, and other Soviet and local leaders, along with doves, vigilant workers, and so on. The war camp floats featured hydra creatures that combined images of Western leaders like Harry S. Truman, Charles de Gaulle, and Konrad Adenauer along with images of Uncle Sam, rich financiers (in at least one instance with antisemitic overtones), and swastikas.[96]

The Stockholm Appeal continued long after May Day celebrations. Czechoslovak activists created a "Peace Train," which journeyed to seven towns across the country. In each town, a peace congress was held and on the train "sketches, songs and dances" illustrated "the fight against the warmongers of the world."[97] Elsewhere in Czechoslovakia, "men and women organized peace brigades, arranged peace playgrounds for children, planted trees of peace and gave streets and squares the lovely name of peace."[98] Peace campaigning could also be worked into the more quotidian spaces of everyday life. According to the WPC journal *In Defence of Peace*, "In all the cinemas of Poland, before the show begins, a loudspeaker calls on the public to sign against the atomic bomb."[99] Some Polish bakers decorated their loaves with the slogan "Fight for Peace," calling on shoppers to support the Stockholm Appeal.[100] Simply put, peace messages were everywhere, whether on the street, in the workplace, or even on the breakfast table. As the Polish national peace committee wrote in its report to the WPC, "No one can stay outside this great movement, can remain deaf to the call for safety from the horrible danger that looms over mankind."[101]

But the Stockholm campaign was not limited to speeches, slogans, and pageantry; activists from each country pursued signatures from all social groups. In Poland, activists set out in groups of three to visit every home, spreading out into villages to reach peasants on their farms.[102] The activists were bolstered by "artists and entertainers of local cultural groups, country sports committees and traveling cinemas," who were also enlisted to spread the message.[103] In Czechoslovakia, pairs of activists recruited from members of the Czechoslovak Federation of Women, the Sokol gymnastics organization, and the Czechoslovak Federation of Youth were charged with going from house to house to get signatures, especially in villages.[104] In Hungary, youth activists took up stations outside factory gates to corral workers on their way in and out to sign the Stockholm Appeal.[105] Activists in Romania, in addition to going from house to house, set up tables on the street and at bus and tram stations to encourage pedestrians and commuters to sign.[106]

Another tactic was to involve members of the clergy. In Romania, the Stockholm Appeal was endorsed by Patriarch Justinian, head of the Romanian Orthodox Church, and the Councils of the Catholic Church; priests were encouraged to mention it in their sermons. Activists set up tables outside churches so that when people left the Sunday service, they could immediately sign the petition.[107] In Hungary, the local Budapest peace committee was headed by eight priests and a peace pilgrimage was organized by the Society of the Holy Crown. Czechoslovak and Polish clergy also issued statements supporting the Stockholm petition.[108]

According to official statistics on the Stockholm campaign, the petition drive was astoundingly successful. It was perhaps even too successful, as commentators in the West noted that the number of signatures some of the People's Democracies claimed to have garnered was larger than the adult population.[109] Internally, Czechoslovak peace campaign workers complained that some people signed twice, skewing the numbers.[110] It is certainly possible that the totals were padded at various points during the process, but it is unlikely that this accounted for a particularly large percentage of the total number of signatures. The intent of the campaign was to require participation, not to fake it.

In Czechoslovakia, organizers of the signature campaign received detailed reports every few days on the number of signatures in different districts. These reports not only gave precise numbers of petitions signed; they also carefully noted pockets of resistance. For example, a report dated May 16, 1950, claimed that all citizens in the village of Čeradice had signed except for one woman, noting by way of explanation that her farm had been expropriated by the state. For the city of Bratislava, the report mentioned incidents where families had yelled at the peace activists who went to their homes or had refused them entry. These cases were, however, investigated and found to be the work of "former capitalists and class enemies."[111] In the area around the city of Gottwaldov (formerly Zlín), a number of people refused to sign, apparently mostly former members of the Czechoslovak People's Party, a Catholic political party. Similarly, in the village of Hluk (in the Uherské Hradiště district), the whole town of seven hundred persons refused to sign under the influence of the local parish priest, named Černík.[112] The detail given in each of these cases strongly suggests that such moments of refusal were, in fact, relatively rare and that a majority of people signed the petitions without incident.

Research shows that, in Czechoslovakia and Poland, resistance to the Stockholm Appeal was concentrated in the countryside, not coincidentally the location of much dissatisfaction with regime policy. Many peasants in 1950 opposed the collectivization of agriculture and hoped to forestall it. Some Polish peasants refused to cooperate with anyone they identified as a state actor, including census takers and peace campaigners, because they did not want to be recorded as supporting the state in any way. According to the historian Dariusz Jarosz, some peasants tried to avoid peace activists by running into the fields. If caught, some still refused to sign; others did so only when the threat of fines, arrests, or other penalties persuaded them to rethink their initial reluctance. Some wrote, "I want peace," on their petitions without signing their names. Still others agreed to sign only "on the condition that their district did not have a cooperative."[113] Although opposed to the Communist regime, the peasants in this last group decided that being counted as members of the peace camp was worthwhile if it allowed them to keep their farms. By signing, they signaled that they would accept the state's power to define the truth if they were not forced to join a collective farm.

As this last example suggests, there were many forces pushing people to sign the Stockholm Appeal. In Poland, the magazine of the peace movement, *Pokój zwycięża* (Peace is winning), published a letter from the actor Aleksander Zelwerowicz begging permission to sign the petition even though the signature drive had concluded. Zelwerowicz had been hospitalized for several months and missed the chance to add his name during the original campaign. Although he still could not manage to climb a flight of stairs, Zelwerowicz pleaded to be allowed to "fulfill this cardinal obligation" and "ease his civic conscience."[114] Zelwerowicz made the stakes of a simple signature clear. Signing the petition showed that one was a loyal citizen of the socialist camp. Those who did not sign were enemies; they would live under the weight of all that implied. This is not to suggest that most people signed the petition out of fear. We can't know why most individuals signed; it could have been out of terror at the consequences of not signing, enthusiasm for the regime, or a desire to end war that had little to do with either.[115] In the aggregate, however, the emotion behind the act was less important than the fact of the signature itself. The fact that some people, like the Czech pastor Ernberger from the town of Holice, first refused to sign, but were convinced after repeated visits and discussions with activists to reverse their decision, indicates that they realized their signature indeed had meaning.[116] Although it did not necessarily indicate what a person believed, signing did signal that an individual had accepted the peace movement's essential truths about the warmongering West and the peace-loving East.

The peace campaign continued to be a vehicle for popular mobilization well after the conclusion of the Stockholm Appeal. Peace became a means of extracting not only signatures but labor from the population. This was the substance of the speech given by the Polish president, Bolesław Bierut, at the February 1951 meeting of the Central Committee of the PZPR (Polska Zjednoczona Partia Robotnicza, or Polish United Workers Party). For Bierut, the struggle for peace was inextricably tied to work for Poland's Six-Year Plan. He said, "There is a constantly growing awareness that the struggle for peace concerns each and every person and is most closely bound up with the everyday work of the whole nation, with the substance and aims of this work."[117] As part of the peace campaign, workers were exhorted to work faster and harder, to take on extra shifts as "volunteers," or to contribute their wages to peace loans. For example, during the Stockholm Appeal campaign in Czechoslovakia, the mine "Václav" in Nýřany agreed to complete its quota for the second year of the Two-Year Plan early, as did the "Good Luck" mine in Dobřany.[118] Villages also pledged to work harder in the name of peace, promising to deliver more eggs more quickly or to produce more grain or plant more potatoes than their quota demanded.[119]

The peace campaign also became a way of encouraging women to enter the workforce. In Czechoslovakia, President Gottwald gave the women's movement the slogan "Build the homeland—you will strengthen peace."[120] Across Eastern Europe, Communist leaders tried to use the rhetoric of peace to mobilize women as workers. In Czechoslovakia, annual celebrations of International Women's Day were designed to stress the connection between world peace and the physical labor of Czech and Slovak women. Their primary goal, planners of Women's Day admitted, was to encourage as many women as possible to enter the workforce, preferably in heavy industry or animal husbandry.[121] Women's Day organizers used all means at their disposal to persuade women that their sweat in the fields or on the production line would make the world a safer place for their children. They took their message of work for peace into every community, plastering the landscape with placards that declared "work—the weapon of peace" and "women in production—fighters for peace and happy families."[122] As they spoke about

"Each ton of steel wounds the warmongers." A 1954 Czechoslovak poster shows how hard work in the factories will confound the forces of Western imperialism. The molten steel forms the word "peace." *Poster by Lev Haas, All-Trade Union Archive of the Bohemian-Moravian Confederation of Trade Unions, poster collection*

the need for world peace, they presented honorary diplomas to women who had distinguished themselves by overfulfilling their work quotas.[123] By 1951, Women's Day events were being held in even the smallest towns and villages across the country, as well as in thousands of individual factories. Party officials estimated that 2.5 million people attended formal celebrations of Women's Day in that year.[124]

The way the peace campaign was used to draw women into paid labor and activist work highlights the way this movement more generally became a mechanism for mobilizing the bodies of East Europeans in support of regime goals. In practice, the peace movement was both ideological and pragmatic. Like show trials, the peace movement illustrated the new realities of the Cold War world and explained to East Europeans which side they were now on and what that might mean for their lives. But while show trials merely demanded acceptance of those truths, the peace movement insisted that good citizens be willing to commit their labor to building socialism. The peace movement was not the only way that Eastern Europe's Stalinist regimes tried to encourage their inhabitants to toil in service of the planned economy, nor was it necessarily successful in this goal. Many individuals were more willing to sign a petition than take a factory job, if they could help it.[125] But the peace movement revealed what the region's Communist leaders hoped to achieve: a population devoted to building a socialist utopia.

A Complete Hoax

At the Wrocław World Congress in 1948, the British delegate A. J. P. Taylor complained that the Soviet participants and their Communist allies had set themselves up as "monopolists of truth."[126] Certain of their rightness, they refused to entertain ideas that diverged from their beliefs about the West. But such fierce conviction about the nature of the enemy was a common Cold War trait. Many in the West easily fell into this same pattern. Believing that Communists were inherently untrustworthy, they were convinced that the WPC existed only to ensnare unwitting Westerners and prepare the ground for Soviet domination of the globe. Whereas in Eastern Europe, governments made enormous efforts to push the population into the peace campaign, in the West they did everything in their power to prevent their citizens from taking part in WPC activities. This was particularly true in the United States, where peace groups were vociferously attacked as potential Communist-front organizations. According to a report compiled by the House of Representatives Committee on Un-American Activities (HUAC), the WPC was "the most dangerous hoax ever devised by the international Communist conspiracy." HUAC warned that "the master conspirators in the Kremlin" wanted to use the peace cause to "deceive" and "ensnare" honest Americans. It dubbed the WPC's peace proposals mere shams and claimed that the Stockholm Appeal had been devised "to establish a huge Red mailing list which can be used for the circulation of Communist propaganda." Unless exposed, the WPC would trick unwitting Americans into helping the Soviet Union and "convert" them to the enemy cause.[127] According to HUAC, it was a fact that any peace group connected to the WPC was really only interested in abetting the Soviet drive for global hegemony.

Unlike East Europeans, citizens of the United States and its allies were free to express opinions or join organizations as they wished. At the same time, however, officials in the United States and Western Europe did what they could to frustrate the activities of the WPC, including refusing visas to peace activists from Eastern Europe who hoped to attend conferences in the West.[128] They also impeded the efforts of Westerners to cooperate with it. In October 1949, the WPC decided to send delegations to the parliaments of major world powers to speak in favor of banning atomic weapons and ending the arms race. They proposed sending to the US Congress a group composed entirely of West Europeans, including Pablo Picasso, the Reverend Hewlett Johnson (the so-called Red dean of Canterbury), and professors, scientists, and politicians from France, Italy, Switzerland, and Belgium. The entire group was denied visas by the US State Department. Senator Tom Connally (D-Texas), chair of the Senate Foreign Relations Committee, defended this decision by asserting that the members of the delegation only wanted "to infiltrate, to propagandize, to harass, and to annoy the Congress of the United States." The Senate minority leader, Kenneth S. Wherry (R-Nebraska), agreed, likening the WPC to the "bubonic plague."[129] If allowed to cross the borders, it could find unwitting hosts, infect the population, and decimate the innocent masses. Not wanting to lose the opportunity to paint its rival as a country that opposed freedom of speech, the Soviet Union gleefully accepted its delegation from the WPC and even allowed an American, O. John Rogge (described by HUAC as "a pliant American stooge"), to address the presidium of the Supreme Soviet.[130]

HUAC attacked peace groups operating in the United States as dangerous threats to national security. Its 1951 report named numerous organizations and listed their members (sometimes including their hometowns and occupations), insinuating that they were all Communists or Communist sympathizers and enemies of the United States. The first American group established to work with the WPC, the Peace Information Center, was forced to disband after less than a year. Its chair was the noted African American activist W. E. B. Du Bois. By the time he agreed to head the Peace Information Center, Du Bois had already been fired from a frightened NAACP for his socialist leanings. The Justice Department, operating under the assumption that a group that advocated peace along with the WPC could only be working for the Soviet Union, demanded that Du Bois and four other officers register as foreign agents under the Foreign Agents Registration Act of 1939. To avoid that, Du Bois dissolved the organization, but he and the other officers were nonetheless indicted and brought to trial as undeclared foreign agents. The government's legal case was slight, and the judge dismissed the charges a few days into the proceeding. Even without a guilty verdict, the case sent a clear message. Though it was not illegal, showing too much support for the WPC could lead to serious repercussions.[131]

HUAC similarly attacked the Congress of American Women (CAW), the American affiliate of the Women's International Democratic Federation (WIDF). CAW was founded in 1946 with the goals of working for peace, international cooperation, women's equality, social justice, and antiracism; it attracted a membership of 250,000 within a year. The organization's refusal to see Soviet peace activists as enemies and its skeptical stance on the Truman Doctrine as a force for peace just as rapidly attracted the notice of HUAC. HUAC claimed both CAW and WIDF were Communist front organizations and sought to prove this by noting that their activities had been described admirably by media outlets like Moscow radio, the *Daily Worker*, and *For a Lasting Peace, For a People's Democracy*, the journal of the Cominform. HUAC used coverage in such suspect publications or connections with WIDF or CAW to also cast aspersions on other women's peace groups, such as Minute Women for Peace and the Committee of Philadelphia Women for Peace.[132] No less an authority than Eleanor Roosevelt warned Western women of "Soviet inspired" peace groups like WIDF, who wanted to "infiltrate and maneuver women's groups in various parts of the world," luring them to take part in "false peace propaganda."[133] For Roosevelt, WIDF was an enemy organization that lied to women about its true nature and real goals.

One result of this persecution was to make the Communist orientation of Western peace groups a reality. Members who were not Communists quickly felt compelled to end their participation and even hide their former involvement, leaving behind only a tiny core of members who were committed Communists. In turn, the hard-line stance of these remaining peace activists discouraged those who did not share their sympathies from working with them. Within a few years, "peace" had become identified with Communist politics, not only in the United States, but also in Sweden, Denmark, the Netherlands, and France.[134]

A Monopoly on Truth

For Communist peace activists, working for peace was like fighting a battle. Peace had clearly defined enemies—the imperialist warmongers—and the goal of the peace movement was to defeat them. For the most part, these activists were not interested in building coalitions across ideological divides. Instead, they aimed to convince the masses that their way of seeing the world had the status of truth. At WPC events, non-Communists who differed with received knowledge about the nature of the West met with a cold reception. Within Eastern Europe, these dissenting opinions were ridiculed as the cant of enemy forces.

Like show trials, the peace campaign used fear to inspire and mobilize the population. Peace activists presented the West as violent and rapacious, with no qualms about using incendiary bombs or bacterial weapons on civilian populations. Western leaders promised to "liberate," but they really hoped to exploit and destroy. To combat this danger, East Europeans were pushed to support the peace campaign with their signatures, their presence at rallies and events, and their labor. The vast majority complied. It is impossible to know precisely what compelled their participation, except that fear in some form—whether fear of the West or fear of the consequences of noncompliance—was a likely motivating factor.

In the West, government officials turned the tables, labeling WPC sympathizers enemies and calling peace campaigners dangerous Communist subversives. Citizens were exhorted to refuse to participate in the peace movement, and the Stockholm Appeal's proposal to ban atomic weapons was vilified as Red propaganda designed to take advantage of Western sympathies. As in the East, most insisted that there was only one truth, but for them it was the truth of Communist perfidy.

3 BATTLING THE BIG LIE

In the midst of the 1952 American presidential campaign, John Foster Dulles published an article in *Life* magazine advocating a new direction for US foreign policy. The Communists, he said, were winning the war of words. The United States could no longer allow their vicious slander to go unanswered. Americans, he declared, "should be *dynamic*, we should use ideas as *weapons*; and these ideas should conform to *moral* principles. That we do this is right ... but it is also expedient in defending ourselves against an aggressive, imperialistic despotism."[1] Dulles's candidate, the future president Dwight D. Eisenhower, openly promoted psychological warfare as a strategy in the Cold War. The United States would show the world that the glorious future promised by Communists was a sham. It would convince the uncertain that the freedom offered by the West was the only path to happiness.

Although Eisenhower pledged to take a more vigorous approach in this battle for hearts and minds, the idea that the United States needed to fight Communism on an emotional and intellectual level was not new. Propaganda had been part of American foreign policy since the beginning of the Cold War. In 1947, the National Security Council charged the newly created Central Intelligence Agency (CIA) with the task of carrying out covert psychological operations to halt the spread of Communism.[2] Throughout the Cold War, the United States worked both overtly and covertly around the world to counter Soviet propaganda. It funded radio stations and periodicals, supported anti-Communist cultural organizations, established libraries, and created scholarship programs and cultural exchanges to support this cause.[3]

American officials during the early Cold War openly talked about the need to influence global public opinion in favor of US policy, but they shunned the term "propaganda." Though initially value-neutral, the word had become associated with America's totalitarian enemies: first Nazi Germany and then the Soviet Union. For many Americans, "propaganda" meant spreading lies and false information.

Edward Barrett, assistant secretary of state for public affairs in the Truman administration, recalled, "American congressmen, like Americans in general, were suspicious of anything that could be labeled propaganda."[4] To get away from this unsavory label, US officials instead spoke of "psychological warfare" or the "battle for hearts and minds," as they still do today. From their perspective, this distinction was justified. They believed that what they were doing was intrinsically different from the parallel Soviet effort. The Soviets used propaganda to fool the world about their evil intentions; the Americans merely countered these blatant Soviet lies with the truth.

The belief that the West spoke the truth while Communists merely lied played a fundamental role in the way the United States approached the task of psychological warfare during the early Cold War. In a speech to the American Society of Newspaper Editors in April 1950, President Harry S. Truman proposed a new "Campaign of Truth" to fight Communist advances around the world. Although Communist propaganda was powerful, Truman claimed it could "be overcome by the truth—plain, simple, unvarnished truth—presented by the newspapers, radio, newsreels, and other sources that the people trust." The truth was, Truman said, the only real defense against Communist lies.[5] From this perspective, it was pointless, and perhaps even pernicious, to engage in serious intellectual debate with Communists. Communists had no valid ideas; their promises of a better life were only lies masked by clever and insidious propaganda. Communist "ideology" consisted of dictatorship, terror, and oppression. The American task was to debunk the lies and reveal this truth.

Eastern Europe was a crucial battleground in this effort to counter Communism's lies with American truth. According to both the Truman and Eisenhower administrations, the idea that East Europeans had joyfully joined the Soviet camp was a lie. The truth was that they had been taken prisoner and turned into helpless slaves. The Communist governments of Eastern Europe were foreign occupiers who ruled by terror, leaving their populations powerless in the grip of their all-encompassing fear. This idea of East Europeans as captive peoples was essential to the way American officials portrayed Eastern Europe at home and abroad. It was, however, not solely the creation of American propagandists. It was nourished by East European émigrés, who were happy to serve as experts on the subject of their homelands.

East Europeans—whether they had fled as political exiles shortly after Communist takeovers or illegally crossed the border to the West years later—shaped how American officials, journalists, and academics thought about life behind the Iron Curtain, helping to create what Americans would see as the truth of Eastern Europe. East European émigrés also played a crucial role in exporting these truths back into the Soviet Bloc. These exiles helped develop much of the

American propaganda directed at Eastern Europe, particularly radio broadcasts. Through a complicated interplay of interactions that stretched back and forth across the Iron Curtain, East Europeans were key players in the creation and dissemination of knowledge about their region. Their expertise, however, was generally used in ways that supported, rather than challenged, existing anti-Communist assumptions about Communist oppression. East European émigrés would help those assumptions take on the weight of fact. To show how this process worked is not to deny the oppressive nature of Eastern Europe's Communist governments. Rather, it reveals the ways in which certain ideas and beliefs about Eastern Europe took on the status of truth for American anti-Communists and their allies, eliding or discounting other experiences of life under Communist rule.

Battling the Big Lie

The battles of American psychological warfare were supposed to take place abroad, where the US government would counter the false blandishments of Communist propagandists with the truth. In the United States itself, there was ostensibly no need for government-run media; the free press would do the job of getting the truth out. The Free Europe Committee (FEC) was an institution that belied this distinction.[6] Ostensibly a group of private citizens, the FEC was actually organized with CIA involvement; it was covertly monitored and funded by the CIA until 1971.

The FEC's goal was to get the truth (as its members understood it) to the residents of the People's Democracies. In order to transmit this truth directly to the region, the FEC created Radio Free Europe, a radio station that broadcast to the satellite countries in their own languages. But although its primary mission was abroad, the FEC played a key role in shaping the ways many Americans thought about Eastern Europe. The FEC established the Free Europe Press, which published scholarly reports about the region as well as a magazine, *Notes from Behind the Iron Curtain*. These publications, many of which were written by East European exiles who had been given positions at an FEC-funded research institute, the Mid-European Studies Center, would shape the thinking of many journalists and academics about the region.[7] But the FEC's most direct contact with the American public was through its domestic fundraising campaign, the Crusade for Freedom.[8]

The Crusade for Freedom served a dual purpose. It provided a cover for the CIA's financial support of the FEC by making it appear that Radio Free Europe (RFE) was a private enterprise funded by donations. In reality, although the campaign did raise some funds, RFE could never have operated without substantial CIA support.[9] But the campaign itself was a public relations tool, reinforcing the goals and presuppositions of US foreign policy. From 1950 to 1960, the Crusade for Freedom reached out to ordinary Americans for a few weeks every year and asked them to help send the truth to Eastern Europe. While the success of the crusade waxed and waned over the decade, it would have been hard for most Americans to be unaware of its existence. It was announced nationwide in print ads, on billboards, in film shorts, and in radio and television spots created by the Advertising Council, the nonprofit organization devoted to creating ads for public service campaigns (it was begun during World War Two to promote war bonds and used many of the same techniques for the Crusade for Freedom).[10] Organizers worked to involve local civic and religious organizations in the campaigns, and local communities often held rallies and parades in support.[11] Given the extent of the crusade's visibility, one historian claimed it was as familiar to 1950s Americans as "Ivory soap or Ford automobiles."[12]

The first Crusade for Freedom campaign was launched in September 1950 with an address by Dwight D. Eisenhower, then president of Columbia University. The speech was carried live on all the major radio networks; it would also be

Radio Free Europe sends truth through the Iron Curtain in this billboard from the 1954 Crusade for Freedom campaign. The billboard was mounted above Cottrell's clothing store in Denver. *Photo by Floyd H. McCall / The Denver Post via Getty Images 161991183*

broadcast abroad by Voice of America and the fledgling Radio Free Europe. Much like Communist leaders, Eisenhower presented a Manichaean vision of the world. America represented "freedom, opportunity, human happiness," while behind the Iron Curtain there was "political wickedness," "cold-blooded betrayal," "godless depravity," and "secret police and slave camps."[13] Under Communism, said Eisenhower, life was full of terror. An individual had no rights. The government had complete "mastery of his life and soul." But perhaps the biggest danger of Communism was its lies.

Communists lied about themselves, promising prosperity and equality, when they would bring only misery and oppression. They also lied about the United States, claiming that it "had nothing to offer the world but imperialism and exploitation." For Eisenhower, nothing could be further from the truth. This illustrates one of the tensions that would characterize much of the Crusade for Freedom rhetoric throughout the years. Eisenhower characterized Communist claims as "specious," "incredible," "fantastic," and "twisted." In short, they were ridiculous lies and were not to be taken seriously as a viable critique of economic or social relations. And yet they were somehow entirely believable to large portions of the world's population. For Eisenhower, that something so ridiculous and so false could also be so believable was simply due to the "clever" and "calculating" nature of the lies and the skill behind their distribution. Rather than consider any validity behind Communist claims, the United States needed to work more effectively at countering them with the truth. For Eisenhower, truth was a weapon and Radio Free Europe was its delivery device.

The urgency of Eisenhower's appeal was amplified by the Korean War, which had broken out a few months earlier. Eisenhower began the speech by saying, "Americans are dying in Korea tonight," giving their lives for American ideals. But those ideals, he claimed, were being misrepresented in Communist propaganda, which turned God-fearing American soldiers into warmongering imperialists. This made the stakes of the battle for truth clear. Communist lies cost American lives by encouraging people to support America's enemy. They dishonored America's dead by slandering American GIs. If left unchecked, they could help Communist forces win the war in Korea and attract enough allies to bring the Communist war of aggression to American shores. The forces of Communism would not stop, Eisenhower declared, until they had "destroy[ed] human liberty and control[led] the world." By supporting the Crusade for Freedom, ordinary Americans would help fight Communism's "big lie" by allowing RFE to broadcast the "big truth" about the United States and its allies.

During this first year of the Crusade for Freedom, organizers urged all Americans to send in donations of "Truth Dollars" and sign "Freedom Scrolls," in which they affirmed their belief in freedom as a God-given right of all people.[14] In Washington, DC, there was a campaign to get a hundred thousand residents to sign the scrolls. Four hundred volunteers went door to door to obtain signatures. Civic organizations rallied their members to assist the drive. The Board of Education authorized the distribution of the scrolls to schoolchildren. Seeing people lined up to sign the petition at the kickoff of the drive in front of the District Building downtown, local resident Margaret Sweeney asked, "Is that to fight Communism?" and then eagerly joined the line. The resemblance of this campaign to the Communist-led drive to encourage people to sign peace petitions was not completely lost on the American crusaders. Speaking at the kickoff of the campaign in Washington, a former US ambassador to Japan, Joseph Grew, said, "The only peace Stalin offers is the peace of the police state, the peace of the prison, the peace of the tomb." Americans, Grew argued, needed to mobilize against Communism's "vicious propaganda" and "get the truth behind the Iron Curtain."[15]

By the end of the campaign, organizers claimed a total of 16 million signatures on the Freedom Scrolls. They also raised about $1.3 million in donations, but the money was never the main point of the Crusade for Freedom. As Thomas Braden, one of the CIA officials that oversaw the Free Europe Committee, wrote in 1954 to Arthur Page, then chair of the Executive Committee of the FEC, "While we [the CIA] consider the amount of funds raised to be important, we think 'amount' is secondary to 'breadth.'"[16] As far as the CIA was concerned, large corporate donations to the FEC were fine, but it was preferable for the crusade to concentrate on involving as many Americans as possible, even if each could give only a dollar to the Cold War cause.

The symbol of the 1950 campaign was the Freedom Bell, modeled after the Liberty Bell. As part of the publicity campaign, the bell made a tour of eleven US cities before it was sent to Berlin, where it was installed in the Schoenberg town hall, surrounded by heaps of signed Freedom Scrolls.[17] In the well-turned phrase of Drew Middleton, reporting from Berlin for the *New York Times*, the pealing of the bell "echoed the vigorous sounds of Western democracy."[18] The installation was presided over by General Lucius Clay, former military governor of the US zone of occupied Germany, architect of the Berlin airlift, and national chair of the Crusade for Freedom. Speaking to the crowd, Clay said the moment had come for a "spiritual airlift" to carry truth to the East. Clay echoed Eisenhower by taking it as a given that the inhabitants of Eastern Europe were deprived of all freedom and lived solely on a diet of Communist lies. He was seconded by the mayor of West Berlin, Ernst Reuter, who spoke of the need to reach "the scores of millions of slaves and oppressed peoples who are looking towards us full of hope." The story of the Freedom Bell was made into a short film, *The Bell*, narrated by

Henry Fonda, later made available by the Advertising Council to theaters and television stations for the 1951 Crusade for Freedom campaign.[19]

Although they varied by the year, the Advertising Council's ads for the Crusade for Freedom reliably presented Eastern Europe in the same fashion. This was a land of fear, lies, terror, and oppression. One particularly striking print ad from 1952–1953 was titled "Mr. and Mrs. Murderer." The image depicted a couple seated at a table, drinking. The man was off to the side and in shadow, while his blond wife sat in the center of the frame, lit by a hanging lamp. She held a cigarette and its smoke rose around her face. Although she was rather beautiful, with heavy, dark eye makeup, her face wore a hard and cruel expression. According to the text, they were "Mr. and Mrs. Margineau," collaborators with the Securitate, the Romanian secret police. Each night, the ad claimed, they took part in "blood orgies," where innocents were beaten as the Margineaus and other members of the "government gang" drank and sang. Radio Free Europe, declared the ad, had exposed the couple as Securitate agents in its broadcasts (naming agents on air was a common theme of early programs).[20] Though the ad claimed that broadcasts naming supposed Communist torturers gave people the power of the truth (and the ability to avoid or shun those so named), it also reinforced the very fear it claimed to alleviate. Ads like these, and the RFE broadcasts on which they were based, sent the same message to both Americans and East Europeans: the inhabitants of the Soviet Bloc were at the mercy of ruthless sadists.

A 1952 ad, "Hungarian Tragedy," gave a similarly bleak picture. Also based on a story broadcast by RFE, this ad told the tale of Mrs. X, a Hungarian woman whose husband had been sent to work in the mines.[21] One day, Mrs. X was given an assignment in a labor brigade and told she must leave her young son behind. The state, she was told, would raise him instead and give her three thousand forints in compensation. After being forced to give up her son, Mrs. X threw herself in front of a train in despair. The ad claimed that by broadcasting the truth about Mrs. X and others like her, RFE would keep hope alive in the People's Democracies. It is difficult, however, to see how this particular story could inspire much optimism in Hungary. Mrs. X, after all, had found no option other than suicide. Her son would be raised by the Communist state, and her husband was still stuck in the mine. But by portraying East Europeans as cowed and powerless slaves, the ad persuasively showed Americans why they should fear Communism. With ads like these, the Crusade for Freedom brought the truth of Communist rule home to Americans, insulating them from Communism's "big lies."

The most inspiring stories told during crusade campaigns were tales of daring escapes from across the Iron Curtain. Although it is true that the borders were sealed and most who wanted to emigrate had to cross illegally, the very concept of "escape" implied that the entire Soviet Bloc was a big prison camp.[22] Most of

The Crusade for Freedom taught Americans about the evils of Communism and encouraged them to participate in the fight against it. The campaign created ad templates that sponsors could place in newspapers; this one invites viewers to send a "Freedom-gram" to captive East Europeans. *Courtesy of the Ad Council Archives, University of Illinois*

those who fled the People's Democracies did so quietly, without fanfare and without any notice by the Western media. The escape stories that engaged the press were those about people who fled in spectacular fashion, by cobbling together their own armored tank, flying across the border in a stolen military plane, or the like. Typical was the story of the "Freedom Train," a tale that could not have been more perfect as propaganda for the Free Europe Committee if it had been written by scriptwriters at Radio Free Europe.

On September 11, 1951, coincidentally only a few days after the start of the 1951 Crusade for Freedom campaign, a Czech train engineer, Jaroslav Konvalinka, teamed with a railway employee, Karel Truska (variously spelled Truksa and Truxa in the press), to commandeer a train and flee across the border with their families. Konvalinka had been assigned to drive the train, which was supposed to stop at the border town of Aš. The day before, Truska flipped a switch to enable Konvalinka to take a disused side track across the border. After boarding the train as a passenger, Truska cut the air brakes to prevent the conductor from stopping the train. As Truska pointed a pistol at the Communist fireman, Konvalinka plowed ahead through the Aš station and into West Germany.[23] Of the 108 passengers on the train, 35 chose to stay in the West. Those who stayed were quoted in the US press echoing American assumptions about life under Communism. As one woman, who had, luckily, been traveling with her husband and their two children, said, "I didn't want my children to grow up slaves."[24]

On October 23, 1951, only weeks after it occurred, the incident was dramatized in an episode of the popular CBS television series *Suspense*. The show began with a mock broadcast from RFE, bringing "a message of hope to fellow Czechoslovakians imprisoned in their homeland behind the Iron Curtain." During the programming break, the national chair of the Crusade for Freedom, General Lucius Clay, appeared with the president of Auto-Lite, the program's corporate sponsor, to note that it was the Crusade for Freedom that made RFE possible. At the end of the program, the narrator urged the audience to contribute to the 1951 crusade, reminding viewers, "You can help fight Communism by joining the Crusade for Freedom."[25]

Konvalinka and Truska became short-lived celebrities, with Konvalinka hailed as the "Czech Casey Jones." Although most of the refugees on the train who stayed in the West went to Canada, Konvalinka, Truska, and their families were allowed into the United States.[26] They were sponsored by the Lionel model train company, which promised both men jobs. First, however, they embarked on a six-city tour of the country, where they gave press and radio interviews (via an interpreter).[27] In an interview in Washington, DC, they emphasized the crucial role Western radio played for the people of Czechoslovakia. The two were convinced, said a reporter, "that broadcasts from the free world are causing wider and more widespread cracks in Russia's curtain."[28] Their own stories, however, belied any such optimism. Konvalinka claimed he began to plan for the escape when he discovered he would soon be arrested, and Truska had already spent a few months in a prison camp. As in the story of Mrs. X, their description of life in Communist Czechoslovakia was colored by fear and despair rather than hope. The real triumph in their story was the fact that they had been able to leave, not their success in fighting their Communist rulers.

This was underscored in a sequel to the "Freedom Train" story, when one of the passengers who had returned to Czechoslovakia successfully escaped on her own a few weeks later. Sixteen-year-old Zdenka Hyblová told reporters she had gone back only because she had already promised her boyfriend, Pavel, and her best friend, Alena, that they would flee together, and she could not bear to leave them both behind. Hyblová claimed the three had previously hesitated to leave because they were not sure of the reception they would be given by the American occupying forces in West Germany. The warm welcome and chocolate bars she received after getting off the Freedom Train convinced her it was time for them to make their move. While the apparent ease of their flight called into question the necessity of stealing a train to make it over the border, Hyblová's words breezily confirmed the truth about Communist rule. When asked where she would go now, she replied, "Pavel and I are going to Canada. I have heard you can say what you think there."[29]

National ad campaigns were only part of the crusade's visibility. Each annual campaign was organized on the local level by a network of state and local chairs. Cities or towns might organize a parade, a rally, or a dance in support of the crusade. For example, in 1951, the president of RFE, C. D. Jackson, spoke at a rally of 1,500 people in Reno, Nevada, before an evening of entertainment that included a charity auction officiated by Clark Gable.[30] And in 1954, organizers in Bismarck, North Dakota, held a ticketed dance at the Moose Lodge, with proceeds going to the Crusade for Freedom.[31] Beginning in 1954, prominent crusade organizers were invited to attend study tours in Europe. During trips that generally lasted about ten days, they flew to Munich, where they visited RFE headquarters and met with staffers. So-called trippers might also be taken to the West German–Czechoslovak border to see the Iron Curtain firsthand or participate in a balloon launching, in which large balloons laden with propaganda leaflets in local languages were carried on favorable winds toward Czechoslovakia, Hungary, or Poland. Finally, they went to Berlin to see the Freedom Bell and perhaps meet with local and American officials. They returned home to report their impressions of their brush with the Communist world.[32]

The Crusade for Freedom was the most visible element of the FEC's work in the United States. But the organization also worked to shape American popular perceptions of Eastern Europe in more subtle ways. The publications of the Free Europe Press and the research of the primarily exile scholars at its Mid-European Studies Center helped to form the basic assumptions Americans had about life under Communist rule. Although these exile writers had a variety of political backgrounds and often quarreled among themselves, they were united by their fervent anti-Communism.[33] Many of them had fled their homelands shortly after the Communist takeovers and had no direct experience of Communism, but they still firmly believed they knew the truth about what was going on in the region.

The book *Conquest by Terror* by Leland Stowe provides one example of how knowledge created by these exiles influenced the American media. Stowe was a Pulitzer Prize–winning foreign correspondent, hailed for his coverage of Europe, including the Paris Peace Conference, Nazi occupation, and postwar reconstruction. In 1951, he began to research conditions behind the Iron Curtain. Since visiting the region was impossible, he relied heavily on the various branches of the FEC for his information, including contacts with the committee's affiliated organizations for exiles, scholars at the Mid-European Studies Center, and the resources of RFE.[34] After publishing the book in 1952, Stowe would serve as the director of the RFE News and Information Service until 1954.[35]

In the foreword to *Conquest by Terror*, Stowe decried what he saw as the complacency in American journalism and society about the situation in Eastern Europe. American journalists, he said, had much to learn from their Communist counterparts. The Soviets and their allies filled newspaper pages every day with lurid tales of the warmongering United States in an effort to keep the fight against capitalism urgent and vital. For American journalists, the existence of slave labor camps in the People's Democracies was old news not worth reporting. But, Stowe said, "nobody ever really learned grammar or geometry by skimming through the lesson."[36] Communist journalists incessantly repeated their attacks because they were trying to convince their public to believe lies. American journalists were armed with the truth, but they also had a mission to educate the public about the urgency of the Cold War cause. It was their job to "indelibly" imprint the evils of Communism on American minds.[37] This increased consciousness would galvanize Americans against "the great Red plot" to enslave the entire world.[38] Thus, *Conquest by Terror* was not primarily motivated by a desire to understand the complexities of the region, but aimed to use its plight to illustrate the broader dangers of Communism for the American audience. It would show Americans the horrible fate that would await them in the event of a global Communist victory.

Unsurprisingly, given that his research was guided largely by intensely anti-Communist exiles, Stowe found that conditions in Communist Eastern Europe were worse than he had even imagined. In the book, Communist regimes were portrayed as evil and totalitarian. The defining element of Communism was its omnipotent police force and spy network, consisting, Stowe claimed, of millions of agents. He asserted that "80–90 percent of the population" lived in "a permanent condition of fear, coercion, and privation or destitution."[39] Everyday life was totally controlled by the party. Freedom was "strangled."[40] There was no rule of law, only the arbitrary whims of Communist officials. The reasoning behind these harsh policies remained obscure; there was little in the text about socialism or ideology. In the early pages, Stowe even defined the term "class enemy" as composed of nationalist or religious opposition, aristocrats, or supporters of the region's former regimes, all but ignoring class itself.[41] Deprived of any ideals, Communist governments existed only to enhance their power (or Soviet power) and to transform their subjects into miserable slaves.

Whereas "Communists" represented evil, Stowe saw East Europeans primarily as helpless victims. Various chapters presented peasants, workers, Christians, and youth as the objects of Communist oppression (or, in the case of youth, of its propaganda), never its architects. Stowe admitted that some locals worked with the regime, but he generally excused their participation as coerced and inauthentic. This was, for the most part, a foreign occupation carried out against the will of the local population. The foreignness or strangeness of Communism was integral to his message. But the point was not so much that Communist rule was foreign to Eastern Europe, although *Conquest by Terror* did make that argument. Rather, Stowe implicitly emphasized the ways in which Communist rule was alien to *American* sensibility. He decried Communist regimes for their lack of personal freedom and the amount of state interference in everyday life, noting that governments had instituted many methods of monitoring the population, including the rationing of basic foodstuffs, identification cards, and the requirement to register one's residence with the local police. He remarked in appalled astonishment that permits might be required for travel and that few could afford to travel, as Americans did, in their own cars.[42] That rationing, a low level of personal automobile ownership, and mandatory identification cards were not unique to Communist states did not mitigate Stowe's view that such policies demonstrated how Communism negated capitalism's basic freedoms.

Conquest by Terror's reach was broadened via a twelve-article series by Stowe carried daily in the *Washington Post* from July 28 to August 9, 1952. Each article in the series encapsulated the arguments of one of the book's chapters, leaving out the detail in favor of the basic message of Russian/Soviet evil and East European victimization. The headlines made this clear: for example, "Russians Rule Satellites by Murder, Terror Methods," "Russian System of Control Rests on Vast Spy Network," "Fifteen Million Workers in Shackles," and "Eastern Europe Slaves Exceed One Million."[43] Stowe emphasized the speed with which the

Communists had transformed the countries of Eastern Europe, noting in the first article in the series that this had occurred in part because Americans had underestimated their capabilities. The Soviets, he said, were not very advanced in the production of goods, but they were excellent at "exporting their own slave-state system" and "expanding their police-state machine."[44]

Toward the end of the series (and likewise toward the end of the book), Stowe attempted to qualify the all-powerful nature of the Communist state by noting that East Europeans might struggle to hold onto their national identity or religious faith. But this resistance, if it could even be called that, was only internal. "Popular revolts simply cannot occur against police states holding a monopoly of modern weapons," he wrote.[45] The prisoners of satellite Europe were locked fast in their cells, subject to the whips of their Communist masters, able only to dream of a better life. Stowe offered no solution to their plight other than a total American victory in the Cold War.[46]

While Stowe undoubtedly harbored no ill will toward Eastern Europe, his book offered East Europeans little hope. For Stowe, the tragic fate of Eastern Europe was important primarily because it revealed the larger stakes of the Cold War. The question of how to help Eastern Europe was "merely one aspect of a much bigger question," he wrote: "What can we do to defend all peoples, including ourselves, against Red conquest?"[47] Eastern Europe was America's foil and opposite, what Americans had to fear becoming. In the conclusion to the book and the article series, Stowe told Americans that the Cold War was really a war of ideas in which they must all fight, not to help Eastern Europe, but to preserve their own freedom. If they did not counter Communist lies with American truth, the Communists would win over the hungry masses of Asia, Africa, Latin America, and the Middle East with their "Red seduction" and thereby acquire the means to overpower the United States as well. This call to arms (or call to propaganda) implied that Communists had ideas that could have resonance around the world, which Stowe had up to this point at least implicitly denied, by asserting that Eastern Europe had been taken over by brute force, abetted only by spineless opportunists. But, like all the work of the Crusade for Freedom, it also debunked those ideas as baseless lies, mere tools to aid in the takeover of the world.

The Voice of Freedom

While the Free Europe Committee influenced how Eastern Europe was characterized in the American media, its larger task was to carry out psychological warfare behind the Iron Curtain. Its main vehicle for transmitting ideas to the Soviet Bloc was the radio station Radio Free Europe. By the end of 1950, RFE had established service to Bulgaria, Czechoslovakia, Hungary, Poland, and Romania. The first broadcasts were prepared in New York, but by the middle of 1951 most of the reporting and program production had moved to facilities in Munich.[48] RFE's broadcasts represented a complicated mix of perspectives. The various language desks at RFE were staffed largely by anti-Communist émigrés from the region, while the corporate headquarters, which remained in New York in this period, was composed primarily of Americans.[49] Each language desk had its own staff and its own schedule of programs. The desk editors, hired and trained in New York, had control over their desk's program scripts. They were, however, supposed to follow a consistent policy line. The station's management periodically issued specific guidelines (referred to internally as "policy guidances") detailing how scriptwriters should approach particular events or issues.[50] American policy advisers also read scripts in translation after they were broadcast and wrote reports critiquing programs and offering suggestions for improvement.[51]

As one of its first handbooks declared, the purpose of RFE was to counter Communism's "big lie" with the truth.[52] Giving East Europeans access to the truth meant, on the one hand, offering accurate and substantive news reports that addressed falsehoods or deficiencies in the local Communist-run news media. Cultivating an aura of objectivity and factual accuracy was a way of getting listeners to identify RFE and the West with truth in contrast to Communist lies. RFE characterized itself as a reliable source of knowledge, while delegitimizing the Communist media as mere propaganda.[53] Unlike the BBC or Voice of America (VOA), both of which also broadcast to the region in the local languages, RFE emphasized domestic news, setting itself up as a direct competitor to local news sources.[54] RFE's Czechoslovak desk, for example, concentrated on the accurate reporting of events within Czechoslovakia. RFE's research arm was devoted to finding out information about events behind the Iron Curtain by monitoring the Communist press and radio, interviewing refugees and travelers, and corresponding with residents.

In this period, however, the station was at least equally concerned with showing that Communism was ideologically false. Providing the truth meant countering Communist propaganda with RFE's own. Biweekly reports on broadcasts prepared by the New York–based office of the policy adviser addressed such issues as news quality and language, but also whether programs were effective propaganda. The policy advisers were much more concerned with the quality of the propaganda effort than with the quality of RFE's news programming per se. One early report on Hungarian broadcasts from June 1951 even criticized the Hungarian desk for simply reporting the facts, remarking, "Too emotionally involved to use present events ruthlessly as weapons against the regime, the Desk merely used straight reporting and comment. This, in itself, was well done, but it does not begin to tax the capabilities of RFE. It is crucial moments like this that

RFE should come into its own."[55] RFE's role here was explicitly not merely to report the news, but to use the news to illustrate the greater truths of Communist rule in Eastern Europe. This critique of the Hungarian desk also illustrates some of the differences between what American advisers and East European exile writers considered effective propaganda. The New York office frequently criticized scripts for being too emotional or polemical, as well as too vague, silly, or elitist. New York–based reviewers called for "hard-hitting and vigorous" or "forceful and clear" programs that skillfully refuted Communist claims and attacked their policies with facts rather than just invective.[56]

Along with the news, RFE broadcasts during the early 1950s conveyed a range of truths to their listeners. Perhaps the most fundamental of these was that Communists lied and could not be trusted. This was the foundation of the daily program "Other Side of the Coin," which aired in both Czechoslovak and Polish versions (the programs were alike only in their premise; the scripts for each were original). As the Czechoslovak version of the program declared in its opening seconds, "We disclose lies and swindles in Communist propaganda."[57] Each episode "decoded" the Communist press, telling listeners what the "real" story was. In one early episode, the narrator declared that the Communist press told so many lies that the general rule of thumb was to always assume that the truth was precisely the opposite of what the Communist media asserted.[58] The unstated assumption behind this program (and RFE as a whole) was that truth resided in the West. This idea was reinforced in a special commentary written by the Czech exile writer Pavel Tigrid (who also wrote some scripts for "Other Side of the Coin") to mark the fourth anniversary of the Communist takeover of power in Czechoslovakia. Tigrid began his remarks by talking about how he had met with a group of eminent Czechoslovak exiles a few weeks previously in the United States. All of them agreed that the remarkable thing about the United States was that lying was completely unnecessary.[59] RFE's authority as a source of truth did not come from the fact that it was staffed by exiles, but from its location in the West (the fact that it was funded by the American government was still secret). At home, the same people would be forced to tell lies. But in the West, they told only the truth.

The effect of remarks like Tigrid's was to place responsibility on people's environment rather than on their character. The Czechoslovak exiles had lied at home because they felt compelled to do so, not because they were intrinsically liars. They did not have control over their own actions. For RFE, this powerlessness was characteristic of Communist Eastern Europe. The inhabitants of Eastern Europe were routinely referred to as "captive," "conquered," "oppressed," or "enslaved" peoples, both in scripts and in internal RFE communications.[60] These descriptors were generally used without comment; they were simply standard ways of referring to the populations of the Soviet Bloc. For example, the introduction of the program "Inside Romania" of October 9, 1952, began with an announcer stating, "And now our program continues with news and commentaries on enslaved Romania ... What is being told from one end and to the other of our conquered ancestral homeland?"[61] Occasionally, programs might offer more detailed images. A Polish script from around the same time compared Communist factory controllers who incessantly pressed their charges to fulfill ever-increasing quotas to slave overseers of ancient Assyria or Babylon. While the Communists did not actually whip the workers, the program noted, they held a metaphorical "lash" over them in the form of the security police and its network of informers.[62]

Unusually, the last example portrayed Polish workers enslaved by Polish Communists. More typically, RFE programs deemphasized local responsibility for Communism, equating Communist rule with foreign occupation. Both Communist personnel and ideas were often referred to as alien elements imported from Moscow, with no local roots in the region. East Europeans were merely the victims of a Soviet invasion. An analysis of Hungarian broadcasts from March 27 to April 9, 1952, noted that "the Desk devotes a good deal of time to describing conditions within Hungary and to establishing the Regime's responsibility for them ... The rationale behind most of these polemics is that the Regime is a product of an alien culture, and, as such, evil."[63] A particularly virulent example of this kind of rhetoric appeared in a Romanian broadcast of May 10, 1952 (May 10 was Romania's Independence Day until the Communists took power in 1947). The script began by lamenting the "seven years of Soviet occupation" in Romania and continued, "In the midst of this complete subjugation of the country by Soviet banditism we saw the clear intention of the invader to destroy our national being."[64]

Similar language was used in a Polish script a week later. The program began with the narrator, Anthony Zarzecki, declaring, "The Communist regime of Poland is trying with all possible tricks and the use of violence to force upon the Polish community a Soviet way of thinking and acting ... The living and the dead are supposed to be the executioners and tyrants of the Polish nation, they are to serve the unsatisfied appetites of the Soviet lust for power."[65] The point of this particular show was to decry the way that the Communist regime in Poland was trying to reclaim Polish national heroes, in this case Zygmunt Padlewski, a Polish nationalist who was executed by the Russians for participating in the January Uprising of 1863. To RFE's Polish desk, the Polish Communists were the equivalent of the tsarist overlords of the nineteenth century. The fact that they were ethnically Polish was immaterial. They were the representatives of a foreign ideology and a foreign oppressor and did not represent the authentic Polish nation.

Many scripts, especially those from the period before June 1953, equated Communism with terror and oppression. Programs denounced the heinous crimes committed by Communist regimes, publicized information about prisons and work camps, and reminded listeners that informers could be lurking anywhere. As a typical example, a series of programs broadcast by the Romanian desk was devoted to the sadistic activities of the Communist police. One script from February 6, 1951, consisted entirely of accusations of police cruelty, noting offenders by name and location. "The list of the victims of these criminals is much too long to be read," intoned the narrator. "It is made up of men murdered, men who vanished in the prisons of Bucharest, of patriots who were picked up at home in the eyes of their families, or in the streets, or sent to Russia, or to work on the canal, or to the darkness of the mines at Ocnele Mari, or of the workers beaten up and maimed or disabled for life, of students manhandled because they refused to bow their heads or sell their souls to the Communist beast, or even of innocent women and children accused of being 'reactionary.'"[66] In this script, Communism was not about ideas, but only about the murder of innocent people at the whims of thugs and gangsters.

This kind of language was common in broadcasts from the early 1950s. One reviewer at RFE's policy office remarked in 1951 that a "typical Hungarian desk script" was filled with hyperbolic invective denouncing the depravity of Communist officials. A "partial list" of the epithets used in just one script included "cursed pagans; gangsters; depraved scum; ruthless hirelings; ravenous wolves; bastard Muscovite upstarts; callous brigands; bestial bastards,"[67] language that intriguingly echoed the invective used in Communist show trials. It was understandable that RFE's exile employees, who might have fled their homelands under the threat of arrest, would feel compelled to inveigh against Communist terror.[68] But the intensity of emotion in such scripts could be detrimental to RFE's larger goals. As the same review noted, an RFE intelligence report from Hungary claimed that this kind of emotionally heated broadcast "acted 'like a drug on the people,'" causing more stupor than positive action.[69]

Such programs implicitly told listeners that they were facing an enemy that was beyond them. RFE's American staffers were cognizant that this presented a problem for the station. An internal RFE document noted that "by highlighting the scope of this terror, [RFE] unconsciously embarked upon promoting its irresistible power."[70] By bombarding its audience with tales of Communist evil, RFE potentially increased its listeners' sense of vulnerability and weakness. As one internal analysis asked, "As we emphasize the injustices the prisoner peoples are forced to endure, do we not also underline their essential helplessness?"[71] Scriptwriters were directed to compose broadcasts that emphasized Western strength as a counterpoint to Soviet power. The idea was that this could create hope instead of fear. But some analysts worried that this was not an effective strategy because it still emphasized the helplessness of East Europeans themselves. One wrote, "It is possible that we have been courting apathy, apathy born of the implication that the fate of these people is to be decided exclusively in the outcome of the struggle between East and West."[72]

The question of whether to promote active resistance to Communist rule in the region bedeviled RFE. The station wanted to offer hope to its audience, but usually shied away from advocating resistance, fearing responsibility for failed uprisings.[73] A policy guideline written for the Czechoslovak desk dated May 17, 1951, suggested a middle course, advising scriptwriters to emphasize that "liberation when it comes, will come from the West."[74] Some early scripts encouraged listeners to expect the imminent demise of Communist governments, without specifying how that would happen. The Romanian script of February 6, 1951, warned Communist police torturers that the nation would judge them when "the day of reckoning arrives."[75] But such statements could have repercussions. RFE directors feared the cost to the station's credibility if its broadcasts made predictions that did not come true. Accordingly, the 1952 RFE policy handbook prohibited statements promising Western liberation. One memo even asked editors not to quote intemperate speeches by US Congress members calling for armed intervention in Eastern Europe to avoid giving the wrong impression.[76] This policy began to shift after the uprising in East Germany in June 1953 and contemporaneous riots in Czechoslovakia. Programs were still not supposed to advocate revolt, but the desks were directed to encourage listeners to believe in their power to change domestic policy through manifestations of popular discontent.[77] A 1953 Czechoslovak desk policy guideline noted that it was now possible to press people to "contribute" to their own liberation, "to make use of their strength and ingenuity to begin hacking away at the Iron Curtain from the inside."[78] This policy continued, albeit in a slightly more moderate tone, until after the failed Hungarian revolution of 1956.[79]

Captive Minds

On December 22, 1949, US President Harry S. Truman gave a speech dedicating the carillon at Arlington National Cemetery. He spoke of the world's desire for peace, but cautioned that it would remain elusive as long as the world was divided into "free and captive peoples." The "captive peoples," he said, lived in "darkness" so impenetrable that "they cannot see the hand we hold out in friendship." Deprived of knowledge of the world, living in what amounted to a prison, these captives had no agency. They were the puppets of their masters, who "made them" reject the friendly overtures of the West.[80] In his speech, Truman did not specify who these captive peoples were. But the audience would have understood that he was referring to the populations of Eastern Europe.[81] In the early Cold War, the term "captive peoples" or "captive nations" (along with "enslaved peoples" or "prisoner peoples" and other variants) was often used to refer to the inhabitants of the Soviet Bloc; some examples have already been given in this chapter. By evoking the image of a prison or a concentration camp, the term suggested that the peoples of Eastern Europe had no control over their own destiny. Immobilized behind the barbed wire of the Iron Curtain, they sat and suffered and waited to be released.[82]

The term "captive nations" (or "captive peoples") was first used in the 1920s by anti-Bolshevik nationalist governments in exile to protest Communist rule in Ukraine, the Caucasus and other parts of the new Soviet Union.[83] After 1939, the American news media sometimes used it to refer to people living in countries occupied by Nazi Germany. Newspapers were more likely to use "conquered peoples" or "subject peoples" to describe those living under Nazi rule, but "captive peoples" also appeared in this context. There is no evidence that American officials and reporters deliberately began using "captive peoples" in conjunction with Communist Eastern Europe as a means of comparing the Soviet domination of Eastern Europe to Nazi aggression, but the fact that the same term was used for both phenomena subtly suggested a continuity of evil between Nazi and Soviet regimes. RFE broadcasts often made the comparison between the two regimes in less subtle terms for their East European audiences. An episode of the Polish version of "Other Side of the Coin" on April 1952 charged that "the so-called liberation" [from Nazism] was . . . nothing more than a change in the person of the ruthless occupant." The essence of the system, according to this broadcast, was the same: "Their [Nazi] work survived and in [a] new edition with new people serves . . . the same shameful idea of the liquidation and abolition of human freedom."[84]

Behind the term "captive peoples" was the assumption that freedom was the exclusive province of the West. Communists could rule only by crushing freedom and turning the people into prisoners. In his 1952 *Life* article calling for a more aggressive foreign policy, John Foster Dulles described Communism as a society in which practically everyone was enslaved: "On the Soviet side a dozen people in the Kremlin are attempting to rule 800 million human beings—while trying to conquer more. All except a privileged few work under conditions which sternly deny them the 'pursuit of happiness.'"[85] For Dulles, Soviet citizens were no better than slaves, but the citizens of the People's Democracies were even more powerless. These captive nations were ruled by a foreign power, alien to their own way of life. Decrying the state of these captive peoples became a staple of US foreign policy. By 1952, both Democratic and Republican party platforms "looked forward to the day when all the captive nations of Europe and Asia would be free," although neither party cared to specify how this liberation would be achieved.[86] Although the Eisenhower administration was careful not to commit itself to military intervention on behalf of Eastern Europe, it continued to endorse a policy of bringing freedom to the enslaved peoples of the Soviet Bloc.[87] As the White House announced in 1955, "The peaceful liberation of the captive peoples has been, is, and, until success is achieved, will continue to be a major goal of U.S. foreign policy."[88] In 1959, this commitment to the so-called captives of Eastern Europe was commemorated in Captive Nations Week, which the US government continues to observe today.[89]

The label "captive peoples" was avidly grasped by political exiles from Eastern Europe. Just as Dulles used the term to question the legitimacy of Communist governments, exiles used such language to argue that the Communist regimes in their countries were foreign occupiers that did not represent them. They claimed the status of captives as a badge of honor and a sign of their own anti-Communist credentials. But even though East European exiles were eager to jump on the bandwagon of the captive peoples, they were also encouraged to do this by American officials or their surrogates. In 1951, the Free Europe Committee gathered representatives from the region in Philadelphia, where they pressed for the freedom of the captive peoples, arguing that world peace could not be achieved until they had been "released from the shackles of Russian mastery."[90] A few years later, when political leaders from different national groups in exile finally agreed under FEC pressure to cooperate under one organization, they named it the Assembly of Captive European Nations (ACEN). While the different groups often had trouble cooperating with each other, they had no problem accepting the common label of "captivity" and presenting this as their face to the world.[91]

This image of captive peoples and nations was echoed in the title of Czesław Miłosz's classic analysis of Stalinist Poland, *The Captive Mind*, published in English in 1953. The book was written in Paris shortly after Miłosz defected from Poland in 1951. Before his stint at the Polish Embassy in Paris, Miłosz had served in the Polish diplomatic corps in New York and Washington, DC; he was familiar with the Western press and would have known the English-language connotations of his title. Yet it is not entirely clear why Miłosz decided to call his book *The Captive Mind*. Miłosz's earliest correspondence with his American publisher, Alfred A. Knopf, did not mention any title at all.[92] In a June 1952 letter, Philip Vaudrin, Miłosz's editor at Knopf used "The Great Temptation" as a tentative title.[93] But only a month later, it had been changed to *The Captive Mind*. Vaudrin wrote to Miłosz that he thought this title was acceptable, but he believed they could still do better.[94] Vaudrin's letter makes it clear that the title was not his idea but does not say where it came from. In their book about Miłosz and his work, Leonard Nathan and Arthur Quinn suggest that the title came from Miłosz's reading of Simone's Weil's essay "Human Personality." Their evidence is circumstantial: Miłosz was open about Weil's influence on his work, and Weil's essay did use the term "captive mind" in ways echoed by Miłosz's own work.[95]

For many later readers, *The Captive Mind* was the definitive statement about intellectuals in Stalinist Eastern Europe. But the book's reception in 1953 did not equal its later influence or predict its longevity (it is still in print). About eighteen months after its publication, *The Captive Mind* had sold only 2,600 copies, despite being favorably reviewed in major publications and lauded by figures such as Hannah Arendt.[96] It is only possible to speculate about the reasons. It could simply be that few Americans cared to read about the fate of East Europeans. It might also be that the subject matter of *The Captive Mind* was especially challenging to the American audience. The book examined how intellectuals (particularly writers) responded to Communism. It could be argued that the title "The Great Temptation" was a more accurate description of the text than "The Captive Mind." One of Miłosz's main themes was the attraction Communist ideology had for intellectuals. Unlike most American or exile writers, Miłosz was willing to engage with Communism as a set of ideas and not only as system of terror.

Four of the book's nine chapters analyzed why particular writers (referred to by pseudonyms) were drawn to Communism in some way. Miłosz depicted them sympathetically; three of the four can be seen as tragic figures (one was portrayed as an opportunistic hack). They were intrigued by the ideology of dialectical materialism (or Diamat), which offered a comprehensive way of looking at the world and analyzing its problems. They had doubts and misgivings, but eventually they chose to accept the Diamat rather than resist it. They began to work with the regime and delighted in a system that held intellectuals in such high esteem. They were published, became famous, and had comfortable lifestyles. But then they began to feel trapped by the Diamat, which, while offering certainty, stifled creativity. Gradually, they were convinced to betray their artistic convictions in the name of the regime.

Despite this, none of them renounced Communism or broke with the government, although one committed suicide.[97] While they were forced to make artistic compromises, they convinced themselves that they were better off in the East than in the West. If they had become captives, they were in a prison they had helped build and entered willingly. These were not heroic intellectuals thrown in jail for refusing to toe the Communist line. Nor were they powerless victims, even if they felt oppressed by the mighty ability of the Diamat to structure thought. Their situation did not fit the image of the captive peoples usually portrayed in the American media. It was more complicated, more nuanced, and not so easy to understand in a culture that, like Truman in his speech, wanted to divide the world into two distinct sides.

Probably the most influential chapter in the book is about the idea of Ketman. Miłosz took the term from a book by Arthur de Gobineau about Muslims who preserved their heretical beliefs in the face of opposition by acting in public as if they had disavowed them. It was more honorable to live secure in the knowledge of one's secret enlightenment than to die in fruitless open resistance. With respect to Communist Eastern Europe, Ketman was often taken to mean simply acting as if one supported Communism when one really did not. This interpretation was consistent with the understanding of captive societies by Americans or exiles during this period: no one truly accepted Communist ideology, but many were forced by fear to behave as if they did. Dissembling was indeed an integral part of Ketman; as Miłosz wrote, "He who practices Ketman lies."[98] But Ketman was not as simple as that. To adopt Ketman was not exclusively the province of anti-Communists; it indicated opposition to a part of the ruling culture. It could be used by both the most convinced "pure" Communists and their opponents alike.[99]

Ketman indicated a form of resistance to dictatorship, but it was simultaneously a form of accommodation of the self to that dictatorship. When a person had practiced Ketman for a while "he c[ould] no longer differentiate his true self from the self he simulate[d]."[100] Ketman did not merely cloud the self; it changed it. The practice of Ketman, Miłosz speculated, became a way of making meaning for the individual. Ketman, he said, "means self-realization *against* something."[101] The aspects of the ruling culture against which a person struggled became, in other words, the Other against which they defined themselves. Rather than preserving a preexisting resistant anti-Communist self, Ketman created a new self that was, perversely, dependent on its existing environment. Ketman allowed captives to survive their situation and achieve a measure of agency, but it also meant they might not find the circumstances of liberation truly freeing.

Reviews of *The Captive Mind* in the United States did not always reflect this nuance. Some reviewers struggled not to see the book in the terms dictated by American preconceptions about captive nations and Soviet evil. Peter Viereck, writing in the *New York Times Book Review*, reduced the Diamat to "thought control" and said that Miłosz "reinforced[d] the reader's reverence for individual freedom by showing that the 'captive mind,' no matter how bribed and terrorized and propagandized, can still resist captivity." Viereck was unable to take Communist ideology seriously; it was only a poor disguise for a clenched fist. For him, integrity meant resistance. He referred to "softness against Communism" as "a neurosis of middle-class intellectuals—rich, rootless, guilt-ridden, self-hating"—and repeatedly labeled Miłosz as a fellow traveler because he had been employed by the Polish diplomatic corps.[102]

In the *Washington Post*, Edwin D. Gritz gravitated toward even more florid language, writing that *The Captive Mind* "goes far beyond the familiar terrors of communism to reveal man's far more terrible struggle against intellectual perversion to Red tyranny." Gritz was a little easier on Miłosz himself, noting that he worked for Poland "during the period of 1946 to 1951 when many aspects of communism were befogged by skillful propaganda." Like Viereck, Gritz did not willfully misread the text, but his interpretation of it tended to conform to American expectations. Both Viereck and Gritz were convinced of Communism's oppressive, evil nature in a way that Miłosz's subjects (if not Miłosz himself) were not.[103] The character of these reviews was noticed by Miłosz's editor, Philip Vaudrin, who wrote to send him the early reviews and remarked, "Not all reviewers seem to have seized on the real point of your book, and some would seem to have deliberately avoided the real point. But the important thing is that your book is being received over here as a really significant contribution to our understandings of the life of the mind under Communism."[104]

Some reviewers were better able to see beyond the image of shackles and jails that the book's title suggested. William P. Clancy noted in *Commonweal* that, although Miłosz's writers had to pay a price, "the reward was great—public peace, usefulness, and the knowledge that one has made his peace with 'history.'" Miłosz made it clear, Clancy admitted, that, for some, captivity was "a plausible price to pay."[105] In a long, perceptive essay in the *New Yorker*, Dwight MacDonald lauded the book's "wit and elegance" and "original and penetrating" treatment of its subject, saying it was more "subtle and imaginative" than any study other than Hannah Arendt's *Origins of Totalitarianism*. Yet he presciently added, in a way that likely had Philip Vaudrin gnashing his teeth, that it probably would not sell very well. The reason was that the author "has refused to employ any of the popular approaches to this kind of thing." Part of the difficulty, MacDonald pointed out, was that Miłosz insisted that East European intellectuals could be understood only on their own terms, not through the lens of captivity imagined by the West.[106]

The Captive Mind was controversial among émigrés from the region, devoted as they were to a certain image of captivity. Some Polish exiles were violently opposed to the book, which they considered an apologia for Communists (and Miłosz a closet Marxist).[107] Their opposition was one factor in the US State Department's refusal to grant Miłosz a visa during this period; in 1960 he would finally leave Paris to become Professor of Slavic Studies at the University of California at Berkeley.[108] Despite the controversy, Miłosz made an agreement with RFE to translate and adapt (unspecified) portions of the book for use in broadcasts on all the language services except the Polish.[109] Although *The Captive Mind* apparently did not get to Poland via RFE, print copies were read and discussed there.[110] The book also made an impression on at least some RFE staff members. An RFE research report about architects in Poland analyzed their situation as an expression of Ketman.[111] Ketman similarly helped a BBC Audience Research staffer, Dr. Z. Grabowski, to frame part of his interview with a Mr. P, a recent Polish refugee in Berlin.[112] Thus, *The Captive Mind*, written by a Pole in the West to describe a phenomenon in Eastern Europe for a Western audience, could potentially influence how East Europeans (both in exile and not) interpreted their own experience.

Satellite Mentality

In the early years of the Cold War, the American media usually referred to the Communist countries of Eastern Europe as a cohesive bloc, making little distinction between them. All Communist countries were perceived as essentially the same: totalitarian dictatorships characterized by terror, oppression, and fear. The only thing that made Eastern Europe distinct from the Soviet Union was that it was doubly subject, its governments beholden not only to Communist priorities but to Soviet demands. The region's different languages, religions, histories, cultures, even alphabets, all seemingly ceased to matter; most Americans did not even know they existed. In crucial ways, the satellites were the same, an idea also inherent in terms like "captive nations." Even Miłosz helped to solidify this impression. In *The Captive Mind*, he referred to "Central and Eastern Europe" as a unit, with distinct attitudes and characteristics that developed out of its inhabitants' similar response to directives coming out of Moscow (or "the Center").[113]

The idea that Communism had created a similar culture and similar patterns of behavior in Eastern Europe was manifest in *Satellite Mentality*, a book published in 1956. This volume analyzed about three hundred interviews carried out in 1951–1952 with Poles, Czechoslovaks, and Hungarians who had recently fled their homelands; most were interviewed in German and Austrian refugee camps within weeks after their arrival in the West. The interviews were conducted by International Public Opinion Research (IPOR) at the behest of Voice of America. The interviewers were less recent, well-educated exiles who used a script prepared by IPOR. The interviews were extensive—most transcripts were twenty to thirty pages long in English translation—and dealt with a variety of topics of interest to VOA, such as radio listening habits, perceptions of the United States, and knowledge of current events. VOA then contracted with the Columbia University Bureau of Applied Social Research to conduct an extensive analysis of the material.[114] The bureau's report was released to VOA and the State Department in 1953, but not published until 1956.[115] The report was coauthored by Siegfried Kracauer, now renowned for his work on the cinema and visual culture in Weimar and Nazi Germany, and Paul L. Berkman.

The VOA interview project was conceived and executed by individuals—including Kracauer and Leo Lowenthal, who served as chief of the Evaluation Division of the International Broadcasting Service of the State Department—who were central to the development of totalitarian theory, and this perspective informed all aspects of the project.[116] As scholarly researchers, Kracauer and Berkman made every effort to be sensitive to the potential biases in their data. They cautioned that "to explore the interviews as a source of knowledge is a precarious undertaking," citing the skewed nature of their sample: predominantly poorly educated young men from the ages of seventeen to thirty who hailed from border regions and belonged to the peasantry or working class. The authors also noted that recent exiles living in refugee camps might feel compelled to cast their own stories in what they imagined was a positive light, exaggerating the extent to which they had been persecuted or changing the reasons they had fled. Though respondents were explicitly told that their answers would have no bearing on their applications for emigration visas or work prospects, they still might tell their interviewers only what they believed they wanted to hear.[117] In turn, the refugees' sense of what the interviewers expected could itself have been shaped by what they had heard on Western radio stations like VOA and RFE.[118] To account for such bias, Kracauer and Berkman's method was to focus on the contradictions in a person's story. A respondent's true feelings, they hypothesized, emerged in these unguarded moments.[119]

However, although they were careful to account for the bias on the part of the interview respondents, Kracauer and Berkman did not question their own assumptions about the workings of Communist regimes with the same care. The authors ascribed great power to Communist propaganda, which they assumed was based on lies. As they said in a preparatory set of hypotheses they developed for VOA in January 1953, "Communist propaganda has a way of insidiously influencing minds exposed to it . . . [It] sticks in the mind. It is tacky. And should its ever-repeated slogans even be disapproved, they nevertheless succeed in structuring attention and outlook." In time, they postulated, these Communist presumptions would "sink themselves into the deep psychological layers" and become inextricably fused with the personality.[120] Although many contemporary historians might agree with the idea that the surrounding culture inevitably shapes a person's subjectivity, for the authors this was something peculiar to Communist or totalitarian regimes. While they avoided using the term "brainwashing," Kracauer and Berkman did label Communist propaganda "thought control," "mind manipulation," and "indoctrination."[121] It was a weapon cleverly designed to deprive individuals of their free will.

Respectful of their data, the authors noted that most interview respondents did not seem to care much about the ideas being promulgated by the state. Most of them were badly educated young workers or farmers, who tended not to engage with Communism as an ideology at all. What they really resented about propaganda campaigns was not the ideas they expressed but how they were forced to give up leisure time to attend boring political meetings or participate in extra weekend brigades without pay.[122] But rather than seeing this as evidence that Communist propaganda had failed (Communists did hope, after all, to make people enthusiastic about their ideas), Kracauer and Berkman claimed it heralded success. Using their method of looking for contradictions in their sources' stories, the authors emphasized moments when even these committed anti-Communist refugees seemed to have "succumbed" to Communist propaganda.[123] Remarking that capitalists were influential in the United States or that Americans did not enjoy a social welfare state was, for the authors, proof that Communist propaganda was working, sneaking its way into even anti-Communist hearts.[124] That such comments might have a factual basis was of no significance.

One of the things that surprised the authors was that many of the interview respondents did not say that they hated all Communists. They had imagined that the refugees would express only disgust for their oppressors. Instead, the respondents made distinctions between different kinds of Communists and expressed sympathy with those who had joined the party just to keep their jobs or stay out of jail and even with the ideologically committed who had been party members in the interwar period. They were less forgiving of those who became party members opportunistically; some claimed such people were likely to denounce others to get ahead. The way to explain this unforeseen phenomenon, Kracauer and Berkman theorized, was by invoking what they called the "occupation concept." "Satellite non-Communists," as they called them, thought of their countries as colonies of Moscow. They were therefore able to transfer all of their hate and resentment to the Russians/Soviets and view most of their own compatriots, even those who had joined the party, sympathetically. Those Communists who were completely subservient to Moscow were denationalized and viewed as Soviet stand-ins rather than "real" Hungarians, Czechoslovaks, or Poles.[125]

Quite perceptively, the authors noted that such beliefs might have been strengthened by Western radio broadcasts that emphasized the foreign nature of local Communist regimes. Kracauer and Berkman even remarked that many satellite citizens might have been ideologically disposed to support Communism if they did not see it as an instrument of Russian domination. For the authors, this indicated that radio broadcasts emphasizing the concept of captivity or occupation were successful tools for the West.[126] Yet, although they lauded its usefulness as a propaganda device, Kracauer and Berkman did not critically analyze the idea of East European captivity itself. Instead, they accepted it as describing a self-evident reality. Terms like "captive peoples" and "captive populations" were sprinkled liberally throughout the text as self-evident descriptors. The authors saw no need to comment on their use of these terms or to treat them as manifestations of a particular ideological perspective, even as they showed how the concept of Soviet "occupation" was spread by exiles and the Western media to Eastern Europe. From their perspective, it was totalitarian societies, not the free world, that infected and warped people's minds with propaganda. If Western radio inspired some East Europeans to see their Communist rulers as foreign occupiers, this was simply telling them the truth.

Whereas the free world exalted the individual, Communism, Kracauer and Berkman believed, tried to destroy the self. Following Hannah Arendt's analysis in the *Origins of Totalitarianism*, they claimed that Communism was an "atomizing force" that worked to turn "the individual into a mere automaton." A free and independent self could only be "a threat to a Communist regime, even if [that self belonged to] a convinced Communist."[127] This analysis led the authors to valorize passive resistance as a means of maintaining the free self. They labeled many activities, including telling jokes about Communist officials, going to church, and not buying newspapers, as manifestations of passive resistance and argued they meant that the Communists would not win their battle to eliminate individuality.[128] Kracauer and Berkman accepted without question the contention of many respondents that active resistance was simply impossible. In this, they joined the many exiles and Westerners who claimed that a lack of resistance in Eastern Europe did not indicate support for Communism, but only reflected the reality of the awesome power wielded by Stalinist regimes. The authors did not consider whether this sense of powerlessness could also have been at least in part imbibed from Western radio programs. Instead, the book validated the refugees' assertions of their own powerlessness and even invested that powerlessness with a kind of power: the power to save the soul in the face of totalitarian onslaught.

This totalitarian perspective similarly shaped Kracauer and Berkman's analysis of fear. The authors stated early in the volume, "We take it for granted that the Satellite peoples live in a state of fear." This fear, they believed, was "ubiquitous" and "intense—so intense that in effect many despair of putting up with it."[129] Although they rigorously questioned interviewees' statements about their susceptibility to propaganda, their images of the United States, or their feelings about different kinds of Communists, the authors did not examine their statements about fear critically. They simply accepted them as proof of what they already believed to be true about Communism. At times, their careful and intelligent analysis of the interviews caught some contradictions that could have qualified their own blanket assertions about the ubiquity of fear in Communist

Eastern Europe. The authors noted that many interviewees claimed that fear had strained friendships. Not knowing who might be an informant for the secret police, they could no longer behave normally even around their friends. This left them, Kracauer and Berkman contended, in "a cocoon-like state of isolation that inevitably paralyzes the will." But they also observed that some of the refugees admitted elsewhere in their interviews that they did in fact maintain close friendships and even remained friends with party members. Kracauer and Berkman suggested that such friendships might be a refuge from the regime. But, although they acknowledged the contradiction in the respondents' statements, this did not lead them to consider that the fear interviewees reported might not be as ubiquitous as they imagined. It was, it seemed, impossible for them to imagine that life under Communism was not always carried out under a layer of oppressive fear, even when their own sources suggested this might be the case.

The Fact of Fear

There is no question that Communist brutality in Stalinist Eastern Europe was real. East Europeans did not portray themselves as powerless captives simply because they heard terms like this Western radio broadcasts. At the same time, we can see that the American conviction that there was only one truth about Eastern Europe privileged certain kinds of stories and experiences over others. Many Americans, including committed journalists like Leland Stowe and brilliant academics like Siegfried Kracauer, could understand Eastern Europe only through a totalitarian framework. Because they believed so firmly that Communism was no more than a big lie, they had a difficult time taking its ideas seriously. And because they knew already that East Europeans spent their lives in the grip of an atomizing and paralyzing fear, they were unable to see the ways in which refugees' own stories nuanced this totalizing picture. Looking at the sources they used from a different perspective suggests a much less clear-cut story. At the time, however, the work of men like Kracauer and Berkman provided the foundation of objective knowledge that supported totalitarian theory.

4 THAT FUNNY FEELING CREEPING UP YOUR BACK

In June 1951, an unnamed source from inside Hungary told Radio Free Europe (RFE) researchers, "Two fears haunt the people of Hungary, the so-called 'bell fear' and the 'uniform fear.'"[1] The bell fear, the source explained, was the terror people felt whenever the doorbell rang, thinking the sound meant the police had come to take them away. The uniform fear was the rush of anxiety Hungarians experienced when dealing with uniformed state employees, whether police officers, soldiers, railway conductors, postal workers, or gas company inspectors. Uniforms, according to the source, symbolized state power and conjured images of house searches, arrest, and torture. The source emphasized that it was completely rational for Hungarians to be living in this state of extreme fear. Everyone knew, he said, that the police tortured innocent people indiscriminately. Without providing such specifics as names and dates, the source gave some examples: an elderly woman whose teeth had been knocked out in police custody and another woman who died of "internal burns" after being given injections of boiling water during an interrogation. The informant then listed numerous other forms of torture "everyone" knew were used by the security service, including electric shocks, beatings, ice-cold water baths, and forcing prisoners to stand for hours at a time. The bell fear and the uniform fear were rooted in this common knowledge. The report suggested that Communist efforts to awaken fears of spies and saboteurs from the West had come to naught: Hungarians, said the source, were much more afraid of Communist police agents than of Western warmongers.

Radio Free Europe collected many research reports like this one. Most were based on interviews with refugees who had recently fled their homelands; a minority contained information sent by correspondents who still lived in the region. These RFE reports, known internally as "Information Items," were filtered through many layers of mediation. Especially in the years before 1954, the format of individual "Items" was idiosyncratic. RFE interviewers often did not use standardized or prepared scripts, nor did they record their conversations as they took place. The interviewers did not always identify themselves as RFE employees, but might engage subjects in casual conversation without telling them that their responses would be reported to RFE. They wrote reports about their conversations after the fact, often from memory, and included only the information they thought would interest the RFE staff.[2] Although it is difficult to determine the precise impact an employee's ideological biases had on the composition of any particular report, the strongly anti-Communist orientation of RFE undoubtedly influenced what interviewers and analysts found interesting or believable.

During the years before 1956, RFE researchers composed tens of thousands of these reports or "Information Items." So-called Items were first filed in the original language of the interview, with summaries, commentary, and subject headings in English. Some were fully translated into English or German for use by workers from any of the RFE language services.[3] Together, the Items formed a source database that could be used by RFE analysts and scriptwriters for research purposes.[4] Each contained a brief evaluation comment by an RFE analyst assessing the report's value as "objective" information. Did the Item contain reliable facts, and could its information be corroborated by other sources? RFE's evaluators made the process of verification seem straightforward, but the task of sorting fact from fiction, or truth from lies, was actually quite complicated.

The RFE analysts who evaluated the report about the bell fear and the uniform fear were concerned primarily with whether it was factually accurate. They noted that while the source had been reliable in the past, the information in this particular report could not be independently verified. Nonetheless, they remarked, "This report contains well-known facts of the last three to four years. Not newsworthy."[5] The RFE team judged the report to be fact, despite its lack of names, dates, or other specific details to corroborate its accounts of torture or widespread fear among the population. They classified it as "not newsworthy" because they agreed with the source that the brutality of the Hungarian security service (Államvédelmi Hatóság, or ÁVH) and the oppressive fear it inspired had already been so conclusively proved that it had achieved the status of old news.

But how did this information about the ÁVH's methods and the fear they inspired become common knowledge? How did the existence of something as subjective as fear take on the status of fact, so taken for granted that references to it could be assumed to be true, even without the usual corroboration? Unlike pieces of discrete information, such as the price of eggs or even the name of a secret police commandant, claims about emotions were hard to verify. Because they came from personal experience, claims about emotions like fear were generally taken at face value, especially if they met preexisting Western expectations about how people should feel under a totalitarian dictatorship. Once they were captured on paper, reports about fear and other emotions could corroborate future reports based on ostensibly similar personal experiences. As these reports accumulated, they were transformed into evidence about everyday life behind the Iron Curtain, helping to provide a scientific basis for Western knowledge about totalitarian societies.

It was easy to see the knowledge created from informants' personal experiences as providing an uncomplicated window into Communist society in Eastern Europe. However, even in the early years of the Cold War, East Europeans did not live in a vacuum, exposed only to the ideas presented by the local Communist-dominated media. Western radio stations could affect the ways East Europeans interpreted their own experiences. Information gathered by RFE, like the report on the bell fear and the uniform fear, informed broadcasts that were transmitted back into Eastern Europe.[6] Listening to the radio, East Europeans heard about the brutality of their police and the ubiquity of police informers; they might even be told their names. This does not mean that Communist terror was merely a fantasy concocted by RFE or its competitors. This terror was certainly real and many people personally experienced it. Western radio stations did, however, become an additional source of information about police informers and their influence. For those not directly touched by state violence, Western radio might even be the primary source of such information. Western broadcasts took fears about informers and transmitted them to broader audiences, tacitly or explicitly encouraging their audiences to interpret their lives through the lens of these fears. In this way, the knowledge East Europeans created from their own experiences was not conceived in isolation, but in dialogue with the broadcasts they heard on Western radio stations.

Documents based on refugee interviews, whether conducted by RFE, VOA, or some other organization, are therefore very complicated, created through an intricate network of interactions back and forth across the Iron Curtain. Expressing their fear of being watched or spied on became a way for East European refugees to articulate and give meaning to a variety of experiences. Such fears were easily recognized and provided a basis for communicating other ideas and emotions, including feelings of powerlessness, disappointment with social change, and the despair of not fitting into a new world. Worry about watchers—children, neighbors, companions on the train—became a lens through which many people interpreted a rapidly changing world and allowed them to develop strategies for getting by in this new environment.

They Are Watching Us

An RFE special report called "Letters from Czechoslovakia," dated December 1, 1952, highlighted a communication from an unnamed Czech correspondent identified only as a young man. The youth claimed the fear of arrest was so pervasive in Czechoslovakia that "an atmosphere of fear envelops everything," like an incurable fever moving rapidly through the population. The correspondent continued, "You must feel it for yourself, in your own bones, and then you know there is no escaping it." What caused this paralyzing fear? The report implied that the young man had no particular reason to believe he was of any interest to the police; as far as we know, he was not involved in an opposition group and had not done anything to attract notice. His fear appeared to have originated from a seemingly arbitrary act of police brutality. A boy from his town, he said, had been arrested and was sweeping the street in front of the prison under the eye of a guard. As the correspondent watched, the boy "probably made a sudden or unexpected move" and the guard shot him, then kicked the motionless body. There were several witnesses, he said, but no one, including the writer, did anything to help the boy. Later, seeing the police conducting an identity card check on a train, the correspondent claimed to have been paralyzed with terror. He told RFE, "I felt the fear creeping up my back, a funny feeling of weakness and helplessness . . . You see, you never know if they are not just looking for you."[7] Having seen that the police could kill, this informant imagined they might use their power on anyone, including himself.

The young Czech man's story presented a society under what amounted to military occupation, with identity card checks on trains and armed security forces empowered to shoot civilians in the street. His portrayal echoed that of American officials and RFE broadcasters, who claimed that the countries of Eastern Europe had been occupied by foreign invaders, rendering their populations no more than captive slaves. The vast majority of refugee interviews (no matter who conducted them) echoed this basic presumption and claimed it as an essential truth. "No one" or "hardly anyone" supported the Communists, and 80–90 percent of the people wanted a change of regime, they declared.[8] Communists held power not by the force of their ideas, but by the terror they wielded. The security services were not merely a symbol of Communist power but its very substance. Like an invading army, it was their task to infiltrate and neutralize the population. Fear was one of their most useful weapons, refugees asserted.

Stories about police terror and brutality circulated widely across the boundaries between East and West. Western officials or propagandists were an eager audience for such narratives. Particularly in the years before 1953, RFE collected many stories of police violence and torture. Many of these reports echoed what prisoners recounted in later memoirs published abroad or after 1989; a source in Bulgaria reported that a friend had been arrested and subjected to continuous interrogation for more than twelve hours, just as survivors of show trials reported the use of such tactics when they were under investigation.[9] Other reports verged more toward the fantastic, like the story of a high school teacher from the Sobieski gymnasium in Krakow. An informant alleged that the teacher was given a "special treatment with gas": his hands were bound behind his back, and he was suspended from a kind of a crane so that only the tips of his toes touched the floor. A mask was then attached to his face so that a gas could be administered to induce him to confess. The source claimed the torture brought complete agony while leaving no marks. RFE evaluators noted that it was "impossible to ascertain" the extent to which this description was dramatized.[10] But whether or not the story accurately reflected police methods, through its retelling it became part of a body of knowledge about the frightening capabilities of the Communist security services that existed in both the East and the West.

Many interviewees attributed extraordinary powers to the security services, imagining that they had a miraculous ability to observe anyone at any time. One Czechoslovak source declared in 1951 that the Czechoslovak state security (Státní bezpečnost, or StB) had agents in all workplaces, coffeehouses, pubs, restaurants, movie theaters, and places of amusement. With every utterance against the regime, the source said, people expected to be sent to a concentration camp.[11] His claims were echoed by a young Hungarian electrician who fled the country in December 1954. This source told RFE, "The number of spies in the country cannot be figured. If someone makes an unequivocal remark he will be arrested immediately and will be tortured."[12] In turn, the electrician's remarks sounded eerily similar to those of a Bulgarian exile in 1952 who said, "In Sofia, there are more secret police agents than flies. They are everywhere, at every corner of the streets, in every public place."[13] RFE analysts took such claims seriously. RFE evaluators noted on the Bulgarian report that the source's story "corresponds with similar information," indicating that they had received numerous claims of this sort and accepted their credibility. And indeed, another report asserted that, in 1951, fully 20 percent of the Bulgarian population worked for the secret police, leaving everyone "surrounded" by agents, which RFE considered to be "probably true."[14]

Stories and rumors about the surveillance capabilities of the secret police were present throughout RFE's interviews. Some were fantastical. An older Prague woman who had been active in the French Resistance during the Second World War while her husband was in the Czechoslovak army in the West told an RFE informant she was convinced the StB had placed listening devices in all the chimneys in the city, enabling agents to hear what was going on in anyone's house. She claimed that several resistance groups had been discovered in this way. When the informant suggested to her that rumors like this were the result of widespread fear or had perhaps been deliberately spread by the police to create such fear, she vehemently rejected the idea and asserted that "all Prague" knew the StB was capable of such extensive surveillance.[15] The RFE informant's report suggests that this woman sincerely believed her claims. Her faith in the StB's power likely stemmed from her position as a strong anti-Communist of an older generation. The informant visited Prague in September 1952, more than four years after the Communist takeover of power, two years after the trial and execution of Milada Horáková, and after the arrest of thousands of members of the non-Communist opposition. For the woman, a belief in fantastic listening devices helped her to understand these events and explained the remarkable ability of the StB to infiltrate and eliminate opposition groups. Like many of RFE's sources (and RFE's analysts as well), she imagined that her beliefs were widely accepted as facts and was convinced that everyone thought as she did. Yet even the RFE informant realized that this was not the case. During his trip, he observed young people on the train gaily and openly chatting about their social lives. He concluded that "they were not worried about the lack of freedom or Communist outrages."[16] This carefree attitude among young people, however, did not shake the older woman's belief in the StB's power or the universal fear of it.

These narratives show how fears of informers or watchers were a way for interviewees to make their feelings or experiences intelligible, to themselves and their compatriots, but also to interlocutors in the West. Describing her life in Budapest, a sixty-five-year-old housewife who legally left Hungary in May 1952 to join her daughter in London, said, "One is always scared. One lives in terrible, constant fear. One fears the inhabitants of the house [apartment building], the neighbors in the street, old friends and family members, the so-called 'house responsible' and the party agitator-propagandists who are molesting the whole population of the city without any interruption." These comments made it seem as if such fears were simply in the air, like a germ spread from person to person. The housewife continued, "They come under various pretexts, they check your room thoroughly, and so it is not surprising that eventually you lose your nerves. People at my age are complaining that they are suffering from various symptoms, such as they are hallucinating, do not see or hear well and there is no medical explanation for these troubles." Though she did not elaborate, it seems likely that the housewife's fears stemmed from a very particular interaction. She, or someone she knew, had experienced a house search and felt afraid. This fear then became a basis for how she understood and interacted with the world around her. It inspired her to see potential enemies everywhere, be wary, and keep to herself. The RFE evaluators again simply took her story at face value, as confirmation of the kind of society they believed Communist Hungary to be, writing, "Although this gives no substantially fresh details, we release it as it seems to us to be a good round-up of description of present life in Budapest."[17]

In many of the interviewees' narratives, the fear of being observed by unseen and unknown enemies became the basis of a strategy for surviving this tumultuous time. As a source from Czechoslovakia noted, "There is no proof that your every move is watched ... and, of course, it is ridiculous to imagine that all the millions of people can be watched 24 hours a day." "Nevertheless," he continued, "if you want to go on living in comparative peace you must imagine that you're being watched continuously."[18] This source described a life lived in a state of constant tension, where every move and every utterance had to be intensely monitored. For this person, the secret police was a shadowy force that somehow existed outside of society but was also firmly embedded in it. Its agents could be masked and hidden, even among the ranks of one's close associates. This source's comments showed how beliefs about the ubiquity of informers could take on their own reality. His belief in the presence of informers (he also repeated a rumor about a restaurant outside of Prague that had escaped privatization by agreeing to have microphones installed under all its tables) had succeeded in obviating the need for any to actually exist. The source served as his own observer, watching and cataloging his behavior for anything that might be seen as suspicious. A Jewish widow from Slovakia who emigrated in 1955 echoed this man's assertions. Overt opposition in Czechoslovakia had been destroyed, she said, because the StB had "managed to create such an atmosphere of mutual distrust that nowadays nobody knows whether his best friend is not a police agent." The widow calculated that "the actual number of police spies is relatively low." But, she said, it did not matter how many there actually were. As long as a hidden network of informers existed, people would be afraid of trusting each other.[19]

Such behaviors were not necessarily irrational, but they were based on speculation and rumor as well as fact. The period from 1948 to 1956 did see tremendous growth in the size and reach of the security services (often referred to as the secret police) in each country of the Soviet Bloc. Formed under the guidance of Soviet advisers, the security organizations around the bloc tended to use similar methods and to have a similar sense of mission. It was their task to safeguard the socialist regime against both internal and external enemies. To this end, they certainly did monitor the population, and they used clandestine informers to do so.[20] The exact number of informers is difficult to calculate and assess; numbers could fluctuate and might be deceptive. In Poland, the number of informers and agents dropped by more than half between mid-1948 and the beginning of 1949, because Bezpieka (Polish security service) officials believed many of them were worthless. After this purge, the total gradually increased.[21] Still, given the available data, it is reasonable to say that the extent of informer/agent networks did not even remotely match the claims of some RFE informants. In the Polish case, the number of informants/agents in mid-1948, when the total was at its peak, was approximately 1 per every 465 inhabitants. Although the situation varied by country and date, the data suggests that the number of informers in this period did not equal even 1 percent of the population in any of the countries in the Soviet Bloc, let alone 20 percent, as some RFE sources alleged.[22] Indeed, though the period before 1956 is widely considered the era of terror in Eastern Europe, the security services tended to have greater capability, both in the number of agents/informers and in general surveillance ability (via telephone tapping, the use of listening devices, photography, etc.) in the 1980s.[23]

However, while their power to observe may have been greater in the 1980s, in the early 1950s the security services had much more power to arrest, interrogate, physically abuse, and convict suspects. Tens of thousands of people in each of the countries of the Soviet Bloc were arrested or sent to labor camps for political offenses during the years between 1948 and 1956, charged with treason, espionage, sabotage, subversive association, or the like. Again, it is difficult to come up with reliable figures for such persecutions. Records are spotty, incomplete, and contradictory.[24] Rather than enter into these complicated debates, it is simpler to say that given the scale of arrests, convictions, and deportations, it would have been clear to all of the inhabitants of the People's Democracies that the security services had the power to attack those they considered to be enemies of the state. The very public show trials of major opposition figures as well as high-ranking Communist officials explicitly sent the message that no one was immune to prosecution.

Fears about the repressive power of Communist regimes existed in a dialectical relationship with Western radio broadcasts, particularly those of RFE.[25] Radio Free Europe set itself up as the source of the truth about Eastern Europe. Its broadcasts portrayed all of the region's Communist governments as brutal, illegitimate regimes that held power only through terror and Soviet support. Throughout this period, but especially in the years before 1953, RFE exhorted listeners to be wary of possible spies or informers in their midst. Some programs revealed suspected informers or closet Communists by name, fueling beliefs about the ubiquity of hidden police agents lurking among the population.[26] These programs proved very popular. A twenty-six-year-old man from Wrocław told the BBC in 1953 that RFE's broadcasts naming informants were widely influential. When he was living in the town of Bolkow, he said, some residents were named on the air as informants by RFE. They were so frightened of retaliation that they asked for police protection.[27] Similarly, when asked about his favorite radio programs, one of the VOA interviewees, a young Pole named Ryszard Rekowski, suggested

VOA should follow RFE's model and do its own version of such programs. "You know in Poland we are very afraid of the State Police," he said. "There are many 'spies' among the population, many Communist Poles who work against non-Communist Poles. The names of those 'spies' should be broadcast because then maybe they would be more afraid and the population would believe much more in the VOA."[28]

A Hungarian man named K.A., from the village of Suttor near Sopron, also told VOA that his favorite radio show was Bálint Boda's program on RFE. He was especially taken with a series in which Bálint Boda named all the informers in the Sopron area, including Suttor. "He named several persons we would never have thought were informers," K.A. remarked. Whenever Bálint Boda named informers in the area, K.A. said he wrote down their names. He even once went by bicycle to a nearby village to tell some relatives the names of people RFE alleged were informers in their village.[29] K.A. did not doubt Bálint Boda's knowledge of the informers' identity. Though some of the names surprised him, he still believed RFE told the truth about them. Quite a few other Hungarian VOA interviewees mentioned their fondness for Bálint Boda's program, indicating that they listened to it regularly and with great interest precisely because Bálint Boda named informers.[30]

K.A. claimed he was surprised by the names of some of those RFE claimed were informers. Yet K.A. knew well that anyone might find him- or herself in this position: K.A. himself had been asked to be an informer. A few years before he left the country, K.A. was investigated for wasting timber. Because he was not a member of the Union of Working Youth (Dolgozó Ifjúság Szövetsége, or DISz) and his father was an independent craftsman, the police informed him that he was a reactionary. Presumably under the threat of arrest, they told him to join DISz and report goings-on in his village and at his workplace, and especially to name anyone who listened to Western radio stations. His interview does not make it clear whether he actually informed, although he apparently joined DISz.[31]

Many refugees claimed they had been asked to become informers under the threat of their own arrest or incarceration. Prisoners or suspects were indeed often recruited to be agents in this period.[32] In a typical example from the RFE archives, a Hungarian woman found herself in a tight situation with the ÁVH after having a few drinks with a man on Baross Square in Budapest. She paid the bill and then left with her companion to move on to another establishment, where they hoped to get a glass of rum. Two ÁVH agents followed them and demanded an explanation of their behavior. When they found out the woman was unemployed, they ordered her to report to their office the next day. The following morning they interrogated her, asking how she could afford to purchase drinks without any source of income. She said no one was willing to hire her because she was from "an aristocratic landowning family." The officer then offered her a job as an informant and warned her that if she did not take it and could not provide proof of employment within a few days, he would imprison her for "loafing" (not having a job could warrant arrest in this period). She told RFE that the incident inspired her to flee to Austria the next day.[33] Like this woman, most interviewees who admitted being asked to be informers claimed they refused the offer. It is difficult to know how many accepted the deal. Few would have been willing to admit later that they had actually spied on others; certainly refugees hoping to gain visas to Western countries would not have wanted to admit working for the police, which could mark them as untrustworthy or Communist sympathizers. Records from police archives indicate that these tactics were often successful, although it is not clear how useful such coerced informants turned out to be.[34]

What these stories indicate is that the ways in which people spoke about informers often did not match their personal experience. In interviews, respondents generally spoke about informers in draconian and unforgiving terms; they were pariahs who acted out of self-interest or malevolence and betrayed their community. Yet many of these respondents knew from their own lives that reality was often more complicated; informers could be ordinary people forced into service through no fault of their own. Admitting this challenged the framework in which many refugees wanted to see their societies. They preferred to imagine informers as part of a faceless and oppressive state that was distinct from the population, its victims. If informers were ordinary people put into difficult situations, the ostensibly clear dividing line between the state and the people (or us and them) dissolved.[35] This was undoubtedly why people like K.A. could not only never admit to having worked as informers, but also felt compelled to emphasize their willingness to isolate and shun those who had been publicly identified as part of the enemy.

Keeping Up Appearances

Several refugees interviewed by RFE admitted that the actual number of police informers on the streets was probably not nearly as high as many people asserted. However, they said, since it was impossible to be sure who was an informer and who was not, it was best to act as if one was surrounded by enemies at all times. Many refugees spoke about the ways in which their fear of being watched in public changed their behavior. Their strategies generally involved a retreat from engagement with the public sphere. People stayed at home and shunned the pleasures of modern urban life such as dining out, meeting friends in cafes, or going to nightclubs. When they had to leave the house, they tried to become small, insignificant, and unworthy of notice. Whereas before they might have put energy into looking their best, now they tried to simply be invisible. Everywhere they imagined hateful eyes upon them. It is striking that, although in other contexts most refugee interviewees claimed that only a small percentage of people in their home countries were committed Communists, they nonetheless imagined that the public sphere was pervaded by spite and ill will.

For RFE, these stories had a transparent meaning: they showed how Communism drained all of the color from once vibrant streets, turning everything dull, gray, and drab. Helena, a university student who left Czechoslovakia in September 1952, described Prague as "listless, lifeless, lackluster." There was "an all-over feeling of depression. You feel it everywhere. People hurry along the streets in silence, their eyes glued straight ahead. There is little laughter or gaiety; one seldom goes to a party or a dance . . . In restaurants or cafes people eat and drink in silence, afraid to discuss more than the most general things, and then there is the presence of the SNB [Sbor národní bezpečnosti, or National Security Corps]—everywhere."[36] An RFE report from Poland made similar comments. "Everyone is afraid to be seen in public with one's friends," the source claimed. In cafes, "people sneak in," have their coffee and cake, read the newspaper, and "leave quickly without exchanging as much as a word."[37]

Although many of those interviewed by RFE emphasized the desire to remain silent, many also reported their desire to remain unseen. According to a young Polish bookkeeper from Wrocław, "If someone appears on the street better dressed than average, everybody turns and looks." It did not take much to stand out, he said, since most of the clothes sold in the stores looked the same. In 1951, the source received some sport shirts from his parents in New York. With their distinctive checked pattern, patch pockets, and zipper, the shirts stood out. The first time he wore one of them, the bookkeeper was asked so many times where he had got his new shirt that he grew uncomfortable and went home to change. He never wore the shirt on the street again. His parents also sent him some ties, which he never dared to wear in public. Although they were not "really screaming colors," he was afraid they would receive unwanted attention. Even socks could not escape notice. On a train to visit relatives, the bookkeeper wore nylon socks sent from New York that caught the attention of a fellow passenger. Asked where he had got them, the source stammered that he had brought them back after a stint as a forced laborer in Germany. The man said nothing, but "watched him suspiciously. Source said he was glad when he could leave the train." The bookkeeper was undoubtedly reluctant to admit his clothes came from his parents in the West, but his anxiety over how to keep his secrets led him to imagine that everyone around him wished him ill. He was afraid that his socks marked him as an enemy, when it was equally likely that the man on the train was reacting to the bookkeeper's story about having got them in wartime Germany, if indeed he did continue to notice the bookkeeper at all. For the RFE evaluators, the bookkeeper's report merely "depicted well the atmosphere of drab and dull hopelessness."[38] They did not question the bookkeeper's unstated assumption that the people who noticed his clothes wished him harm.

As the story of the bookkeeper suggests, sartorial style had political overtones. The bookkeeper was afraid that his clothes would cause others to see him as an enemy, in his case because they suggested a close relationship with the West. But clothes were also a marker of class. An 1953 RFE report from a Bulgarian exile who claimed to be in close contact with friends back home mentioned a number of garments that would mark their wearers as "fascist bourgeoisie." These included ties and soft caps for men and fur coats or hats for women. If anyone wanted to send clothes to friends in Bulgaria, the exile recommended socks, since they would be hidden under trousers and would not make the wearer susceptible to unwanted attention (although the Polish bookkeeper might have disagreed with that assessment).[39] The Bulgarian report was echoed by another from Poland, which similarly cautioned that wearing hats or clothes from abroad could mark a person as an enemy.[40] Implicit in both of these reports was the sense that the streets were full of watchers and that these watchers were not benign.

Conspicuous clothing could indeed attract the notice of the police. One young Polish sailor returned home with some clothes he had bought while on shore leave in Rotterdam. They were of finer quality than was generally available in Poland at the time. At home in the interior of the country, where the inhabitants were less accustomed to seeing Western goods than residents of the coastal cities where sailors docked, he proudly wore his new finery to the opera. But his new shoes and white silk shirt attracted the attention of an agent of the UB (Urząd Bezpieczeństwa, or Office of State Security), who intimated he had smuggled his clothes into the country. When informed that his quarry had bought his garments legitimately, the agent derided the sailor for being a Western propagandist. The incident would likely have come to nothing, but the exasperated sailor retorted by calling the shabbily dressed UB agent a "lice-infested bastard." That got him promptly hauled off to jail to cool his (stylishly shod) heels for seventeen days before he was finally released without charge.[41]

In these reports, people worried about what their external appearance would say to a potentially hostile world. But this world could also invade their homes in the form of visits from Communist activists. In these moments, people felt even more compelled to prove that they were not enemies of the regime. One Hungarian woman recalled how she and the other housewives in her building were "literally terrorized" by activists known as people's educators who came to speak to them about shortages of basic household goods. Though the activists were ostensibly there to hear complaints from the housewives, instead the women wracked their brains to try to give what they felt were the politically correct answers to queries about the reasons for the empty store shelves. To avoid these meetings, the women tried to pretend they were not home, but the janitor was pressed into service to round them up. The housewives were willing to try to hide, but were too afraid to simply say they were busy or to give vent to any actual frustrations with the Hungarian government's poor performance at provisioning in such a setting, where their names and addresses would be known.[42]

A female Hungarian émigré who had trained to be a party activist (a "people's educator") told a similar tale. As part of her course, she went on home visits, encouraging anyone she found at home to purchase party-sponsored newspapers, make contributions to a peace loan, or sign up for memberships in one of the various state-sponsored mass organizations (trade unions, women's organizations, youth organizations, and such). On one of her stops, she realized that the inhabitants—an old woman, her son, his wife, and their two children, and a second son, a crippled war veteran—had carefully prepared for such visits. The family had subscribed to the Communist party newspaper (*Szabad Nép*, or Free people), the grandmother and son had joined the appropriate mass organizations, and they had (in the trainee's opinion) memorized lines showing the correct attitude toward political questions. Curiously, the trainee noticed that all four studiously avoided mentioning where the children's parents, who also lived in the house, were employed, only saying that they were translators. Then one of the children accidentally blurted out the truth: his parents were employed at a Western embassy. This incident illustrates how fear of persecution compelled outward conformity and an unobjectionable outward appearance. This family knew quite well what the people's educators wanted to hear and they tried to perform the parts of good Communist citizens, even acknowledging the regime's attitude toward the West.[43] In this case, the translators continued to work for a Western embassy even though they knew it was considered dubious, undoubtedly for financial reasons, and they hoped to safely hide behind their family's ability to say what their visitors expected. In other situations, it was easier to simply shun contacts with the West than to risk any consequences, much as the Polish bookkeeper decided to never wear his parents' gifts out on the street.

In 1954, a middle-aged Czech émigré illegally returned home to visit. He reported to RFE that when he tried to see old friends and family members, they slammed the door in his face, afraid of what might happen if they spoke to him. He mentioned in particular an old friend who had been in an illegal partisan group with him during the war. This once brave man, he said, now refused to meet him or shake his hand, despite their long history together.[44] Whether or not they actually believed that the West was their enemy, the Hungarian translators and the Czech émigré's old partisan friend publicly accepted this view of the West (either by lying about their place of employment or ignoring their old friend). Their priority was not to disagree, but to prove that they were not enemies themselves.

The fear of being watched in public was a fear of being publicly identified as an enemy of the state. It could thus be closely tied to anxieties about social transformations under Communism, particularly class inversion. A story told by a woman in Warsaw illustrates this dynamic. In a letter of 1952, the woman detailed her frustrations after an evening in the Polish Theater on Obezna Street. She had taken pains to dress nicely for the performance and felt as if everyone else in the audience was looking at her accusingly for trying to maintain former bourgeois standards of decorum. She was discomfited by her neighbors' stares and took them to indicate ill will, imagining they disapproved of her because of her class status. Yet she also criticized the man sitting next to her, complaining that he came to the theater in his work clothes, smelling so badly of acetylene that she could "hardly stand it." Others nearby picked their teeth throughout the performance such that, she said, "all through the show I heard that horrible noise which gave me goose pimples." She lamented the days when properly dressed "gentlemen" went to the theater, showing her acute discomfort at the destruction of former class hierarchies and her own loss of status. In former times, she might have stared accusingly at a worker who dared come to the theater in his coverall or perhaps who dared come to the theater at all. Now she was (at least she imagined) receiving this treatment, and it made her both angry and afraid. She vowed that the next time she went to a play she would make a point of dressing as poorly as possible.[45]

Unlike the Polish sailor with his shiny silk shirt, the woman at the theater on Obezna Street was not actually harassed by the police, nor did any of her neighbors in the theater say a word to her about her appearance. Her sense that she had attracted unwanted attention was confirmed only by her own interpretation of her neighbors' glances. Nonetheless, her experience at the play inspired her to consider changing her habits to conform to what she believed was the new norm. This source, like most RFE sources, took a position that was overtly anti-Communist and regarded Poland's Communist regime as alien. Yet her story shows how many East Europeans, whatever their political inclinations, were slowly accommodating themselves to the requirements of their governments, in this case hiding former class origins and class-based resentments. Whether they wanted to or not, even those who classified themselves as opponents of the regime, as this woman did, could not simply remain isolated from it. They negotiated with their new world and, indeed, helped to create and shape it with their public actions.

The fear of being watched also became a way of expressing fears of social change in an interview conducted in Stockholm with a Polish woman in her mid-sixties who had legally immigrated to Sweden. The widow of a prosperous doctor, the woman began her story by talking about the harsh glances she had received on the train as she left Poland for good. She believed both the police and her fellow passengers had watched her with contempt and suspicion. But while she first talked about her discomfort at being observed, it quickly became apparent that the core of her discontent was the lack of respect she felt she had received in the new Poland. The widow identified this rudeness with "Soviet" ways that had emboldened the young to disregard "the basic rules of civilization." According to her, the young people who now ruled Poland only wanted her to die. They cheated her in the stores and refused to help her get on the bus. They also, she claimed, considered the old to be the most likely spies and saboteurs for the West and therefore kept them under watch.

She was subjected to this even in her own home. Together with her elderly aunt, the widow had been relegated to the former maid's room of her large Warsaw apartment after local officials settled seventeen people in its other rooms. Though she thought most of the tenants were good people, she thoroughly disliked the two university students who had been lodged there. One of them, Jerzy, openly read her mail, saying it was his duty as a member of the Association of Polish Youth (Związek młodzieży polskiej, or ZMP). Although many people did not agree with this complete lack of respect for the elderly, she claimed, they were all too afraid to say anything, not knowing what might happen if they crossed one of the "young rowdies."[46] In her story, the fear of being observed and reported on merged with her more personal existential fears about being left behind by a changing Poland and feeling like an old person in a young person's world. She felt betrayed by the changed power structure that took away her status as a member of the bourgeoisie and as an older woman, making these qualities suspicious rather than esteemed. For her, this social reversal was indeed the sign of the end of civilization.

Little Communists

For the doctor's widow, the real problem was the "young rowdies" that the Communist state had empowered well beyond their years. She resisted the way in which, she alleged, these young people had redefined her as a drain on resources and a potential spy. Her horror that Communism had enlisted the young to monitor the old was reiterated in many other interviews. In a 1953 report described by RFE as "very good" and "moving," a Slovak man alleged that Communist terror had awakened so much distrust among people that parents were too afraid to speak openly in front of their children. He recounted a visit to a friend in Kremnice during which the man's little daughter came into the room and greeted him with a common Communist expression: "Honor to labor!" The friend was embarrassed, remarking that now even "innocent children are being poisoned by Communist venom." He explained that he was too afraid to tell his daughter that "good day" was a more appropriate salutation. "Just the other day," he told the source, "she came home from school and proudly began to sing a song praising Stalin. You just have to tell yourself that you will explain everything when she is older." After a minute, the man looked up with eyes full of tears and told the informant a story about a miner he knew whose fourteen-year-old son came home from a meeting of the Czechoslovak Youth Federation (Československý svaz mládeže, or ČSM) and gave his father a new Communist prayer for miners to read instead of the old Christian one. The angry father boxed his son's ear. After the son related this incident at his next ČSM meeting, the father narrowly avoided jail.[47]

This report illustrates a common theme in refugee interviews: children who became either witting or unwitting informers against their parents. As with the story of the doctor's widow, the idea of a child being granted the power to determine her parents' futures became a vehicle for expressing discomfort with the social upheavals that had accompanied the Communist takeover of power across the region. In this report from Slovakia, the Communist state offered the daughter a place within it, which her father felt powerless to reject on her behalf. The state usurped his parental authority, inserting itself into the private space of the home and making him feel that he had to lie to his own daughter. While he ostensibly hoped he could talk to her more openly when she was older, implicit in his tears and his recitation of the second story was the fear that even then this would not be possible. Like the miner's son, his daughter might embrace the role the state handed her and abandon her parents in favor of building a new Communist future.

An RFE report about a Polish youth expanded on this theme, suggesting that the first generation to be educated in Communist schools was intrinsically different from its predecessors. This young man was from a well-to-do family of hard-nosed collaborators. His parents "kept their heads above water" during the war and continued to run their wholesale business under German occupation. After the Communist takeover the firm was confiscated. Within a short time, however, the father obtained a well-paid managerial position and was able to supplement his generous salary with the illicit sale of goods the family had somehow managed to retain from its former business. As befit the scion of such a family, the son sought to ingratiate himself with the regime. He became the ZMP secretary of his school (a preparatory high school for the Silesian Institute of Technology) and was always ready to "blare out a speech on Western imperialism." But his enthusiasm was just a useful pose for the benefit of the family. His younger sister, however, had grown up under Communist influence at school. Unlike her siblings, she was a true believer, and her loyalty was to the regime rather than her parents. Her brother claimed she would walk without hesitation "over the dead bodies of her family" to get to the glorious socialist future. The rest of the family tiptoed around this "true Red" and spoke openly only when she wasn't home. RFE analysts commented that the sister was "deluded" and recommended that the source's comments about her be given special attention.[48]

Children who were brainwashed by Communist teachers to adore the Communist state above even their own parents became a recurring motif in RFE's collection of Information Items. These reports speak to the fear, especially prominent among exiles and refugees, that children and young people would become ideologically invested in Communism.[49] The refugees interviewed in the West tended to claim that adults were rarely swayed by Communist ideas, even if, like the collaborationist Polish family, they were compelled to negotiate with the regime out of necessity. Adults merely submitted to police terror, but children and youth were malleable. Under the influence of their teachers, they could be turned into unthinking supporters of the state.

In the early 1950s, the RFE research department circulated reports about education that spoke directly to these fears, highlighting the "lies" children learned and the helplessness of parents who were too afraid to correct them. One report recounted the experience of a sportswriter from the Czechoslovak city of Brno, whose son came home from school saying things like, "You know, Daddy, the Americans are our enemies and the Russians are our friends. The Americans must be evil people." The sportswriter tried to gently provide a different perspective, not contradicting the school but telling his son about the virtues of prewar Czechoslovak presidents Tomáš Masaryk and Edvard Beneš. His son accepted this information, but continued to talk about how much he wanted to be a Communist Pioneer and wear a little red scarf.[50] This man was more willing to act than one of his compatriots, a former clerk, who was appalled to hear that his children not only practiced mathematics by working problems about how many hours of work it would take a shock worker (an exemplary laborer who worked much faster than his or her peers) to fulfill his or her quota, but learned that Americans were warmongers and that President Masaryk had authorized the shooting of workers. Afraid that his child would inadvertently say something to his teacher if his father contradicted what he had learned, the clerk remained silent.[51] In similar fashion, a Hungarian architect who was able to move his whole family to Denmark claimed it was fear for his son's mind that motivated him. The boy, said the architect, was "powerless" in the grip of his textbooks, teachers, and youth organizations. His very vocabulary (and hence his way of making meaning) had been shaped by the regime.[52]

According to this line of thinking, the children of Eastern Europe were no more than raw clay, waiting to be molded by their Communist teachers. But, although parents characterized their children as powerless in the face of relentless propaganda, their fear more accurately stemmed from the apprehension that Communism had empowered their children in dangerous ways. An RFE interview with a gymnasium student who had attended school in eastern Slovakia exemplified anxiety over this potential shift of power from old to young. It detailed how student leaders at the school had conducted a public review (*prověrka*) of their teachers. The teachers were forced to stand in front of their assembled students and submit to public criticism that questioned their loyalty and methods. As a result of this incident, the school principal and his wife, a teacher of languages and literature, both lost their jobs; the principal was sent to work in the mines. For the RFE evaluators, this was a "shocking" illustration of how Communism perverted the natural order of things.[53] The evaluators undoubtedly found such a story shocking, but it was also the case that RFE had an interest in publicizing such incidents precisely because of the fears they would evoke. Communist regimes around the region did indeed work to mobilize the youth, and they achieved some success in this regard: young people were more likely than their elders to support Communism.[54] Communist governments also tried to use their young supporters to attack less enthusiastic but more senior professionals, with more success in some places than others. Czech Communist university students, for example, wielded significant power over their professors during the first years of the Communist regime, much more than Polish students did.[55] Still, in most environments, established hierarchies, not only of age but also of gender and class, were actually much more resistant to change than the overheated fears of RFE analysts and their informants allowed.[56]

Expressing fear about children being turned into Communists was a way of expressing a more general anxiety about one's own loss of power and the sneaking suspicion that this loss might be permanent. This is clear from the recollections of Francieszek Jarecki, a young Polish pilot who flew a MiG-15 to Denmark on March 5, 1953, as a novel means of escape from the country. Jarecki noted that young people in Poland eagerly took the opportunities for independence the Communist party handed them. Teenagers, said Jarecki, would boldly announce that they were off to a ZMP meeting, knowing that their parents would feel powerless to stop them, no matter what time of day or night. Then they would head off to the movies or do whatever they wanted. Their independence was also ideological; young people, said Jarecki, had radical beliefs about social justice and scorned both the economic and political systems of prewar Poland. For Jarecki, young people's distrust of capitalism was simply the result of successful Communist propaganda and the dwindling influence of their parents or the Catholic Church.[57] He, like the RFE evaluators, could see such beliefs only as the result of lies and intellectual coercion.

Editors at RFE constantly worried that young people supported Communist regimes, and they discussed the best way to win them over to the anti-Communist cause. But, although they discussed the need to not talk down to those in the younger generation and to treat them as mature and intelligent individuals, they did so only because they thought this would make more effective propaganda, not from any real desire to take young people's views seriously. A 1951 policy guidance memo for the Czechoslovak desk noted that the Gottwald government had offered its youth opportunities for rapid career advancement, new social status, and the feeling that they were part of a positive movement for social change. But tellingly, the RFE editors refused to take Communism's ideological appeal seriously. Their planned response was a program "as lively and cheerful and relaxed as we can make it." The new youth program would initially consist of nonpolitical content like swing music, jokes, sports, and reports on youth activities around the world. Once it had attracted a young audience the scriptwriters would "insert into it matter of a propaganda nature." Because they saw Communism as ideologically worthless, the RFE editors did not believe they needed to challenge it on the level of ideas. They merely had to counter its malicious propaganda with their own. In taking this approach, however, they steadfastly refused to see young people's dreams, hopes, or concerns as significant.[58]

A 1955 report on a young Polish woman who had traveled to Sweden for medical treatment showed the persistence and the limits of these assumptions. The woman did not know she was speaking to an RFE informant, who made a record of their conversations only after the fact. According to the informant, the woman described a gradual shift in her beliefs that led her toward Communism. Although her intellectual transformation had, she said, "moments of strain and conflict," she now thought, "The future of the world undoubtedly belongs to Communism. I believe in it and I want to believe in it." Those who disagree, she charged, "should have something better to offer. So far, they have shown they have nothing to offer but dollars—and this is not enough. People should be concerned with their prosperity but must believe in something besides." The RFE evaluator called her opinions "rubbish" and said she must be either "an incredible goose" or "a shrewd young schemer"; presumably she was a goose if she actually held such rubbishy opinions and a sophisticated operative if she did not but nonetheless conveyed them so convincingly. For RFE, it was impossible to take this young woman and any of her beliefs seriously. The RFE evaluator dismissed her as naive or brainwashed by the party because she claimed Poland had democracy, which for her did not need opposition parties and was compatible with the dictatorship of the proletariat, and because she said she loved Stalin. RFE analysts considered both sentiments ridiculous. Yet this young woman could also be quite reflective about practices in Communist Poland, remarking, "The manner of putting Communism into practice sometimes hurts me. But I try to think that it is necessary... even here I sometimes have doubts." These comments implied she was much more considered in her beliefs than the RFE evaluators wanted to admit. For RFE, it was easier to write this young woman off as a childish goose swayed by propaganda than to concede that the ideology she espoused might actually have meaning for young people.[59]

Can't We Be Friends?

Many refugees claimed that fears of police terror and informers had a pernicious effect on friendship and social ties within local communities. They described a situation that aligned with the totalitarian model then being developed in the West, in which the fear of constant, unseen surveillance broke old social bonds and created a society of atomized individuals who were afraid to trust one another with their real thoughts. An Iranian citizen who had lived in Poland for decades before leaving the country in 1953 told RFE that in the town of Zabrze "everyone is afraid of everyone else and lives only for himself. Social life as it used to be in former times does not exist any longer, all this is the result of reciprocal distrust."[60] The source speculated that this feeling might be particularly strong in Zabrze, which was located in the territory Poland received from Germany after 1945 and thus had a high percentage of recent immigrants and fewer people with long-standing community ties.[61] This may have been the case, but many others from regions outside contested or borderland territories made similar claims about the atomizing effects of Communism. As Jerzy Wierzbowski, a Polish fisherman, noted, "People are afraid and talk little about that [Western radio broadcasts]. Because one never knows who the other fellow is, whether he works for the UB or not." Wierzbowski did venture to say that one might be more open with a very trusted friend, but even here, he said, "one talks, but very cautiously."[62]

A young Czech woman from the town of Varnsdorf narrated a typical story of this kind of siege behavior. A hairdresser, she described the goings-on in her salon, which was under the direction of the state hairdressing enterprise. In her town of twelve thousand people, all private barbershops and beauty salons had closed, leaving only two nationalized enterprises to provide all grooming services. The woman's salon was open only until 5:30 pm each day, which meant that the lines from 4:00 until closing and all day Saturday were long and full of irritable, tense people concerned that they would not be accommodated before closing time. Despite the crowds, however, the salon was usually "as quiet as a church," with the silence only occasionally broken by discussions of innocuous topics, like food or other aspects of daily life. According to the young hairdresser, the once robust public space of the beauty salon or barbershop was drained of any meaningful interaction. People were too afraid to say anything of substance to each other. Rather than a social center, the salon had become simply a place to wait and be groomed.[63]

Wladyslaw Tomczynski, a young Pole who fled because he got a draft notice and was afraid that "they would turn me into a Communist in the army," similarly claimed in an RFE interview, "There reigns such an atmosphere of mistrust in Poland generally that everyone is afraid of his own shadow." He felt this made establishing relationships with young women particularly difficult. He would go out with a girl, he said, but even after seeing her several times would not be able to tell whether she favored the Communists and how much he could trust her. The gendered conventions of appropriate feminine conversation made this dilemma worse for him. As he noted, "Women, when you go out with them, always agree with men, they listen, try to understand you, but you are afraid to say what you think." Certainly, this delicate dance in getting to know a potential romantic interest would have been familiar to young people on both sides of the Iron Curtain. But Tomczynski claimed that in Stalinist Poland the stakes in romantic relationships were different. If you opened yourself up, he opined, and then broke up with the girl, she would head straight to the UB and denounce you.[64]

When Voice of America (VOA) conducted its interview project in 1951–1952, a question about friendship was part of the interview script. Respondents were asked, "On what basis do people form friendly groups in Poland today?"—as neighbors, at work, or as people with shared political views? They were also asked if this differed from the past and how.[65] While the question was not (at least on paper) framed in a particularly leading manner, the very fact that the question was included suggests that the interviewers expected respondents to talk about the negative impact Communism had on friendship. And most recorded responses met these expectations. A large majority of respondents who addressed this subject claimed that, at the very least, the sphere of friendship had been invaded by politics. As the Hungarian B.T. said, "You pick your friends according to their political views."[66] It was impossible, many claimed, for Communists and non-Communists to be friends; their opposing interests made it difficult to sustain trust. As another Hungarian refugee, Mrs. I.K., described it, "Between Communists and non-Communists there is a cat and dog friendship," an eternal battle between genetic adversaries.[67] A Czech accounting clerk, J.R., claimed that the only real friendships that could be formed were between anti-Communists. Communists, he said, were incapable of making or keeping friends.

"Every Communist," said J.R., "... will send any friend down the drain who is in his way." Joining the party to gain financial security, he intimated, came at the cost of giving up friendship.[68] A Slovak villager, J.M., agreed with J.R's assessment, telling the interviewer, "Certainly no non-Communist is friends with a real Communist, because he would feel ashamed before the whole community."[69]

For J.D., a Czech man, the issue was not political affiliation but political realities. J.D. had owned a flour mill in the Slovak village of Záhorská Ves. After it was nationalized, he said, "I made no secret of my hatred for the Communist regime." He was promptly labeled a dangerous reactionary. J.D. claimed that under Communism "many friendships have become insincere or were broken up." He said, "I had a friend who was not a Communist, but who asked me not to visit him anymore because I had become politically undesirable. He feared my visits to him might jeopardize his chances of peaceful existence or cause his persecution." J.D. continued, "It is my opinion that fear caused many friendships between anticommunists to become insincere." Later, J.D. explained that an insincere friendship was one that had become a mere matter of appearances. The friends no longer trusted or talked to each other seriously, but would occasionally greet each other and exchange pleasantries just to maintain the fiction that they were still friends.[70]

J.Z., a Czech in his mid-twenties from eastern Moravia, echoed J.D.'s remarks. According to J.Z., "Since the Communists came to power in Czechoslovakia friendship has become very superficial and people grew distrustful in their mutual relations." J.Z. believed this applied to all friendships, regardless of whether the friends were Communists or not. For J.Z., the problem sprang from the Gottwald regime's determination to vanquish all opposition to Communist rule. To foil any possible resistance, he said, the Communists coerced people into providing them with information. As he put it, "They use human weakness or hardship to know all their opponents and learn what everybody is thinking."[71] Many claimed that it was almost impossible to make new friends because it was too hard to ascertain a new acquaintance's real character and motives. V.K., a Czech export clerk, argued that the fear of informers inhibited his ability to form new friendships. According to him, "When two people want to become friends they have to watch each other for a long time first, to see how the other behaves and reacts, what he says and who his friends are."[72]

Some respondents argued that very close old friends could still trust each other, as long as they were not divided by political differences. Maintaining such friendships had become more difficult, however. Many asserted that gatherings of more than a few people were out of the question because they would draw suspicion. The Hungarian S.L. told VOA, "There is hardly any place left today where friends could meet confidentially in greater numbers. In the nationalized restaurants, the employees watch every word."[73] Others noted that food shortages made it impossible to entertain at home. While the bonds of these old friendships might remain, they did not function in the same way, because social contact with friends was limited.

Stories about the destructive effects of Communism on friendship were so pervasive in the VOA interview project that it would be easy for anyone reading the answers to just this question to conclude that social atomization was the inevitable fate of all East Europeans.[74] However, reading these answers in conjunction with the answers to other questions places this narrative in a different light. This was the case in the interview of I.V., a Hungarian. I.V. came from a village (indicated only as "H.") that was ceded by Hungary to Czechoslovakia in 1947. Before the transfer, I.V. had worked as a clerk at the local IBUSz (Hungarian tourist and transportation agency) office. After H. became part of Czechoslovakia, I.V. worked on a large farm in the village with other members of his family. He fled with his wife and child in order to avoid being deported by the authorities from Slovakia to the Sudetenland region. When asked about the impact of Communism on friendship, I.V. said, "Beyond a certain limit, intimate, friendly contact between people had disappeared from the people's democracies." The surveillance of the authorities, he said, made gatherings of friends almost impossible.[75] Yet, when asked about radio listening habits, I.V. told another story. "In the village," he said, "people used to widely discuss the foreign political views heard over the radio the previous night." I.V. himself said he often talked about what he had heard on Western radio programs with local farmers. This behavior was not limited to those who shared anti-Communist political views. As I.V. recounted, "I often heard the four or five Communists in our village talking about the Western radios, when I went to the town hall on official business ... When the one blushed and tried to protest, the others used to say: 'Don't try to deny it, my neighbor told me you were listening to it yesterday, too.'"[76]

To put I.V.'s story in context, privately tuning into foreign stations like the BBC, RFE, or VOA was not illegal in any of the People's Democracies. Yet governments around the region made it clear that the Communist party did not agree with such practices. Western radio stations were often mentioned disparagingly or ridiculed in the local press. In a typical article, the Czechoslovak newspaper *Lidové noviny* (People's news) claimed that anyone who listened "gets near the camp of the warmongers" and charged that even seemingly "passive listening" was an active decision to move against the state.[77] Propaganda campaigns branded those who listened enemies of the people.[78] These campaigns were so widespread that some of the VOA interview respondents believed that private listening was actually against the law, or as one survey respondent from Romania claimed, "Listening to Western stations is not officially prohibited but [it is] punished as if it were."[79] A number of respondents had heard stories about others who had been arrested for listening to the radio or had this fact used as evidence against them when they were arrested for a different offense. One Polish interviewee said, "It seems the authorities are fomenting and starting such rumors to keep the people in a panic and to discourage them from listening."[80] However, although private listening was not against the law, listening in groups larger than the immediate family was forbidden in most countries, as was talking about the information in broadcasts with others: this was considered spreading enemy propaganda and was an actionable offense.

I.V.'s story thus contained a contradiction. I.V. claimed that the fear of the police made friendship much more difficult. Surveillance eliminated the possibility of social gatherings, which were not illegal but might be considered suspicious. Yet I.V. also claimed that many people in the town openly talked about what they had heard on Western radio stations the night before, either with him or in front of him, even though doing this could be considered grounds for arrest. As he told it, even the Communist officials in the village openly spoke about what they had heard on Western radio, with each other and in his presence, even though he was someone who had been labeled an enemy of the regime. (I.V.'s land had originally been scheduled for confiscation and his family for deportation in 1949; he remained in the village on reprieve until 1951, when he fled after suspecting that the deportation was about to proceed.)

The kind of contradiction evident in I.V.'s story was not uncommon among the VOA survey respondents. A set of early reports based on the interview data that dealt primarily with radio listening was prepared by the Columbia Bureau of Applied Social Research a few years before Siegfried Kracauer and Paul L. Berkman did their analysis of the same set of sources. According to these reports, all but a very few of the 421 respondents said they listened to Western radio stations. Most reported listening to several different stations, and more than half of the respondents listened to each of these stations several times a week.[81] A large percentage (73 percent in Poland) listened in groups of two to five people, precisely what was most illegal and most dangerous.[82] Yet many of these same people also claimed that Communism had made it impossible for people to trust one another. Listeners did say that they took precautions while tuning into foreign stations. They kept the volume low, locked doors, and closed windows, and quickly turned the knob to another station if anyone knocked at the door. Some had two radios playing at the same time, with one set to a domestic station as cover. And while they did listen with others, most restricted the group to those they knew.[83] But this caution could be tenuous. S.L., a sometime tailor's apprentice and clerk described by his VOA interviewer as above-average in intelligence, asserted that people were extremely cautious in talking about Western radio programs with strangers because "they could never know if they were talking to an informer or not." But he went on, "For this reason, the conversation usually started with 'Have you heard what the VOA had said?' If the answer was 'I never listen to the VOA' then the conversation generally ended right there, because the man who asked the question felt he should not let himself be turned in for 'spreading rumors.'"[84] S.L.'s supposedly cautionary behavior relied on a great deal of trust between individuals, given that it essentially amounted to an open invitation to discuss American radio broadcasts. It is hard to imagine that a real informer would not feign interest in the VOA in order to draw the speaker out.

Some might argue that such contradictions indicate that interview respondents consciously answered questions about friendship in ways they believed would be welcomed by their interviewers. While this is a possible explanation, there is no evidence to support it. The interview transcripts generally record many responses the interviewers would not necessarily have wanted to hear: respondents often admitted they preferred other radio stations to VOA or that they thought Americans were less cultured than Europeans or cared only about money and so on. Rather than being deliberate lies, these responses more likely reflected how individuals often acted in multidimensional, ambiguous, and even contradictory ways.[85] The refugees who said Communism had created social atomization and destroyed the capacity for maintaining friendship believed this to be the truth when they said it. Their interpretation was based their own experience, but filtered through the surrounding culture, including anti-Communist friends, other refugees, and Western radio stations. Regardless of how this belief was formed, it became a key part of how they characterized the states they had fled. Yet, although they believed that paralyzing, oppressive fear and distrust were integral parts of the larger truth about Communism, these emotions did not encompass the entirety of their everyday experience. So, when asked about specific practices or moments, their answers were different. In their minds, these moments of solidarity or community did not negate what they believed was the essential nature of Communist rule. One Polish respondent, the young miner Jerzy Szopa, realized this very well. When he was asked whether people talked with each other about Western radio broadcasts, he replied, "Yes, they talk about it amongst themselves, but only amongst those they know (well), because otherwise, if someone squeals on a guy like that, then he (the latter) will get several years in prison. But still, they talk."[86] In his telling, people certainly did believe they lived in a society of terror and informers, but this belief did not always shape their actions.

The example of Szopa suggests that totalitarian narratives describing a society of atomized individuals paralyzed by fear had more coherence as a set of beliefs about what Communism did to society than as a description of most people's everyday lives. This was apparent in the story of the Hungarian tailor's apprentice mentioned earlier, S.L. His wife had emigrated to England in 1947, and so he perhaps missed the lack of opportunities for friendship more acutely than others. S.L. had said that older people like himself relied on friends they had made in school or in the army and noted that it was hard to meet them in restaurants because the employees were all spies. He continued, "There is only one way of finding new friends. You have to find out what's inside a person while drinking."[87] In the presence of alcohol, S.L. implied, people would let down their masks and you could see if you really shared similar views and opinions. The idea of true friends being made in the company of a bottle or two was certainly a time-honored one. But it is also striking that someone who claimed to be wary of informers would suggest that getting drunk with a stranger and sharing confidences was a likely way of making friends. Cautious behavior would seem to require drinking only at home and only with trusted companions.

Incidents of public drunkenness exemplify how people acted in ways that belied the fears they claimed governed their lives. Getting drunk in public places was a common event according to many refugee narratives, and such stories appear in both VOA and RFE sources alongside claims that no one spent time in cafes or restaurants anymore because they were afraid of being overheard by informers. The VOA interviews did not ask about drinking or other such habits, but some respondents mentioned it when comparing their countries with the United States. Zygmunt Machinowski stated that Americans had higher standards of behavior than Poles. "Now in Poland," he said, "people become boors ... They beat women on the puss ... even in public places. I do not think that the Americans would do it ... I do not know, maybe it's that the Poles drink much liquor."[88] Another Polish respondent, Jozef Wrobel, said the difference between Americans and Poles was that, whereas Americans would save their money and buy a house, Poles, seeing no point in saving, would just spend it on drink.[89] Many RFE sources also claimed that public drunkenness was on the rise. One Swede who visited Poland on a business trip in 1952 commented that everyone seemed to be drinking heavily as a way of escaping the cares of everyday life, noting that "the number of drunks one sees on the streets is appalling."[90] A Czech man who had resided in France for years went home for a visit in October 1956 and was shocked at the money everyone around him was spending on alcohol. Even women, he said, were going out and drinking with abandon.[91] A Polish waitress also said that drunkenness was "a common sight on the streets" and even in workplaces. When she asked her friends why they drank so much, they answered, "What else have we got in life? When we have drunk some vodka we forget about everything!"[92]

The very same waitress also claimed that people were wary of going out to cafes for fear of being observed by UB agents. Yet they were apparently not nearly as concerned with being publicly inebriated, despite the well-known effects of alcohol on the tongue and the general fear of agents and informers lurking about on the streets. Drunken remarks could indeed attract the attention of the security police or their agents.[93] During the days just after Stalin's death in 1953, Czechoslovak police arrested quite a few individuals, like Josef Dominik from Gottwaldov. Dominik was found late at night drunkenly singing on the street. When asked to quiet down, he said, "You bastard, don't you know that we are celebrating the death of Stalin?!" Dominik, who had been a member of the Czechoslovak Communist Party since 1945, was arrested.[94] But despite the obvious danger associated with drunken behavior, few people mentioned their fear of police informers in connection with drinking in public. It is impossible to know what went through an individual's mind when making the decision to consume alcohol recklessly in a public space or to travel home from a private party while in a state of drunkenness. What is clear, however, is that the fear of agents and informers existed in balance with decisions to consume alcohol in public environments.[95]

But alcohol was not always needed to loosen tongues in public spaces. A VOA interviewee, Zygmunt Ostrowski, worked as an assistant in a butcher shop. Every day, he said, people stood for hours in line in front of the shop, hoping to purchase some portion of the small daily delivery (generally 50 kilograms). They lined up as early as 3:00 a.m. and stood waiting until the delivery arrived, sometimes not until after 11:00 in the morning. As they waited, Ostrowski remembered, "they talk in the lines (especially) the women, they talk. And these women do not pay attention to the police, but talk about what poverty (there is). How bad (it is) in Poland, how life is good in America."[96] Ostrowski's story closely paralleled another told to RFE a few years later. In June 1953, shortly after a series of worker demonstrations in East Germany, a student from Gdansk Technical University was called to a meeting of the Association of Polish Youth (ZMP). At this meeting, a UB agent declared that American agents had tried to start a revolt in the GDR and called on the ZMP members to do their part to counter such an attack in Poland. The student was asked to serve as a temporary UB agent; his task was to stand in the line in front of a butcher shop the following morning and report on what was said. He arrived in front of the butcher's at 5:00 a.m. and immediately began to be questioned by the old men and women who were already waiting. Young men, he soon gathered, were not often seen in lines, and the people were instantly suspicious of his intentions. The student tried to make up a story about how his mother was ill and had sent him to do her shopping, but no one believed him. Not caring that he was undoubtedly there to report on them, the waiting people complained about how tired they were and groused about how stupid it was to be in line when no one could be sure there would be anything to buy once the doors opened. They lamented that all the meat was being sent to Germany or to party big shots and bemoaned the injustice of this. Some added that things had been better before the war. One old woman shouted at the student until he finally retreated to the end of the line, but the people at the back were equally rude to him. The student would have had plenty of material to report to the UB, had he cared to do so. He claimed, however, that he did not feel right turning people in, so he did not.[97]

This incident took place in somewhat extraordinary circumstances. The people in line may have been emboldened by rumors of the demonstrations in East Germany, where workers had demanded better food supplies and prices. They may also have been inclined to ignore or even openly berate the young and inexperienced student because he undoubtedly looked uncomfortable and not dangerous. Yet these kinds of incidents were not limited to such moments—another Polish RFE informant claimed that line heckling was a popular activity in early 1953. Housewives outside the line, this informant claimed, would target a low-ranking party member (low-ranking enough to have to stand in line for bread or other foodstuffs) and as the line snaked slowly by would loudly say to each other things like "Isn't life in the people's democracy of Poland wonderful? At last we have got everything we want thanks to the people's democracy! Have we ever got our bread as fast as we do these days . . . ?" and so on. According to this source, the hapless PZPR (Polska Zjednoczona Partia Robotnicza, or Polish United Workers Party) member would not be able to respond to such sarcastic but outwardly nonoppositional comments, nor would he or she be able to leave the line. The line, according to this source, had become a "vertical coffeehouse without coffee." It was, at least in this telling, a paradoxically safe space, where neighbors chatted and exchanged information, including what they had heard on foreign radio broadcasts.[98]

This characterization of the line is a far cry from the depiction of public space as a zone filled with spies that had to be traversed as carefully as a minefield. Here, the line became a place for shared solidarity in the face of a regime that promised but failed to provide for its citizens' basic needs. The knowledge that such safe spaces even temporarily existed or that people got drunk and yelled profanities in the street or listened to forbidden radio stations with friends does not mean that the fear of informers was not real. It does, however, complicate the ways we should think about this fear. One Bulgarian refugee claimed, "Terror penetrates everything like dust and infests every bit of the air."[99] But this image, though compelling, is too all-encompassing to accurately describe the ways in which this fear operated. Even in Stalinist Eastern Europe, people were not consistent in their behavior and could act in contradictory ways. The fear of being noticed or watched might take hold in some moments and recede in others. We need to hold both the existence of the fear and the limits of that fear in balance, realizing that the one does not negate or invalidate the other.

That Feeling of Helplessness

In the report about the bell fear and the uniform fear, the informant and his Western interlocutors believed that universal and ever-present fears of the security services and their networks of informers were the inevitable result of living in a Communist society. A closer look at these stories about the immense power of the police presents a more nuanced picture. The police in Eastern Europe did have extraordinary power in the years before 1956. But, although instances of police terror were very real, the fear of the police and informers had multiple, crisscrossing referents on both sides of the Iron Curtain. Fears of the informers and police came not only from actual experiences with these instruments of state oppression, but also from rumors, Western radio broadcasts, and even campaigns around show trials. All of these sources combined to create an aura of fear, which many took to be the truth of life under Communism. This "truth" did not effectively encapsulate the complicated reality of everyday experience, but it did provide a means of conceptualizing and understanding these regimes, both for some of those who lived under them and for those who fled. Central to this understanding was what the young Czech informant described as the feeling that creeps up your back, that "funny feeling of weakness and helplessness." Even though many people's stories reveal moments when they acted without fear, most refugees characterized themselves as powerless in the face of Communist terror.

5 SOPORIFIC BOMBS AND AMERICAN FLYING DISCS

Communist peace activists constantly told East Europeans that the West was the land of imperialist warmongers. Magazines, newspapers, posters, and radio broadcasts all emphasized the rapaciousness of the Western military. If the socialist camp was not vigilant, the Communist media proclaimed, Western leaders would wage war to devastate the socialist countries of Europe. But according to refugees who fled from behind the Iron Curtain, few at home feared a war with the West. Instead, refugees claimed, most East Europeans hoped for an American invasion. In an interview with Voice of America, B.T., a young Hungarian tractor operator, was asked why people in his village listened to Western radio broadcasts. B.T. replied, "People listened for news that would tell them that the war broke out. The little room at the State Farm where we listened to the radio was so full that you couldn't squeeze any more people there. People wanted to hear when the Communist regime would be defeated. People talked about the news of battles between East and West and about the preparations for the great war. They liked to hear this kind of news."[1] According to B.T., his coworkers on the state farm hoped for war rather than peace. They did not respond to news of Western rearmament with dread; instead, they cheered the idea of a strong Western military. War with the West, they thought, would not bring destruction and death, but liberation. In their minds, war was the only way the Hungarian Communist regime could be removed from power.

Attitudes like this were extremely common among those interviewed by Radio Free Europe (RFE) or Voice of America (VOA). A large majority of respondents claimed they hoped for war as the only path to liberation. Western analysts noted the ubiquity of this claim at the time. In *Satellite Mentality*, Siegfried Kracauer and Paul L. Berkman explained the desire for war among interviewees as a symptom of both the success and the failure of the Communist peace campaign. The campaign had not inspired the respondents to fear war, but it did illustrate the influence of Communist propaganda. The interviewees had fixated on Communist claims about Western military preparations and aggressiveness and believed them to be true. They were convinced that war was imminent and were disappointed to discover after crossing the border that Western war preparations were not as advanced as they had believed. In an aside, the two authors noted that Western radio broadcasts might have also contributed to this assumption.[2]

Despite their perspicacity in noting the influence of the "reciprocal influence" of Western broadcasts, Kracauer and Berkman limited their observation to the interpretation of the peace campaign and beliefs about Western militarization.[3] For Kracauer and Berkman, the dream of liberation followed quite naturally from the circumstances of totalitarian dictatorship. They did not see a connection between the Western concept of East European captivity, which they themselves used uncritically, and refugees' need to believe in liberation from abroad. Yet the reciprocal influence of the peace campaign and Western broadcasts went deeper than Kracauer and Berkman allowed. In talking about their dreams of a coming war, refugees showed that they had internalized a belief not only in Western military preparation and power, but in their own position as captive slaves, lacking the ability to do anything but hope for freedom.

These feelings of powerlessness turned war into an object of fantasy and wish fulfillment. War fantasies offered a way to imagine a future in which individuals who felt powerless had their agency miraculously returned. In the safe arena of dream and fantasy, war could bring liberation rather than chaos and carnage. Those who fantasized about war imagined that an all-powerful regime had rendered them helpless. This does not mean these regimes were as omnipotent as their citizens sometimes asserted. However, whether or not East Europeans really lacked agency to the extent they claimed, many experienced the feeling of extreme powerlessness and fantasized that only war would enable them to vanquish their enemies.

We Are Only Waiting for Liberation

From the beginning of the Cold War, the American media had characterized East Europeans as helpless captives to their Communist overlords. As conquered peoples, they were forced to submit to the whims of their leaders, whatever their own beliefs or desires. Refugee interviews reflected and reinforced this discourse of East European powerlessness. A twenty-seven-year- old Bulgarian pharmacist interviewed by RFE in Italy on his way to Israel in 1953 eloquently expressed this attitude. He claimed that "the more that is being exacted from the people, the more they seem to accept it." Bulgarians had decided it was impossible to resist the regime, no matter what it asked. They willingly worked overtime shifts, stood in endless lines, contributed to the peace campaign, and tolerated any amount of interference in their daily lives, all without complaint. Inwardly, the pharmacist said, Bulgarians disagreed with the regime on every point, but outwardly they simply did what was asked of them. Everyone realized, he said, that "one cannot kick against a God. It is utterly useless to resist and attempt to upset the regime from within."[4]

The Bulgarian pharmacist's picture was related to the concept of Ketman in Czesław Miłosz's book *The Captive Mind* (published after the interview had taken place), but with a crucial difference: in Miłosz's book, those who practiced Ketman believed their deception was in the service of some higher goal. They imagined themselves superior to their masters because their subterfuge allowed them to achieve their own ends. But for the pharmacist, pretending to embrace the regime and believe in Communism was simply a requirement for survival. It did not give a feeling of superiority, nor did it allow the practitioner to outwit the master to his or her own benefit. It was merely the price the system exacted from all of its inhabitants.

In the Bulgarian pharmacist's story, most people had been reduced to bystanders in their own lives. Their only actions were coerced and inauthentic. They smiled or cheered on cue because they felt powerless to display any dissent. Many interviewees insisted on their inability to affect the world around them. In one interview, a Romanian emigrant of Armenian heritage told a dramatic story of the consequences of such powerlessness. This man claimed that beginning in the fall of 1955 Romanian security police conducted a brutal crackdown around Bucharest. In February 1956, he witnessed the police kidnap a victim off the street. While walking to the grocery store, he passed by the Church of St. Gheorghe. Suddenly, a 1953 Buick pulled up to the curb. Five men jumped out and grabbed a man who was walking along the street and began to drag him to the car. The interviewee, who recognized the victim as Matei Malamuceanu, a lawyer, heard him scream, "Save me, brothers, I am innocent!" The interviewee wanted to do something, but he was paralyzed "against his will" by thoughts of his family and images of corpses dancing through his head, and did nothing.

Although he wished he could have helped Mr. Malamuceanu, the interviewee did not blame himself for his inability to act. In his account, he himself was also a victim, the victim of a dictatorship that had created a society in which a citizen was afraid to help another in need. He described Romania as a "captive country," held hostage by the Communists, which he equated with a foreign power. His own victimhood, which reduced him to a state of "prostration and terror," absolved him of any personal responsibility to overcome his fear and act against this brutal tyranny.[5] RFE evaluators did not castigate the Romanian source for his inaction, merely noting other sources who confirmed police reprisals during this period. In his situation, the source could undoubtedly have accomplished little. But as RFE staff members realized, their own programs had contributed to the overriding sense among refugees that they were powerless to act on their own behalf. Broadcasts emphasizing the brutality and terror of Communist regimes were in some ways too effective; they encouraged those who opposed Communist governments to believe that nothing could be done, even to ameliorate their worst excesses.[6]

In talking with Western interlocutors, many respondents (whether refugees or correspondents) mirrored the ways the Western media talked about East Europeans as captives. Like the Bulgarian pharmacist, they claimed that what appeared to be enthusiastic support for Communism did not represent the truth. The masses did not really endorse their Communist leaders, interviewees argued; they only pretended, because they were powerless to do otherwise. Communist terror, such as the Romanian Armenian witnessed, had made overt resistance untenable. Refugees claimed, however, that inwardly the population held itself apart from the regime and waited for its demise. One RFE report from Czechoslovakia was tellingly titled "How Gottwaldov's Population Is Waiting for Liberation." The source, a thirty-one-year-old refugee who spoke to RFE in Salzburg, claimed that most of the city was against the regime. They were all "waiting from one year to the next for the liberation, in the way in which a prisoner waits for the day in which he will be released from prison," he said.[7]

As this source presented it, the residents of Gottwaldov had internalized their status as captive peoples and took refuge in the idea of their own passivity. By seeing themselves as prisoners, they positioned themselves apart from the regime that governed them and refused accountability for any of its failures. They went about the motions of everyday life, but saw themselves as just marking time. Many people, claimed the source, took refuge in various pseudo-scientific and religious theories that seemed to predict liberation by outside hands. Proponents of the "Pyramid Theory," for example, believed that calculations based on the length of the corridors in Egyptian pyramids proved that Communism would end on August 20, 1953. Adherents of the "*Titanic* Theory" claimed that Communists would suffer the same downfall as the designers of the *Titanic*, who mocked the power of God by claiming they had built a ship that was unsinkable. All these theories predicted that Communism would suffer an inevitable fall, requiring no action on the part of ordinary people. RFE's evaluators also interpreted the kind of passivity noted by the source as evidence of widespread anti-Communist feeling. They noted that people also took comfort from pseudo-scientific prophecies during the Nazi occupation of Czech lands, suggesting that this "proved the similarity of both regimes."[8]

The source from Gottwaldov likened Communism to prison. Janos Jasko described his experience in Hungary as a form of slavery. Jasko, a worker at the Rákosi Matyas factory, was interviewed by VOA in September 1951 at Camp Asten, near Linz, Austria. Jasko had fled Hungary a few weeks before, when officials discovered that he had been living under an assumed name since a fracas with the police in 1945.[9] Jasko charged that Hungarian workers were no better than slaves, because they were not free to speak their minds and could not freely decide how to spend their time. They were forced to work long hours to fulfill impossible quotas and were not paid enough to maintain a decent standard of living. "The Communists would like everyone to work for nothing, eat community food, and live in slums," he remarked.[10]

Hungarians also qualified as slaves because they were under the control of the Soviet Union. The "Russians" provided raw materials but then took away the finished goods "and even the machine that was needed for the manufacturing," all without paying "even a kopek" to the Hungarians.[11] As slaves, Hungarians had surrendered control over their own destiny. Whipped and starved into submission, they could never rise up against their masters. Only outside intervention would release them from captivity. Jasko hoped that an American-led UN force would come to the rescue, as it had done in Korea. "The work of the sons of the little nations has no result," he said, and "there is not even anything to eat if Communist violence holds sway over them. We wait for the United Nations to free Hungary from this desperate situation."[12]

Many of the VOA interviewees insisted that Communist regimes in Eastern Europe would fall only with American assistance. L.J., an ethnic German vineyard worker from Sopron, believed that only military intervention by the United States could change the situation in Hungary. He remarked, "If the Americans were to occupy Hungary then we would return to the old conditions as they were before. That would be very good. Hungary is not able to do that. Hungary alone is not able to change the situation; they are not capable to do it."[13] X.Y., a young Hungarian worker who fled the country "because of hunger and misery," wanted the Americans to take all the initiative in determining Hungary's future. When asked by VOA whether he believed the United States harbored global ambitions, X.Y. replied, "The Americans should occupy Hungary and set up a regime in which a worker may have a human life. Normal life would [return] then."[14] As this comment made clear, X.Y. had internalized the superpower dynamic of the Cold War. He believed Hungary must belong to one of the two camps; it was simply a question of which one. From this perspective, an American occupation was the only solution to the Soviet domination of the country.

X.Y.'s vocabulary, like that of many other interviewees, was telling. All spoke in terms of occupation and liberation, indicating that local populations were merely acted upon by outside forces. As Kracauer and Berkman noted in *Satellite Mentality*, such responses showed the influence of what they called the "occupation concept," which was fostered at least in part by Western radio stations. According to the occupation concept, Communism was a foreign ideology that represented the interests of the Soviet Union. Domestic Communist parties were merely the tools of the Soviets.[15] But a corollary to the occupation concept (not noted by Kracauer and Berkman) was the conviction that liberation, like Communist domination, also had to come from abroad. Virtually all interviewees believed that East Europeans would never achieve their own liberation. This attitude is apparent in a long formal interview conducted by RFE with an older Bulgarian woman who left the country in 1955. According to this respondent, "Western powers and the United States do not interfere enough in Bulgarian affairs." If they did, she said, "Bulgaria would be freed from the Communists much sooner. The Bulgarian people would also have more hope and faith in the future." For this woman, Bulgaria was always acted upon from the outside. Just as she believed that the Bulgarian Communist government could not act without Soviet approval, she could only imagine that Bulgaria would be freed, not that it would free itself. Even the hope and faith of the Bulgarian people were dependent on outside sources. Later in the interview, the woman declared, "Bulgarians are tired of waiting to be liberated." But for her the only option other than waiting was giving up hope and resigning oneself to Communist rule.[16]

Implicit in this Bulgarian woman's comments was the fear that the West would decide Eastern Europe was not worth liberating. When Western radio stations asked refugees what they wanted to hear on the airwaves, they frequently asked for reassurance that the West would not forget them. Stanislaw Mitkowski, a former Polish railway employee, told VOA in 1951 that "Poles want to be reassured as often as possible that other people sympathize with their plight, that other people understand the whole horror of existence in the present day Poland, that other people are our true friends on whom we can rely and from whom we can expect help and assistance in the future."[17] As Mitkowski described the situation, Poles felt alone and abandoned. Trapped behind the Iron Curtain, they worried that the West had forgotten them. They needed to hear that their sorrows were known in the West, believing that if their plight was visible, the West would have to take action to help liberate them from Communist oppression.

This fear that the West might leave the captives to rot in their Communist jail ran through many interview testimonies. The Hungarian P.H, an independent shipper, told VOA, "It would be shocking for the Hungarian people if they were to hear over the VOA that the U.S. was ready to leave Hungary a victim of Bolshevism . . . The expression of even the slightest hint towards that end through the VOA would provoke the worst possible opinion about the U.S. in

Hungary."[18] This sentiment was echoed by his compatriot I.V., who said, "Should this attitude crystallize in the U.S . . . it would be desperate for mankind because it would mean that it (mankind) has lost any hope that Communism would cease to exist."[19] A third Hungarian respondent, D.Sz., echoed these concerns when he told VOA that its broadcasts should ideally convince Hungarians they "should be hopeful and be assured that the free world would not abandon them and they will be free from Communist rule."[20] For all of these men, East European hope was dependent on Western encouragement and reinforcement. If the West ceased to care about the inhabitants of the Soviet Bloc, they would be left with nothing more than their despair.

When Will the War Come?

I.H., a laborer in a Hungarian vineyard, had also internalized the idea that the Hungarians were a captive nation whose capacity for hope rested on outside forces. When he spoke to VOA in 1951, he remarked, "When I said that the hopes of the people lied with the West I meant that the way people live now is no life, but slavery. They take it as if they were in jail, and that it cannot last forever, and that one day they will become free."[21] But how would Hungarians finally be liberated from their prison? For I.H. there was only one possible way: war. The vast majority of his fellow interview respondents shared his conviction. For refugees, the hope of liberation was inextricably linked with the possibility of war.

In the VOA interview project of 1951–1952, the questionnaire included a question about the likelihood of another war. Respondents consistently replied that they believed war would break out soon in Europe. Convinced that the United States would eventually win any contest, they claimed they longed for war as the vehicle of liberation. This desire for war was not affected by the respondent's gender, age, educational level, or country of origin. It was simply ubiquitous. O.P., a monk from Slovakia, declared that "everyone" agreed war was the only way to bring freedom to Czechoslovakia. Violence and destruction were not deterrents. According to O.P., "People are well aware of the consequences of such a war but they will rather bear the horrors of war than to go on living without freedom."[22] Jan Osiewicz, a Pole from Szczecin, made similar claims about the widespread desire for war. "The Poles wish the war to come because they don't wish or desire to continue living under the present regime anymore," he said. "Everyone in Poland is already fed up with it. They would like it to end once and for all."[23] Respondents did not see war as an opportunity for glory; many had experienced the effects of wartime violence. Yet they recognized war's potential to overturn their governments and rearrange the balance of power in the region, as it had already done during their lifetimes. As war had enabled the Communist takeovers in Eastern Europe, they hoped it would enable the destruction of those same Communist regimes.[24]

In many interviews, respondents claimed that the vast majority of people (i.e., "most Poles" or "the population") desired war because they believed it was the only way to achieve liberation. It is possible refugees consciously made such statements to convince the West that its armies would be welcomed as liberators. However, there is no hard evidence of such intentions. Rather than seeing these kinds of claims as preplanned interventions, I am more inclined to consider them indications of what a speaker hoped or believed to be the truth. Whether or not such claims had an evidentiary basis, they do indicate what the vast majority of interviewees believed about their world, particularly before 1953. For them, it was a truism that "everyone" hoped for war, believing it would mean the end of Communist dictatorship.

Only a small minority of the VOA interviewees registered doubts about the desirability of war. Stefan Birlet, a twenty-eight-year-old Pole, was one of them. Birlet claimed that Poles did not want another war, given their suffering in the Second World War and the loss of 3 million people in German concentration camps.[25] The surprising thing about this sentiment is not that Birlet expressed it, but that so few of his compatriots did.[26] Even Birlet, however, was not consistent. After stating that Poles did not want more violence and death, he declared later in the interview that people realized "their slavery will not end" without a war to destroy Russia. While he did not explicitly say that Poles wanted such a liberating war, he certainly implied that many would see it as beneficial (and, indeed, necessary), despite its costs.

Most did not have Birlet's qualms. In these interviews, more people claimed to fear peace than a new war. People who had convinced themselves that their only path to happiness and freedom was to wait for a war that would remove the Communists from power worried constantly that this liberating war would never come. Z.H., who escaped from Hungary to Austria, was shocked to discover that war plans were not as imminent as he had believed. Although he did not say it, he and other refugees may have imagined that exile was a temporary rather than a permanent solution. Without war, it was not clear how they would ever be able to return home. Z.H. told VOA, "Now that I am in Austria I am afraid that everything will stay as it is" because liberation for Hungary (and therefore also his own return home) seemed so far away. He lamented the complacency of both Austrians and Americans and hoped they would soon realize the danger Communism posed even to them.[27] Those who had not fled were wracked with similar fears. An RFE correspondent in Bratislava wrote in 1954, "A wave of depression is spreading among the non-Communist population of Czechoslovakia. We are passively watching the events taking place in the world.

Nothing shows that we might be liberated soon." She mentioned that the outbreak of war in Korea a few years before had perversely given people hope that liberation might come. But after that war ended, Czechoslovaks feared that the moment for a global war had passed. Now, she said, it was only "depression and hopelessness."[28]

Jaroslav Salivar, a bookseller from Prague, told VOA, "We do not see any other way out of the Bolshevist yoke, except by war." In his opinion, active resistance was futile. The Communist regime was too effective at infiltrating the opposition or co-opting its members with promises of jobs, material advantages, or simply protection from arrest. Resistance crumbled from inside as people became convinced that informers lurked everywhere and no one could be trusted. As Salivar explained, "In the interior we are weak, partly because we do not have arms and partly due to the fact that we are morally undermined. Experiences with resistance groups are bad, because there have always been traitors in individual groups. For this reason no new groups are being established for fear of betrayal." He also cited the effectiveness of arrests and trials in making people feel as though overt opposition were useless, noting that "the best people have either been put in jail or have been executed." Although Salivar spoke only a few years after the Communists had taken over the government, he firmly believed that the regime had already completely obliterated the possibility of domestic resistance. Active involvement in oppositional activities paradoxically only gave the Communists an opportunity to gain informers by threatening people with the choice of cooperation or jail. It was better to sit tight and hope for American intervention. As Salivar declared to VOA, "We are only waiting for help from the outside."[29]

One letter written to RFE in 1951 from someone in Czechoslovakia who claimed to be part of a tiny resistance group registered disgust at the belief that effective change had to come from abroad. The author contrasted the small size of the opposition to the experience of German occupation during the Second World War, when, he claimed, everyone was willing to support the resistance. Now, he said, "80 percent of the people would like a reversal, but easily, without their own effort. They wait for a miracle in comfort, pandering and showing off, even if that is out of fear and disinclination." The source warned that RFE should not think Czechs and Slovaks could ever re-create the old interwar Czechoslovak Republic. If the regime should ever fall, he said, "you will find us tainted by socialism."[30] This man was, however, in the minority for demanding that people who opposed Communism do something other than simply wait for Western warplanes to bring their salvation, as well as for his conviction that a war would not miraculously wipe away the recent past, as if the Communist regime had never occurred. This informant's comments point to why others emphasized waiting rather than acting. Acting implied negotiating with the regime, whereas waiting could be conceived as a form of stasis, an imaginary holding pattern that would keep people the same until the regime fell. This was the key to the fantasy of liberation, that war would wipe away the Communists to reveal a society that was unchanged by their presence.

Put the Communists to Sleep

We are used to thinking about the Cold War as dominated by war fears, not war fantasies. In her book on fear, the historian Joanna Bourke sees the fear of nuclear war as the characteristic or motivating fear of the Cold War in the United States and the United Kingdom. The fear of nuclear war was so overwhelming, she claims, that it evoked only passivity—people could not imagine being able to alleviate the destruction and so they simply did not do anything (like build bomb shelters or prepare for an attack).[31] For anti-Communists in the People's Democracies, however, war was the only way out of passivity. As refugees imagined it, the chaos of war would sweep away the Soviets and allow domestic anti-Communists to take power. But fear of nuclear war had the potential to change this equation. It was hard to eagerly await destruction on the scale of Hiroshima or Nagasaki. After the development of the hydrogen bomb in 1953, the potential for devastation increased exponentially. Most refugees, however, simply discounted these dangers. An RFE report of 1952 based on interviews with eighteen Bulgarian Jewish refugees sojourning in Naples on their way to Haifa claimed that Bulgarians were "reconciled to atom bombing if it will deliver them from the Communist yoke. At least the survivors will have a decent life."[32] Another report based on conversations with the same Bulgarian refugees observed that, although they knew the consequences of another world war would be "catastrophic," they considered it no more dangerous than the policies of the Communist regime, which they claimed "does not hesitate to sacrifice whole generations" in its relentless pursuit of utopia.[33]

Most interviewees did not like to even imagine that war could have these kinds of consequences. Instead, they fantasized that nuclear war could be painless. Many simply ignored the potential dangers of a nuclear conflict, choosing to focus on the expected positive results of a war.[34] Others reckoned with the possibility of atomic weapons, but tried to minimize the impact they might have on the satellite countries. A young Czech air force pilot who had dramatically commandeered a plane to flee the country told RFE, "No one in the ČSR [Czechoslovak Republic] is afraid of atomic bombs. They think that if war broke out the ČSR would not be the main battlefield, because German soldiers would occupy it so quickly that in a few days in would be practically the hinterland ... In the ČSR people expect war as a sure thing."[35]

One could simply refuse to think about the consequences of war entirely. A British woman who fled Prague in 1955 after becoming estranged from her Czech husband claimed, "People constantly talk of 'when we're free.' They don't speak of how they will be freed and don't really care . . . There is little mention of the A-bomb or the H-bomb and possibly people don't even think of such things. The whole problem is to be free."[36] This source believed war would create the backdrop against which a complete rejection of the regime would be possible. She preferred to discount the thought of actual bloodshed, reducing the problem to one of finding elusive freedom, and not actually fighting or dying for it.

Many interviewees insisted that the Americans would not waste atomic weapons on the countries of Eastern Europe. They created a fantasy of atomic bombs as miracle weapons that could instantaneously destroy Soviet power while leaving its satellites untouched. The Soviets would suffer a bloody defeat, but Eastern Europe would simply become free. American atomic bombs could thus be imagined as vehicles of liberation rather than destruction. Boguslawa Smolka-Bauer, a university-educated high school teacher from Poland, believed this fantasy was common among Poles. As she told a VOA interviewer, "People think that America will, first of all, hit Russia with atomic bombs, while U.S. armies will immediately invade the satellite countries." Power would pass easily from the Soviets to the West, with all of the real damage occurring in the Soviet Union.[37] Smolka-Bauer's comments were echoed in 1954 by a group of Polish sailors, who hoped that if a war broke out the United States would use nuclear weapons on major Soviet cities, taking them out and painlessly liberating the Poles in the process.[38] A Romanian student interviewed in 1956 had a similar fantasy. He told RFE, "The Americans will not bother throwing hydrogen bombs over Bucharest or Rumania, where people are ready to fight against Communism, as to launch a few over Russia will be sufficient to sow terror and panic not only in the USSR, but also among the satellite armies. People also say that a war of any sort is to be preferred to continuing to live in terror and misery; at least those who survive will live better."[39] In this optimistic dream, there was no need to worry about the dangers of fallout or any other ramifications of nuclear devastation just to the East. Indeed, some openly relished the idea that atomic bombs would kill Soviets while sparing their own friends and family. N.Z., a nineteen-year-old Hungarian refugee, asserted that Hungarians dreamed of war as a means not only of liberation but of revenge against the Soviets. "They hope," he said, "that maybe an atomic bomb will be dropped on the Russians on Russian territory."[40]

Almost all refugees said they were convinced that the Americans would win any war. The fact that the Soviet Union had come back against enormous adversity to defeat Nazi Germany only a few years before went completely unremarked. To sustain the fantasy of war as liberation, of course, there could be no doubt about an eventual Soviet defeat. Many claimed that the United States had a clear military superiority that would allow it to quickly overpower the Soviet Union. M.V., a Czech viticulture student from Humpolec, said, "In case a third world war should start, we think that Russia will be eliminated by an atom bomb with lightning speed."[41] Refugees consistently asserted that the Soviets were no match for the Americans. The Czechoslovak refugee P., a supervisor at the Jachymov uranium mine, claimed that the Soviet Union was a "giant on earthen feet."[42] In the event of a war, P. claimed, the Soviets would face internal revolt and would be forced to give in to the Americans.

Others refused to believe that the Soviets could match American military technology. They fantasized that Soviet claims of developing an atomic or hydrogen bomb were just lies. K.A., a Hungarian carpenter, remarked to VOA that he could not believe the Soviets had actually developed an atomic bomb, because if they really had one they would have already attacked the United States.[43] In similar fashion, a Hungarian former merchant who fled Budapest for Austria in 1954 told RFE that the "Soviet statement of possessing atomic bombs and plants is certainly only an empty propaganda. The Soviets have nothing; they want to steal the secret from the Americans."[44] A Czechoslovak sculptor declared, "The Soviet Union is considered strong in manpower, weak in quality." Even if the Soviets had made a hydrogen bomb, he said, Czechoslovaks doubted they had the capability to drop it on New York.[45] The belief that the Soviets did not really possess nuclear technology or that even if they did the weapons they produced would not work well (like other shoddy Soviet products, some claimed) served to create an entirely different vision of atomic or thermonuclear warfare. This wishful (or willful) thinking turned the atomic bomb into the vehicle for refugee hopes and dreams instead of the stuff of nightmares.

This need to believe that atomic weapons could destroy the Soviets without also destroying their satellites had an echo in many other far-fetched rumors about mysterious and miraculous American war machines. These fantastic weapons would make it possible to get rid of Communist regimes without any loss of life, or loss of life only among the Communists. One Czech source told RFE in 1952 about a persistent rumor that the Americans had developed a "soporific bomb" that would put everyone not wearing a special mask to sleep; those spared the sudden nap could then easily cut the throats of the comatose Communists.[46] This particular rumor was apparently spread extensively. An émigré who illegally visited Czechoslovakia two years after this report was made claimed that several people he met had earnestly told him that the Americans had developed a special powder they could drop from planes that would put everyone to sleep and enable a clean and bloodless removal of the Communists.[47] Nor was this idea limited to Czechoslovakia. The Hungarian tailor S.L. claimed that he read in the

Communist newspaper *Népszava* (Referendum) that the Americans had used a gas in Korea that put opponents to sleep for twelve hours. The Communists, he said, called this an illegal use of chemical weapons, but he and his friends thought it was quite humane. "Thinking about similar modern weapons made us believe that with their aid a new world war would not last for years."[48]

A middle-aged Hungarian intellectual interviewed by VOA claimed such rumors were cherished by Hungarians who wanted to believe that liberation could come without a war and its attendant costs. He said, "Spoiled beauties and so-called bel esprits . . . believe in a wonder-bomb with narcotic effects. One talked and dreamed of it in Hungary in the past. It is supposed to make enemies sleep for a couple of hours, during which the defenders of Western civilization could conquer their enemies behind the Iron Curtain without the use of destroying weapons."[49] The source scoffed at the gullibility of such people, but his remarks illustrate how a belief in fantastic weapons like the soporific bomb served a very real psychological need. It allowed for hope and optimism in a climate that otherwise provided scant fodder for either. Such fantasies, however, allowed people to put off acknowledging that Communist regimes might last. As long as one believed in the existence of soporific bombs, one could imagine that Eastern Europe's Communist states were living on borrowed time.

Interviewees reported stories of other fantastic American weapons. A Romanian student claimed that during the summer of 1951 Romanians were convinced that they had spotted American "flying discs," a new secret weapon that would be used to drop "atomic powder."[50] It was not clear from this report what "atomic powder" would achieve, but the implication was that it would be a fast and painless way to achieve liberation. Like the soporific bomb, flying discs and atomic powders were not simply miraculous. They bore a strong resemblance to the magical elements in fairy tales, like a bag of magic beans or a lamp containing a genie. Provided by a benevolent if not always trustworthy source (here, the Americans), these magical objects could solve the problem of dictatorship in an instant. The popularity of these wild rumors, which flew in the face of any established scientific knowledge, showed that the population was desperate for something that could completely reshape local conditions from afar. We do not know if those who spread these rumors questioned their authenticity, but the fact that they were so widely repeated indicates that the people who told these tales hoped they were true, even if they had their doubts.

War fantasies could also help combat the feeling of powerlessness by providing an imaginary venue in which people acted out dreams of revenge or self-assertion. In their fantasies, people imagined what would happen once they shed their protective passivity and internally enacted their revenge on the Communist regime. This was the case in the Kilian György apprentice home in Hungary. The source, a sixteen-year-old boy who worked as a glass technician apprentice from 1952 to 1954, described how the apprentices whiled away their free time in the evenings fantasizing about what they would do if a war broke out. They waited for it, the source said, in eager anticipation. It was not surprising that the apprentices fantasized about an event that might improve their condition: their lives were hard, food was scarce, and their hostel was poorly heated. The apprentices clearly saw war as the means of taking control over their lives. They dreamed about how they would use their required military training to fight the Russians. They imagined escaping to join the Americans, not simply to leave their troubles behind, but because this might enable them to enact their revenge fantasies against Soviet troops.[51]

The dream of another young Hungarian man, S.M., who fled the country to avoid military service, is a telling example of how fantasies of liberation related to domestic circumstances. S.M. imagined that after American forces routed the Communists, Hungary would become a colony of the United States. S.M.'s vision of this future American regime in Hungary gave great insight into his perception of the Communist-led Hungarian state. Under American rule, he said, "people would not be oppressed ... Nothing would be taken away from them by confiscation. Maybe some of the wheat would be taken to the US." But, unlike the Soviets, the Americans would compensate the Hungarians for their requisitions. S.M. painted a lovely picture of happy Hungarian workers who willingly worked for an American occupation because they were paid like American workers, which made it possible for them to acquire houses and automobiles. But his fantasy of a prosperous, capitalist (and dependent) Hungary also included the possibility of revenge. He told VOA, "Those who deserved it would be deported, but the thousands of innocent people would not have to fear deportation nor bear its burden." According to S.M., the Communists would pay for their past deeds by suffering the same fates as those they had persecuted.[52]

Political transformation and retribution were also themes in Mieczyslaw Surowiecki's vision of his native Poland after war had freed it. Surowiecki was nineteen when he was interviewed by the VOA in Frankfurt. Before fleeing Poland, he had been a high school student in Jaroslaw. He told his interviewer that he emigrated because he did not want to join the ZMP (Communist youth organization). As Surowiecki observed, war was a common theme in the Polish press. The media tried to stoke war fears to create support for the Communist regime and its Soviet allies, claiming that the Soviet Union would protect the peace that American warmongers threatened. Surowiecki took the opposite approach and hoped that the warmongers would do their work, which he believed would "bring freedom to Poland." While his sketch of the postwar Polish state was vague, he knew it would adhere to "the principles of

American freedom," allow Poles complete national sovereignty, and punish the Communists for their actions.[53]

An Alliance with the Devil?

In their war fantasies, East Europeans imagined that war would bring freedom and the possibility of individual and national self-determination. The new war, they assured themselves, would be painless and quick, nothing like the devastating Second World War. Sustaining this fantasy not only required faith in miraculous weapons; it also meant reconciling with the possibility of a new wave of German invaders. The Bonn–Paris Convention of 1952 proposed that an independent West Germany (formally the Federal Republic of Germany) would join a combined European Defense Community. This did not actually happen: negotiations over West German rearmament stalled, primarily over French doubts about Germans in a combined European military force. The European Defense Community was never formed. Instead, the Federal Republic joined NATO and did not establish its own military until 1955.[54] But West German rearmament was a live and contentious issue on both sides of the Iron Curtain for much of the first half of the 1950s.

The Communist-controlled media of Eastern Europe often linked Western imperialism with fascism, alleging that the West not only mimicked Nazi warmongering but literally allied itself with former Nazis. Speeches, proclamations, and other texts associated with the peace campaign warned that war with the West might mean a return of Nazi aggression and even Nazi rule. As a typical example, the Soviet writer and inveterate peace campaigner Ilya Ehrenburg declared in a 1953 speech to the World Peace Council that the West had "in every way supported the revenge-seeking elements in Western Germany. It has helped to revive military and paramilitary organizations run by the Nazis . . . it has turned Western Germany into an aggressive bridgehead, into an arsenal of atomic and other weapons." Ehrenburg intimated that the American-supported West German government had revisionist plans, hoping to take former German-majority territories from Poland and Czechoslovakia. He also claimed that ratifying the Bonn–Paris accords over German rearmament would be "suicide" for France and suggested that the Soviets would be truer allies to the French than would the Americans and British.[55] In Ehrenburg's presentation, the United States, abetted by its British partners, was re-creating the Third Reich. As soon as these rehabilitated former Nazis were allowed weapons, they would once again be in a position to start an imperialist war. True security, said Ehrenburg, could never be achieved as long as the West treated this revanchist, Nazi-led West Germany as an ally and partner.

Most refugees ostensibly ignored these kinds of warnings and declared that not even the image of West German troops crossing the border slaked their thirst for war. Whatever their misgivings, they claimed that the idea of liberation was worth this potential uncertainty. One Bulgarian engineer, interviewed while immigrating to Israel, said that Bulgarians approved of (West) German rearmament because only a war "could give back liberty and independence to Bulgaria," and they did not think the Soviets could be defeated without German help. Bulgarians would "enter into an alliance with the devil if that would help them get their independence and liberty." In any case, he said, Bulgarians no longer saw the Germans as a threat. However, the engineer noted, Bulgaria had not been occupied by Germany during the previous war, and Bulgarians had no personal experience of German occupation.[56]

The same was not true of Poland and Czechoslovakia.[57] Both countries had been occupied and dismembered by Germany in 1939, with much of their territory remaining under German occupation for the duration of the war.[58] In addition, both had reason to fear German revenge or retribution. Poland had received German territory in recompense for the Soviet annexation of its eastern territories, and Czechoslovakia had expelled most of its German-speaking citizens as collaborators and expropriated their property. In both countries, homes, farms, and businesses formerly owned by expelled German speakers had been given away to new owners. A Western victory meant the possibility of a German return, both as occupiers and to potentially reassert ownership rights over their former land.[59]

RFE researchers were quite sensitive to these concerns. They extensively questioned Czechoslovak and Polish refugees about their views on West German rearmament. Some admitted that Communist warnings about German aggression found their targets. A Slovak told RFE in 1954 that the Czechs feared a German return, and this was the primary reason they supported the Communists. He suggested that in order to quell these fears the station broadcast more information showing that the Federal Republic was a decent and peaceful nation.[60] But most refugees clung desperately to their hopes of Western military intervention and refused to admit that even German participation would prevent Western troops from being welcomed as liberators, although they acknowledged that the idea of German soldiers on their home soil was a matter of concern.

As the United States and its allies considered the issue of West German rearmament in the months before and after the signing of the Bonn–Paris Convention of 1952, RFE stringers asked a number of recent refugees from Czechoslovakia about their attitudes toward a militarized West Germany. Most claimed they would accept a new West German army if it would help bring about the war they believed would liberate them from Communism. A clergyman from Slovakia told RFE that the inhabitants of Prague were "in favor of the establishment of a West German army in the context of a united European defense community, because this was the only way Czechoslovakia and the other so-called People's Democracies could be liberated."[61] According to this man, while some people worried about German revenge for the events of 1945, most saw the West German army as a necessary bulwark against further Soviet expansion.

In a similar vein, a Czech butcher said, "People welcome any action that could mean liberation from Communism." They imagined, he said, that even a new German invasion would have few consequences. He added that even those in the border regions were not worried, because many of them had already lost the property they had gained by moving to the border areas anyway.[62] Others admitted that some in the border regions might be worried, but emphasized that most people welcomed anything that would hasten the end of the Communist regime, even an armed West Germany.[63]

For most anti-Communist Czechoslovak refugees, Czechoslovak–German relations had been irrevocably altered by the German defeat in 1945 and the rise of the Cold War. A Moravian worker who spoke with RFE in May 1952 claimed that Czechs and Germans indeed still hated each other, a feeling that he said was "as old as history" and had only been exacerbated by the previous war and the expulsions that followed it. But this hatred had nevertheless been reshaped by new geopolitical realities. The Communists, he said, wanted to convince Czechs that the East Germans were their brothers, whereas the West Germans were their enemies. For most Czechs, this was ridiculous. They believed all Germans were the same and all might attack Czechoslovakia if they had the chance. But the Germans were no longer their own masters. The Americans, the man continued, would prevent German aggression against Czechoslovakia. Under American supervision, even Germans would be welcome allies against Communism.[64]

The idea that a German army controlled by Americans was at least better than a German army controlled by the Soviets was echoed by an apprentice from Ostrava who claimed that most people said, "If they are building a German army in East Germany, why couldn't they build one in the Western world as well?"[65] (The East German National People's Army was not actually established until 1956.) Both of these reports reflected a sense of powerlessness. For the authors, the fate of Eastern Europe would ultimately be decided by the superpowers. All that was left to Czechoslovaks was to hope for one side to win. But this had the effect of reducing the German threat. No matter what happened, even the Germans would have to act under superpower auspices. For anti-Communist Czechoslovak refugees, therefore, even Germans could be imaginatively mobilized as part of a fantastical war of liberation.

Polish refugees made similar rationalizations that allowed them to imagine a German military assisting in their liberation. A few Polish sailors interviewed by

RFE in North German ports seemed sanguine about West German rearmament. They were certain that the United States would soon drop atomic bombs on Russian cities and end Communist rule in Europe. They hoped that with a Soviet defeat the United States would take its place as the hegemon of Eastern Europe. By taking charge of the whole European continent, they imagined, America would keep the peace. No matter what happened, the sailors believed that the Americans would never relinquish their hold over Germany, and this would keep Poland secure from German aggression. They even imagined that "all Western armies now wore American uniforms and that Germans would also do so when the time came." RFE analysts remarked that the sailors exhibited a "sentimental approach" to politics, but also noted that the report showed how little they had been affected by regime propaganda.[66] The analysts did not consider that the sailors' conviction that war was imminent might itself have been influenced by the constant drumbeats of war that emanated from Communist peace campaigns.

As in other matters, many refugees claimed that their views were representative of the vast majority of the population. We should be careful about taking them at their word. One RFE report (which RFE's analysts said they found reliable) hinted as much. The source was a German citizen of Berlin who visited family members in the village of Dolsk near Poznan. He reported that local memories of wartime suffering were still vivid and that many people continued to hate Germans, without distinction as to East or West. The people of Dolsk, he said, feared West German rearmament and believed this was "a corruption of American policy."[67] Refugees' insistence that West German rearmament would be accepted by their compatriots undoubtedly indicated less about general attitudes at home than about the depth of their own investment in the idea of a liberating war. Their need to keep their hope alive drove them to minimize any possible obstacles to the war they so deeply desired.

War Is Imminent; We Know It to Be True

To many interview respondents, the idea that war would soon break out took on the status of an unshakable truth. While the timing was not certain, the conflict itself was inevitable. Several young Poles told VOA they were so convinced that war was imminent that they escaped over the border to join "the Polish army in the West." Remembering that Polish units in exile fought with the Allies during the Second World War, they wrongly assumed the West must be training a new Polish émigré army to help in the coming conflict. They were saddened to discover that the only thing awaiting them in exile was a refugee camp. Ryszard Rekowski had been a member of the Polish Home Army (Armia Krajowa, or AK) during the Second World War. When he fled to Germany to escape the notice of the security service, he firmly believed he would find a place with the Polish army there. Instead, he told VOA, "I was very disappointed when I came to the West. I thought, when I was in Poland, that here in the West exist very strong anticommunist movements which fight against the Red." Like some of the other Poles interviewed by VOA, he was dissatisfied with conditions in German refugee camps and had begun to wonder if leaving Poland had been the right choice. Even the Polish émigré organizations, he complained, did not really want to help their compatriots or arm them, but only to interview them for "informations about life in Poland."

Rekowski ended his interview by stating his disgust with the lack of preparations for war and assistance for the refugees, saying, "I personally and all the persons I spoke to were very disappointed with the existing situation."[68] Rekowski and others like him had hoped to find a new agency in exile; they imagined that as armed soldiers under Western command they would be able to help shape their country's destiny. Instead, they found only a different kind of powerlessness. As refugees, they had few rights. No one met them with open arms, offering jobs, apartments, and citizenship status. Not officially allowed to work, most wound up in refugee camps for months or years. There they sat, also marking time, waiting for the visas that would allow them to start new lives.[69]

The idea of the Polish army in the West was a fantasy, just like the belief in an inevitable war that would liberate Eastern Europe. These were comforting dreams that allowed some East Europeans to take refuge in the hope that Communism would soon fall, via a deus ex machina in the form of the American military. But, although these fantasies were the product of wishful thinking, they were sustained by the ways people interpreted the messages they received from both local and Western media. It was not that people simply believed what they heard on the news, but that the news reinforced the ideas that they wanted to believe.

War fantasies found support even in Communist peace propaganda. Most refugees claimed that they paid little attention to the domestic Communist media. A Hungarian worker interviewed by VOA said that when the Communist newspaper was read out in the factory cafeteria at lunch, everyone tried to ignore it and "just be noisy with the spoons."[70] Similarly, the young Hungarian X.Y. remarked, "I used newspapers only to wrap my food in them."[71] Some said that they read the papers but dismissed most of the content as mere propaganda.[72] Others claimed that the truth was always precisely the opposite of whatever the domestic media said.[73] Yet, when asked about current events, many respondents gave answers that showed the influence of Communist discourse on their thinking. The conviction that war was inevitable was bolstered, for example, by the two-camps theory that undergirded the peace campaign. The idea that the world was divided into two opposing camps fed the notion that the tension between them would inevitably explode into armed conflict. When asked about the possibility of war, the twenty-two-year-old Pole Wladyslaw Tomczynski said, "Two systems, Capitalism and Communism, cannot exist in the present conditions in the world. The world is too small for these two systems. The communists also stress constantly (the fact) that only when capitalism will disappear from (the world's) surface, all will be well in the world."[74]

The two-camps theory was clearly a factor in convincing Tomczynski that war was inevitable. He was equally confident that that the Americans would win. This kind of thinking was present in many of the VOA interviews, as respondents frequently claimed that the ultimate incompatibility between Communism and capitalism would lead them irretrievably toward war.[75] Many respondents, it should be noted, believed it was the Soviet Union that would start the war, driven by its unquenchable thirst for world domination. As Mrs. I.K., a middle-class Hungarian widow, told VOA, "Despite all of their peace slogans, the Russian leaders are confidently resolved to have war."[76] Even if the Americans wanted peace, this Soviet determination to extend its influence would lead them, and the world, inexorably to war. The Czech J.Z. put it this way, "The Americans don't want to go to war ... Of course, they can already see for themselves that there is no understanding with Communism and so they will have to take a determined step and fight this war."[77]

While respondents were more likely to paint the Soviets than the Americans as imperialist warmongers, they did give some credence to the Communist claim that the West was actively preparing for war. For L.P., a female Czech sculptor, rearmament was one of the factors leading the world to war. She said, "I believe World War III cannot be prevented. My opinion is based on all the war preparations, the ideological quarrels, the rearmament on both sides, and the inflammatory agitation, which will one day ... result in a war."[78] One respondent even opined that the United States was prolonging the war in Korea simply for the chance to try out more of its new weapons. Of course, such ideas did not have to spring from Communist peace rhetoric; some in the West also feared that the postwar atomic arms race would inevitably lead to a new war. But it is clear that, like Ryszard Rekowski, some refugees had become convinced that the West was more militarized than it actually was. Another refugee, Tadeusz Zielinski, was also upset to find that his image of the West did not match the reality. He told VOA that, after arriving in West Germany, "I do not see the West really understands the danger of Communism. I thought in Poland that they have here a strong army or are forming an army and I see now that my opinion was false."[79] Zielinski's belief in Western war preparations turned out to be wishful thinking. But he was able to convince himself of its truth while he was still in Poland, likely at least in part because of his interpretation of the Communist media's portrayal of the West.

Western radio broadcasts also played a role in solidifying war fantasies. The relationship between Western radio and listeners' war fantasies was not simple or direct; listeners did not simply adopt Western perspectives. Most listened critically and did not automatically accept that the content of a broadcast was true just because it originated in the West. Although those interviewed by VOA often claimed that they preferred Western radio because it told them the real facts, they also frequently admitted that they listened to Western stations to receive confirmation of what they either already took to be true or wanted to be true.[80] They tended to accept information that conformed to their existing beliefs and reject what did not. This perspective is exemplified by the comments of T.B., a teenaged Hungarian secondary school student from a farming family who was described by his interviewer as an "extraordinarily clever and intelligent" subject. While he was still in Hungary, T.B. spent a lot of time consuming news from a wide variety of sources, and he was thoughtful about the expectations those around him had of the news media. According to T.B., people were most interested in hearing stories about American war preparations or the defeat of Communists in Korea. He added, "Further news of great interest was that they were able to produce weapons with atomic energy that only kills soldiers but not the [civilian] population. This was the most popular radio news." Clearly, those around T.B. were intent on using Western media to bolster their dreams of liberation by the West. They preferred news that indicated liberation was near and eagerly listened to stories that confirmed their beliefs.

In T.B.'s account, stories of miraculous weapons were given the status of fact rather than rumor because they supposedly had been gleaned from a Western radio broadcast. But this did not mean that people believed anything they heard from the West. The crucial criterion for belief was not the source of the news, but whether it matched people's expectations of the truth. T.B. claimed that people liked stories on VOA that made it seem as if the war would be simple and not difficult. Stories that claimed a new war would last a long time (which he said were commonly heard on the BBC) were "very unpopular." Even more strikingly, T.B. recalled an incident in which a Communist classmate told him he had heard on VOA that the Soviet Union had atomic bombs. "Nobody believed this, neither do I. Nobody believes this in Hungary, even though the Communists are saying the same thing." Here, confronted with an unpleasant fact, T.B. simply denied it could be true, even though it had been publicized by both Communist and Western media. He wanted to believe only the news that supported his dream of an easy, fast end to Communist rule in Hungary. Truth, for T.B. and the people around him, was less a matter of objective fact than of correspondence with their desired reality.[81]

The remarks of Zygmunt Ostrowski, a Polish butcher, show the contradictory demands some made on Western radio. On the one hand, Ostrowski told VOA that listeners tuned into the station to get the real facts about what was going on in the world. Poles, he claimed, believed little of what they read in Communist newspapers, but "America [VOA] always tells the truth." As he went on, however, it became clear that what Ostrowski really wanted to hear was that this American truth conformed to his own hopes and dreams. He said that his favorite programs were about the Korean War, because they challenged Communist reporting on Korea, which he wanted to believe was false. When asked what VOA should do differently, he said, "They should speak more about the war and about Korea, how they beat the Russians and when the great war will come, because people only wait for it to start." Ostrowski did not want to hear about American losses, even if they were occurring. He wanted only stories that told him that the Communists were losing. Similarly, he said, "Sometimes when they [VOA] say that that there will be no war, that they want peace, people curse these Americans and switch the radio off. Women were angry because the men curse and get nervous. Yes, sir, they are all angry. People want to hear about the war there. When it will come and what it will be. People should hear more about that."

Ostrowski's comments make it clear that he was listening not so much to gather facts as to hear stories that bolstered his own war fantasies. When those fantasies were threatened, he preferred to turn the radio off. What Ostrowski really craved was not the news, but evidence that American policy had met his desires. When asked what kinds of programs VOA should offer in the future, he said that VOA should not talk about what life was really like in Poland, because everyone knew this already and it was only depressing. Instead, programs should discuss "how it will be after the war, what the government there [in Poland] will be, how it will be in the villages, how about the shops, whether it will be free or cooperative. They should talk more about the frontiers . . . It will give people more hope that they really think about that in America, and that it is not just bluff."[82] Ostrowski wanted VOA to give him hope, not facts. Because the VOA represented America and America had the power to make its own truth, he wanted the VOA to give voice to his own fantasies and, by so doing, make them real.

You Can't Wait Out Socialism

Like all fantasies, war fantasies could not be sustained indefinitely. These dreams of armed Western intervention were the product of a particular time, as East Europeans struggled to adapt to the new reality of living under state socialism. Strongest in the period before Stalin's death in 1953, war fantasies gradually gained less purchase as it became more and more apparent that they would never come true. For example, a report from a Czech official with the agricultural department of the Karlovy Vary National Committee claimed that in previous years people had often been convinced that the regime was about to fall—it would be by the next "spring or Christmas or October 28 [Czechoslovak Independence Day]." But now, he said, no one thought a war or foreign intervention was in the offing. People did not believe that any local action would matter, as lasting change could only occur if regimes changed in the Soviet Union and all of its satellites.[83] An older Bulgarian woman made similar remarks, complaining to RFE that "resistance to the regime was diminishing daily." The reason, she said, was not that people approved of the government, but that they were "tired of waiting to be liberated and have become skeptical about it."[84] It was starting to look like socialism might be there to stay.

By 1955 or 1956, refugees interviewed by RFE began to express more overt fears of nuclear war. Some of those fears were linked to new knowledge about the destructive capacity of thermonuclear weapons. Several RFE interviewees expressed new doubts about the use of nuclear bombs. A Bulgarian physician who fled Sofia in early 1956 told RFE he thought that the Bulgarian Communist regime was there to stay unless the international situation changed drastically. Many Bulgarians, he said, hoped for a war to dislodge them. But he was not so sure. As he told the interviewer, "I have no doubt about the horrible effects of nuclear weapons and realize that in a possible atomic war there will be no victor, there will only be defeated countries." For this doctor, the probable realities of nuclear war had made the once easy question of whether or not there should be a war an intractable dilemma.[85]

A Hungarian mechanic (of Italian ethnicity) had a slightly different take. Like the Bulgarian physician, he believed nuclear weapons had "reached such a stage that in war they would wipe out a great portion of mankind" but contended that most Hungarians did not worry about this possibility. They still thought, he claimed, that the United States could use its bombs on the Soviets without hurting Hungary in the process. But the mechanic was dubious that a war would break out soon. The superpowers themselves were too scared to start a war now, he told RFE.[86] A Hungarian peasant interviewed at around the same time had similar convictions. He said, "I know nothing about the effect of atomic weapons, except that they would ruin the non-fighting people too and that whole countries would be contaminated." He claimed that "people" still wanted war, but that they "would prefer the future war to be fought with the 'old' weapons."[87] His optimism may have stemmed from the Korean War, in which both sides refrained from using atomic weapons. But it was nonetheless wishful thinking to dream that future wars would inevitably follow this pattern.

For other East Europeans, war began to look less attractive as time passed and lives settled into new routines. Even during the material shortages of the

Stalinist period, people built homes and lives they did not want to see destroyed by war. With the advent of more liberal policies on consumption (in addition to a more general liberalization) after the beginning of de-Stalinization, there was even more worth protecting. One émigré, a Pole who had been a member of the Polish Home Army during the Second World War, claimed in 1954 that another war would be devastating for Poland. Even though he disagreed with the regime enough to have fled the country, he did not want to see a newly rebuilt Warsaw flattened. As he said, "If a new war destroys everything again, no one will have enough strength to rebuild. No one will have enough energy to begin again as before." He maintained that the impetus for change would have to come from something besides war.[88]

A Polish woman visiting London in April 1956 articulated this view even more forcefully. She claimed that after the death of Poland's Stalinist leader, Bolesław Bierut, Poles had lost their taste for war. Five or six years ago, she said, people would have welcomed a military solution, but now they realized how much destruction that would entail and how much they actually had to lose. Émigrés might still want war, but, at least according to this woman, that feeling was not shared by their compatriots at home.[89] The year 1956 was a time of significant change in Poland that made life more livable for many people. The year ended with the successful protests of the so-called Polish October, which brought the national Communist Władysław Gomułka to power and ushered in a more liberal era, allowing many to concede that war was no longer necessary, even if it were possible.[90] Reflecting this new situation, a middle-aged Polish correspondent told RFE in December 1956, "Fear has disappeared for ever—let us hope."[91]

Elsewhere, the failed Hungarian revolution of 1956 crushed hopes for Western liberation. The uprising in Hungary began with student protests on October 23, 1956, and escalated rapidly. Soon, armed rebels were fighting in the streets. To quell the unrest, the Soviets pushed out the Hungarian premier, Ernő Gerő, and replaced him with a reformer, Imre Nagy. But protests continued and radicalized, pushing Nagy to announce that Hungary would leave the Warsaw Pact. A massive Soviet military intervention soon followed, on November 4, 1956. Despite being vastly outnumbered and outgunned by Soviet forces, some revolutionaries continued to fight, spurred, at least in part, by their belief that Western forces would soon come to relieve them. But the liberating army never appeared, and the Hungarian revolution was brutally quashed.[92] Some of those who fled from the Soviet tanks over the Austrian border claimed that Western radio stations, particularly RFE, had told them to expect Western intervention, which never came.[93] Historians have debated the extent to which RFE falsely encouraged Hungarian insurgents.[94] RFE claimed the station had not made overt promises of Western military assistance on the air, although an internal analysis admitted that "certain programs tended to arouse false hopes and expectations of aid from the outside."[95] Considering the prevalence and persistence of war fantasies in the region up to this moment, it is easy to see how even the suggestion of Western liberation could resonate with anti-Communist Hungarian street fighters, convincing them that what they had imagined for so long might finally be realized.

In the aftermath of the Soviet invasion of Hungary, few people in Eastern Europe continued fantasizing about Western liberation. In a striking departure from the tone of earlier interviews, a Hungarian woman who fled to the West in 1959 told US Information Agency interviewers that Hungarians did not look to the West for "morale" anymore.[96] A resident of Prague informed an RFE researcher in late November 1956 that Czechs no longer believed the West would liberate them. They now knew, the source said, that liberation could come only from the Soviet Union. Communism would end in Prague only when it had fallen in Moscow.[97] But it was clear this would not happen anytime soon. And so what would happen to the residents of Eastern Europe? The fantasy of a liberating war had enabled anti-Communists to believe they could wait out socialism. The idea of waiting became a coping mechanism that allowed many people to live their daily lives in a socialist system while imagining themselves to be fundamentally apart from that system, even if the process of everyday life required ideological and moral compromises. The Bulgarian refugee physician who told RFE in 1953 that opposition to Communism was futile held firmly to the belief that, when his neighbors marched and cheered for Communism, they did so only outwardly. As he told RFE, "The general appearance of surrender is only superficial."[98] Whether or not this was actually the case, the physician was comforted by this belief. Indeed, the idea that one could wall oneself off from the regime and not be affected by it was the most compelling fantasy of all. But as Western intervention faded as even a remote possibility, this dream would also have to die.

War Won't Set You Free

The narratives of East European refugees from the first years of the Cold War reflect the influence of the Western concept of captive nations. Many refugees described themselves as powerless prisoners waiting for liberation to come from abroad. Conceiving of themselves and their compatriots as captives allowed them to imagine that they stood apart from the Communist regimes that ruled their homelands. Insisting that they were effectively prisoners allowed refugees to imagine that they remained unaffected by the socialist transformation of society. The idea of their own captivity became a refuge, a place to wait for the war that both the local Communist media and Western radio convinced them was imminent.

That war, they told themselves, would miraculously make all the Communists disappear, allowing the prisoners to emerge from their cells, unscathed by their experience.

Refugees, like Western totalitarian thinkers, imagined that only war would end the oppressive policies of the Stalinist system. They did not consider what might happen if Communist regimes began to change of their own accord. But, after the death of Stalin, it gradually became apparent that change was possible from within, albeit within strictly defined limits. Although the timelines and policies varied, in all of the countries of the Soviet Bloc de-Stalinization meant the end of Stalinist terror, better living conditions, and a more liberal atmosphere. As prisons opened and the threat of arrest receded, fear and feelings of helplessness also faded, if they did not completely disappear. It became possible for East Europeans to imagine, and achieve, a more livable socialism.[99] In this new environment, war was no longer a viable option, even in fantasy.

6 THE POWER OF THE POWERLESS

Before the war, Z.H. was a prosperous textile merchant living in Rakospalota, a suburb of Budapest. In 1945, his shop was taken away. After a few years of trying other enterprises, a stint in prison, and some time in a labor camp, Z.H. fled through Slovakia to Austria. After he got there, he was surprised to see good-quality Hungarian salami for sale in the shops. As he told an interviewer for Voice of America (VOA) in September 1951, he felt this salami represented a pernicious lie. Austrian workers, he said, took the salami as a sign that Communist Hungary was prosperous; if there was enough salami to export, they reasoned, Hungarian workers must be eating their fill. Imagining that Communism brought plenty to the Hungarians strengthened their support for a similar system in Austria. But, Z.H. claimed, such delicious salami was actually unavailable in Hungary. "Hungarians eat potatoes and no salami now," he said. "And even if some salami should be available on black markets in Hungary," he added, "no worker could afford it."[1] If Austrian workers knew the real nature of Communism, Z.H. implied, they would not support it; they would fear it.

For Z.H., the truth of Communism was not prosperity, but deprivation and shortage. Hungarians suffered not only from a lack of freedom, but from a lack of goods, including essential foodstuffs. The Communist media tried to convince the population that they were better off than workers in the West, who were relentlessly exploited by their rich capitalist bosses, but everyone knew these were empty words. The proof was in the salami, or the lack of it. As Z.H. explained in his interview, "At the moment, Hungarian workers are deprived of everything as all goods are exported to foreign countries, mainly to Russia. It is daily hammered into the Hungarian workers by the official propaganda how well off they are and they are invited to enjoy it compared to the misery of the West. The workers feel that this is not true and therefore one should not cease to broadcast the truth about the American living standard."[2]

According to Z.H., if the truth of Communism was shortage and scarcity, the truth of the West, and especially the United States, was abundance. Although Z.H. claimed that Hungarian workers had already internalized this truth, he nevertheless thought that VOA should make it an element of its propaganda. He continued, "People don't doubt that the Americans are actually living like it is reported on the radio. Common people understand only the language of the stomach. In Hungary, the worker today gets no good food, unless he has the money to afford it. Maybe this circumstance along with proper comparisons to American living should be still more emphasized in the radio transmissions."[3] Rather than talking about abstract ideas such as freedom and democracy, Western radio stations, he suggested, should emphasize Communism's failure to meet the material expectations of the masses and contrast this failure with America's success at providing its citizens with prosperity and plenty.

Like Z.H., many of those who left Eastern Europe during the first years of the Cold War talked often about the material deprivations they had suffered at home. As most told it, Communists had promised better lives, but delivered only low wages, long working hours, high prices, and a general lack of consumer goods. While capitalist Western Europe also experienced rationing and shortage during the period from 1948 to 1956, these émigrés blamed the Communist system (rather than the destruction caused by the Second World War) for their poor standard of living. Like Z.H., they adopted a Manichaean Cold War worldview that contrasted East European scarcity with American abundance. For these refugees, who knew they might never see their former homes again, it was a matter of faith that the United States offered a better life than the Communist regimes they had rejected. This dichotomy between American prosperity and Communist poverty was, from their perspective, one of the most essential truths of the Cold War.

East European convictions about American wealth came from a variety of sources. The massive wave of emigration from Eastern Europe to the United States in the late nineteenth century was fueled by stories about migrants striking it rich in the new world.[4] In the early Cold War, these preexisting ideas about American abundance were consciously reinforced by American radio broadcasts to Eastern Europe.[5] As Z.H. noted in his interview with VOA, the radio waves were already full of stories about the high American standard of living; he suggested broadcasting even more of them to help convince his compatriots that Communism had nothing to offer. For his part, Z.H. provided VOA with concrete evidence of Communism's inability to better the material lives of its citizens. In this fashion, Western radio stations and their East European audiences confirmed and reinforced their mutual convictions about the causes and meanings of American prosperity and Communist poverty.

American prosperity was not a myth: citizens of the United States enjoyed much higher living standards than the inhabitants of either the Soviet Union or the Soviet Bloc; this had also been true before the establishment of Communist regimes in these regions.[6] It was also not a matter of dispute that many East Europeans experienced material shortages during this period, although this was not as universal an experience as some claimed. The two sides in the Cold War, however, interpreted that deprivation very differently. Refugee informants and radio stations like VOA and Radio Free Europe (RFE) blamed the centrally planned economies of Communist states for low living standards and inconsistent supplies of basic goods, suggesting that only capitalism could bring real prosperity. In contrast, Eastern Europe's Communist governments framed the scarcity of consumer goods as a temporary sacrifice, necessary for building up their countries' industrial capacity and ensuring a better future for everyone. Like their Western counterparts, the East European media tended to frame economic issues in terms of Cold War rivalries, claiming that shortages were caused by Western sabotage rather than by their own incompetence.

Refugees like Z.H. portrayed themselves as having little control over their material conditions; they claimed they were at the mercy of Communist economic policies that frustrated their attempts to build secure lives. Changing work rules and quota systems meant that workers could never be sure of their monthly pay, while the scarcity of many consumer goods brought stress and uncertainty to the routines of daily life. For many refugees, the experience of not knowing what they might find on store shelves or whether they would have enough money to last the week reflected more general anxieties over the class and gender upheaval that they also associated with Communism. Many refugees worried about the effects Communist economic policies were having on gender relations and family life. They feared that the drive to move women out of the home and into the labor force would destroy the family, but they felt unable to stop this transformation. Refugees' stories about shortages were often embedded in their experience of these larger processes that most felt were outside their control. In this way, refugees' descriptions of scarcity reflected their other claims of powerlessness in the face of Communist dictatorship.

But when refugees focused on the problem of material need itself (as opposed to the social or gender upheaval that was its side effect), they adopted a strikingly different tone. In other contexts, refugees often described themselves using terms like captivity and enslavement. Locked in the prison of their own fear, they were, they said, helpless to act against their oppressive Communist rulers. Though this description might not have accurately reflected the entirety of their everyday existence, they clung to it as an essential truth about their lives under Communism.

But refugees limited this constant reiteration of their own passivity to the sphere of political opposition. When it came to matters of their livelihood, refugees rarely described themselves as either afraid or unable to act. Instead, they bragged about their ability to undermine the state, regarding shortages as something to overcome, not something to fear. To alleviate them, they hoarded scarce goods, turned to black markets, and stole from their workplaces. Rather than just accept unpopular policies, workers complained and even went on strike. But, although refugees told their Western interlocutors many tales of their derring-do in pursuit of a better quality of life, neither Western analysts nor the refugees themselves conceived of their actions as a challenge to their strongly held beliefs about East European powerlessness and fear.

In America, You Can Buy a Car

In July 1952, the Pulitzer Prize–winning reporter Leland Stowe published an article in the *Washington Post* with the headline "Hunger Is a Political Weapon." Part of the series of articles about life in Communist Eastern Europe excerpted from his book *Conquest by Terror*, the article declared that Communist regimes used starvation as a means of subduing the population. "The new Stalinist aristocracy determines both what you eat and how much you may eat. Your stomach and your appetite are absolutely at the disposition of the state," Stowe claimed. He conjured pictures of Communist cafeterias where a favored few received plates heaped with delicacies, most were served a modest portion of potatoes, and others were turned away with nothing.[7] The actual subject of the text was a bit more prosaic: differentiated systems of ration cards that gave some categories of workers (and party members) more access to foodstuffs at subsidized prices. As the article noted, ration cards were generally available only to those who worked in nationalized enterprises. The self-employed had to buy their food on the free market, which was considerably more expensive. Such policies were indeed meant to encourage those who persisted in the private sector to join the state sector. For Stowe, these rationing systems amounted to "slow, deliberately manipulated starvation," since "in all satellite countries food has been desperately and increasingly scarce since 1949 for all but the Red rulers and workers." He illustrated these points with vivid examples, including the situation of a housewife from a "Danubian capital" (presumably Budapest) who described painfully waiting for hours in line to buy only bones and spinach. Stowe's dramatic language and stories of middle-class citizens reduced to penury ("doctors and lawyers" wearing "the same frayed garments week after week") suggested that hunger stalked all decent East Europeans not favored by the "Reds."

Stowe's article was based largely on information collected or composed by exiles and their organizations, including the Mid-European Studies Center (funded by the Free Europe Committee), and Radio Free Europe. RFE's researchers were very interested in economic conditions at home and queried refugees and correspondents extensively about rationing, prices, and shortages. Looking at reports about these topics from the collection of RFE Information Items, it is easy to see how Stowe might have used such documents in his work, although he does not specify his precise sources. One RFE report of August 1952, based on a private letter from a middle-class Hungarian to a friend or relative in Paris, echoed some of Stowe's examples, although it was dated shortly after his book was published. The source had been some kind of professional with her own shop (the report did not make clear what she produced; it could have been anything, from art or clothes to furniture). The store had been nationalized, but the source still continued to work in a studio at home as an independent artisan and therefore had no ration card. While her children had lunch at school, the source ate only tomatoes and fruit. There was no money, she said, for "such luxuries as butter or salami. Once a week we have meat, but it ruins the budget." Mostly they ate "fake goulash" (goulash without meat) or spinach and other vegetables for dinner. Reflecting on this hard life, the source said she had considered suicide, but decided it would just give pleasure to the Communists. Like Stowe, RFE analysts saw the value of such stories as paradigmatic examples of Communist misery. They noted on the report that, although the woman's letter was private, they had translated it for the collection of Information Items because it "might give some inspiration to feature writers."[8]

An equally dramatic report came from an elderly French woman who returned to the West after the death of her Romanian journalist husband. She told RFE in September 1952, in terms that echoed the language of Stowe's article, that "the problem of what and how to eat tomorrow looms large in Rumanian life. Those who have money can obtain anything in spite of the shortages. Those without are slowly dying of starvation." The first paragraphs of the report presented a dire picture indeed. This woman noted scarce supplies of meat, fish, eggs, cheese, butter, and even canned vegetables. She described food lines stretching for more than one hundred meters and claimed that Romanians might wait in these lines for hours, only to receive nothing in the end. Like Stowe's Danubian housewife, the French Romanian widow complained that the only food readily available in the spring of 1951 was spinach, inviting images of plates heaped with nothing but leaves.[9]

A closer look at both reports shows that the stories the sources told were more complicated than what Stowe described. The Budapest woman was sick of eating more vegetables than meat, but she was not going hungry, even though she stubbornly refused to give up her private business and join a cooperative. The root of her despair was more fundamental; she resisted the regime's attempts to divest her of her former class status and privileges.[10] There was a similar dynamic at work in the second report. After her dramatic remarks about dying of starvation, the French Romanian widow noted, "Only non-workers to whom canteens are prohibited or parents of small children eat at home." Canteens that sold subsidized food at reasonable prices to students and employees of both white- and blue-collar enterprises were common across the region. Although the food might not have been of superior quality (the source said as much), having to eat in canteens was a far cry from starving. And that was not all. On the second page of the report, the woman continued, "Bars are usually full on Sundays. People spend the little money they have on food and drinks. It would be futile to attempt to save."

It is hard to reconcile these statements about packed bars with the source's earlier comments about scarcity and starvation. Because RFE did not conduct formal interviews at this time, we do not know what questions prompted her different responses or even if the report echoed the actual flow of the conversation. The way the report is written, however, suggests that deprivation and shortage were this woman's overriding memories of her time in Communist Romania; her most dramatic comments about slow starvation came first, as if in response to a general query about her life. Later paragraphs qualified these remarks, but also suggested that her feelings of want were closely related to feelings of helplessness and loss. Her experience of eating and shopping was closely related to her position as a member of the former bourgeoisie, and her comments reflected middle-class bewilderment at this sudden loss of status. According to the source's comment about bars on Sundays, people were not starving, but they were spending their accumulated wealth on food and watching their former privileges disappear with each bite. It was telling that the source also noted in the report, "Formerly wealthy classes are dressed even more poorly than the workers. Fur coats, jewelry, silk dresses are things of the past."[11] For this woman, dealing with scarcity was closely tied to what she felt was the unfairness of this class upheaval and the loss of her former lifestyle and cultural milieu.

Many RFE informants recited similar litanies about their poor material situation. They reported shortages of many kinds of goods, but most frequently complained of not being able to find or afford meat, milk, eggs, butter, coffee, sugar, or cocoa and bemoaned their inability to purchase new clothes of acceptable quality.[12] These shortages were, to an extent, an effect of overt policy. Governments across the region, following the Soviet model, pushed resources into production rather than consumption. They promised that hard work and sacrifice in the present would be rewarded by prosperity in the future. But for most refugees this promise was nothing more than a hollow slogan. They saw only their unmet needs, which they blamed on the Communist system, refusing to believe that it could bring anything other than scarcity and want.

A young father who worked at a Polish meat-processing plant in Krakow, for example, narrated his life as an unceasing parade of deprivations and expenses, despite the fact that as a worker in a meat-processing facility he had access to much more of that scarce commodity than most. He received two kilos of meat for the family every month, had a lunch in the factory canteen that contained at least some meat every day (there was more meat on some days than others), and could have 120 grams (about one-quarter pound) of sausage during breakfast at the plant every day, albeit for a surcharge of forty złoty per month. But he framed his everyday life as one of constant scarcity and even hunger. He complained vociferously about the scantiness and expense of the meals he received from the factory canteen and claimed that his children were given such a poor breakfast and lunch at their state-sponsored day care and kindergarten that they always came home hungry. Given the costs of day care, food, and public transportation, he and his wife found it hard to save, despite their two incomes. Even after more than two years of work, he said, he had not managed to purchase a new suit. Implicit in his report was resentment that the Communist state had failed to bring workers the kind of prosperity they had envisioned.[13]

Western radio stations were happy to amplify this discontent.[14] When interviewed by VOA, the Hungarian refugee Janos Jasko told a joke that he said was well known in 1951 and that he also remembered being broadcast on VOA. It lampooned the Hungarian government's promises of future abundance. The joke involved a Budapest resident who walked into a Közert (state-run) store and asked for sugar. The clerk replied, "We don't have it now, but we will," meaning that there would be plenty of sugar for everyone once Communist goals for industrialization were achieved and the good life had begun. The customer then asked for potatoes and got the same reply. A request for eggs was met with an identical response. The frustrated customer then bade the clerk farewell with the Communist salutation of "Freedom!"—to which the clerk mechanically replied, "We don't have it now, but we will."[15]

These kinds of broadcasts, to which, at least according to Jasko, listeners would respond with a knowing and rueful smile, did not create discontent with economic conditions under Stalinism. But they did reinforce the belief that scarcity was and would always be an unavoidable circumstance of life under Communist rule. Jasko's own comments helped to reveal this dynamic. He noted that it was generally older people who spread the news they heard on foreign radio stations. In his view, this was because "they had known life before the Communist regime and so their memories confirmed what they heard on the anti-Communist radios."[16] They liked and believed these broadcasts precisely because the stories they heard reinforced what they already believed to be true.

In the West and on Western radio stations, it was axiomatic that Communism meant economic deprivation. This belief was so strong that until the end of state socialism in 1989 it was impossible for many Americans to imagine Eastern Europe as anything other than a place of extreme poverty, even though the quality of life dramatically improved across the region after 1956. This belief was based, at least in part, on the experience of many refugees and their tales of scarcity. But while this refugee experience was often taken in the West as emblematic of the whole, it had significant blind spots.[17] There is little space in the refugee discourse about shortages for someone like Edmund Chmieliński. Chmieliński was born into a poor rural Polish family made landless by the ravages of the Second World War. Unlike most refugees, Chmieliński experienced Stalinism as abundance. He remembered the meal of kielbasa he shared with his new work brigade in Poland's steel town of Nowa Huta in 1951 as the best repast he had ever had. "For the first time in my life," he later wrote, "I became sick from overeating."[18] It is impossible to determine how many people shared Chmieliński's experience. But much of the new Soviet Bloc had been poor for generations, became poorer during the agricultural crises of the 1930s, and was then decimated by war and occupation. Chmieliński was certainly not the only one to see his caloric intake rise rather than fall, even under Stalinism. Those who were satisfied with life under Communism, however, were not likely to illegally flee across the border. As a result, these kinds of experiences were poorly represented in Western reports. Instead, it was the experiences of the dissatisfied that informed what quickly became Western received wisdom about Communist regimes, allowing journalists like Leland Stowe to feel justified in claiming that Communism had given East European workers only "misery and chains."[19]

Most refugees had seemingly internalized a Cold War mentality that insisted the world was divided into two opposing halves, one of misery and another of prosperity. Such a worldview gave them little ability to account for the kind of nuance that a story like Chmieliński's demanded. They were encouraged in this by both the local media and Western radio stations. When Wladyslaw Tomczynski was interviewed by VOA in 1951, he explained how the Polish press encouraged readers to see Poland as offering abundance while the West embodied exploitation. "The Polish press is almost uniform," he said. "There is no paper in which they would not write about the quota, about the plan, in which they would not promise prosperity within the next years. You see all the time that such and such a factory sent a telegram to Bierut about the fulfillment of a plan or about a promise of fulfilling or exceeding a quota." Coverage of the capitalist West emphasized the opposite. According to Tomczynski, the

"More milk!" This 1950s Hungarian poster promises that today's labor will bring future abundance. *Poster by György Pál, Hungarian National Museum*

Polish papers "carried only such accounts which do not say anything good" about the West, offering stories about strikes, worker discontent and exploitation, terrible poverty, and the arrogance of Americans in Western Europe.[20] Like many of his fellow interviewees, Tomczynski accepted the idea that the world was divided into two diametrically opposed halves, but reversed the meanings the Communist press gave to each side, a practice that was openly pushed by Western radio programs such as RFE's "Other Side of the Coin."[21] The West represented the good life, while Communism meant poverty. If anyone were to bring about a high standard of living in Poland, Tomczynski believed, it would be the Americans.[22] Tomczynski rejected Communist propaganda, calling it lies and taking US propaganda as the truth. But he was not able to see outside this Cold War dichotomy or to realize that this very way of seeing the world was itself a creation of propaganda.

For many refugees, Communist claims that socialism would eventually bring a higher standard of living proved that Communism was only lies. This was how P., a Slovak who had been a technical mining supervisor in the uranium mines at Jachymov, described it. As someone with a trusted job supervising political prisoners and dealing with uranium, P. had a privileged position in the Czechoslovak Communist system, with a salary that far exceeded the average. Initially credulous, P. had gradually come to realize that news stories about economic success in Czechoslovakia were false. He said he had read a story about a village that exceeded its quota of farm produce, but later met people from the village who told him none of this was true. The same thing happened when he talked with workers at a factory in Chomutov, who told him everything in the papers about their enterprise was a lie. P. said his evolution was a common one, asserting that many people read stories about abundance in the Communist papers, compared them to their own experience, and decided that Communism was all lies. According to P., "Many of them said: 'They constantly write about our filling standards up to 500 or 800 percent but if I need some pants I can't get them. To get shoes you need a purchase voucher.'" The weight of this experience told P. and those around him that the real truth of Communism was consumer scarcity and not increased production. They quickly came to see Communism as a conspiracy that took their labor and left them with nothing. Trying to puzzle out how there could be empty shelves when goods were being produced, P. reported that he was told, "That's simple, our products go to Wilhelm Pieck [the Communist leader of East Germany]; you know, we just support the Germans again. It is all the same. Everywhere there are the Jews, in Russia and in Germany, and Rakosi in Hungary is also a Jew."[23] Shortages were mysteries that could be explained only by conspiracy theories, in this case involving Communism and Jews, who swindled and lied in order to take all the goods and leave the workers with nothing.

The belief in American abundance versus Communist poverty was a matter of faith for many refugees. This was particularly apparent in the VOA interview project. All respondents were asked a long series of questions about how they viewed the United States and its citizens. Their answers provide a vivid illustration of how refugees tended to see the world in binary terms, making meaning out of what they assumed must be the differences between East and West. Respondents did not merely idealize the United States as a place of plenty, but did so in a way that reflected back on their previous experience at home.[24] Many less educated respondents, who had little knowledge of the United States outside of Communist propaganda, American radio broadcasts, or perhaps letters from relatives, spoke of a fantastic "America" that would remedy all of the perceived economic faults of Communism.

The story of K.J. exemplifies how refugees imagined the United States as the antithesis of Communist society. K.J. was a locksmith's apprentice from the village of Kapuvar, near the Hungarian border with Austria. With only an elementary-level education, he was described by his interviewer as "a healthy peasant-type of youth" and a pleasure to interview.[25] Only nineteen years old at the time of his interview, K.J. had left his village to work in a factory in Budapest. Dissatisfied with factory life, he left his job without permission and returned to Kapuvar, where he worked on the family farm. When he refused to return to his job in Budapest, officials threatened to send him to a labor camp. Instead, he fled across the border.

Like almost all of the respondents in the VOA interview project, K.J. imagined that America offered the material prosperity and abundance that Communism lacked. This perception of the United States as a land of economic opportunity preceded the Cold War, but continued to grow during it. Many respondents reported hearing about American lifestyles from Western radio programs or from relatives or other acquaintances who had emigrated and written letters or sent packages. K.J. did not have a radio himself, although his uncle did and he heard peasants from his village talking about Western radio programs. But even though his access to information was limited, K.J. had a fundamental belief in American plenty. In the United States, he said, ordinary workers could earn enough to buy an automobile. This was "the most tempting thing about America," he said, adding, "I love cars."[26] But American prosperity not only meant a higher standard of living to K.J.; it meant the possibility of independence. K.J., who fled Hungary at least in part because he did not want to be forced to return to the factory he hated, believed that American workers could control their own lives. Within a short time, K.J. imagined, they could earn enough to build a house or purchase a small business like a store or a movie theater, enabling them to be their own masters. And in America, he said, a worker's free time was truly free. American workers did not have to volunteer to work "gratis" for the good of the state. Instead, they had the leisure to go to the movies or ride the motorcycles K.J. imagined they must own.[27]

When asked about the Hungarian press, K.J. said he never read the Communist newspapers, even though he subscribed to one, because he thought they were boring and "I knew that everything was a lie."[28] Yet he believed that the United States was ruled by bankers and manufacturers. Given that he had just discussed how fortunate American workers were, the interviewer asked him, "This means they oppress the people?" But even though K.J. had imbibed enough from the Hungarian press to think the United States was a plutocracy, this did not challenge his more fundamental belief in America as the antithesis of Communist rule. America might be ruled by wealthy elites, but, according to K.J., these elites were so wealthy, they had no need to oppress the people. K.J. did not see their outsize political influence as a problem, because he had no idea that ordinary people could or should have a say in the political process; the only way he imagined workers could have any influence was through trade unions. For K.J., the difference between Communism and capitalism was not free elections, but material prosperity and more autonomy for workers.

The idea that what made America different from Communist states was its material prosperity was echoed by F.P., a twenty-one-year-old Czech from the village of Vojnův Městec in eastern Bohemia. F.P. was an orphan with an elementary education. He trained as a baker, but for health reasons left the trade and worked as an unskilled laborer in a nearby textile mill. He was then ordered to do a stint in the coal mines near Most. After finishing his term, he was told to find another job in heavy industry and took a position at a chemical plant in Semtin. For reasons he did not explain, he began frequently skipping work, not bothering to show up at the plant for days at a time. After his disgruntled superiors finally charged him with sabotage, he fled the country.[29]

F.P. was very open about his view that America was the opposite of Communist Czechoslovakia. Communism meant unpaid work brigades, stupid Russian propaganda films, low wages, and high prices. In contrast, Americans had weekends off, could go to any cultural events they pleased, and were always well paid for their work, well enough to buy six to eight pairs of socks for every one a Czechoslovak could purchase. F.P. was so invested in his idea of the United States as the bastion of material prosperity and security in contrast to Communist deprivation and uncertainty that he ascribed to it a number of social security measures that Czechoslovak Communists had promised but not yet delivered. He claimed America was a welfare state that offered workers guaranteed employment, health insurance, and access to high-quality medical care. He was not sure whether Americans had state-mandated retirement benefits, but this mattered less to him because he believed that American workers could save enough to fund their own retirement, since they were always well paid and had abundant work.

Unlike the Hungarian K.J., the Czech F.P. was certain that the United States was a democracy, but he also cared little about political freedom. F.P.'s comments about how American democracy actually worked were vague, but he implied that representatives to Congress were chosen by political parties rather than by general elections. Despite the power he supposed the parties had, F.P. imagined that most Americans did not belong to them, because they had no need to do so. For F.P., politics was only about self-interest. You cared about politics only if you wanted something and you used politics to get it. Americans were rich and therefore they were happy. This meant they had no need for politics and parties. F.P. did not bother to consider that someone had to be chosen to do the work of governing. America, he said, had "political peace," which meant that few bothered to take part in the political process. Ironically, Americans like Leland Stowe characterized East Europeans like F.P. as oppressed because they lacked meaningful political rights. But for F.P., the ability to participate in the political process was much less important than economic prosperity.

Both K.J. and F.P. were simple men without advanced educations. Interviewees from the intelligentsia usually had more critical impressions of the United States. Boguslawa Smolka-Bauer was a high school teacher with an MA in Polish literature. Smolka-Bauer admitted that Americans enjoyed more political freedoms and a higher standard of living than Poles, but she considered them self-centered, materialistic, and superficial people, capable of making money but not great art. Unlike many other respondents, Smolka-Bauer realized that the United States could harbor great disparities in wealth and opportunity and that not every worker lived the American dream. As part of its drive to convince the population that the West represented warmongering imperialism, Smolka-Bauer recalled, the Polish media often emphasized American racism and the obstacles African Americans faced in their daily lives. She was certain these allegations were true, but most of the people around her insisted that stories about racial discrimination and economic inequality in the United States were just Communist propaganda. According to Smolka-Bauer, most Poles spoke with "considerable conviction about the absolute American democracy, the magnificent prosperity. America is the subject of dreams for 75 percent of the population."[30] More educated than most of the refugee population, Smolka-Bauer recognized that America had achieved a mythical status for many of those who had fled Poland; it was a beacon of individual economic opportunity that could never be home to institutionalized discrimination. Her comments made clear the political stakes of what many interview respondents presented as apolitical choices. Young, poorly educated men like F.P. and K.J. imagined that, when they left the East for the West, they could leave politics behind and concentrate on their material self-interest. What they did not realize or could not articulate was that this very belief was itself a creation of anti-Communist ideology, which assumed material satisfaction could be found only in capitalist societies.

A Shortage of Femininity

In the collection of RFE Information Items, there are many refugee stories about how hard it was to obtain meat, salami, butter, or new clothes throughout the Soviet Bloc during the years between 1950 and 1956. But in September 1952, an RFE report noted a shortage of something unusual: female elegance. According to the report, the economic policies of the Bierut regime had almost eliminated Polish women's ability to appear beautiful. This was, claimed the authors, the result of a conscious decision "to abolish everything 'vain'" or "that which might bring contentment and joy to the life of a woman." Products that would allow a woman to openly express her femininity had practically disappeared from the market, and sartorial habits from the prewar era were denigrated as bourgeois and Western. An elegantly dressed woman appearing on the street would be made to feel embarrassed rather than pretty. Even a woman who sported "pedicured and polished toes" on a beach in Sopot on the Baltic Sea was laughed at by young people who had never seen nail polish before. Under Communism, femininity had been turned into an object of ridicule and scorn.[31]

The attack on femininity was both ideological and economic. Women who wanted to look beautiful were hampered at every turn by the lack of consumer goods. "There is," said the report, "an immense shortage of everything a woman wants to look attractive." Stockings, girdles, bras, dresses, and cosmetics were all hard to find, expensive, and almost inevitably of poor quality. New coats cost more than a month's salary and "looked like sacks." Hats were nowhere to be found. East German cold creams were available, but were costly and caused eczema. It took a month to get an appointment at a beauty salon, and a permanent wave lasted for only a week anyway. Married women, more pressed for time than single girls, had particularly suffered in their appearance. "Their clothes are entirely out of fashion and their hair without luster and dirty," the report claimed.[32]

The Polish woman, once so "soigné and elegant," had become at best "sporty" or "robust," but mainly "not particularly attractive." Yet even in their shabby state, the author of the report claimed, Polish women still had more style than Soviet women. These unfortunate creatures had no feminine grace; they thudded along with "heavy and clumsy" steps and lacked "energy and muscles." Doused in perfume so that they reeked from afar, Soviet women tried to make themselves beautiful but wound up looking like clowns, "with white-powdered face[s] and red circles on their cheeks and heavily over-painted mouth[s]." They had been turned into sad parodies of real womanhood.[33] Polish women had been spared this fate, for now. But how long could they avoid it? The idea that femininity was intimately linked to consumption and that only capitalism could adequately fulfill women's natural desires for goods like stockings and pretty underwear had been a trope of Western critiques of Communism since before the Second World War, appearing, for example, in the popular 1939 Greta Garbo film *Ninotchka*.[34] This RFE report followed in that general vein, implying that femininity, while it might be biological in origin, was delicate and required the right conditions—and products—to flourish.

As this report made clear, consumption patterns had meaning beyond the bare facts of calories consumed or articles of clothing purchased. For the Budapest housewife who complained about being forced to eat "fake goulash," a new vegetarian diet was tied to the loss of class or professional status. For the authors of "The Polish Woman," the more utilitarian garments and hairstyles available to women in the early 1950s were emblematic of a Communist challenge to what they saw as natural gender roles. According to the report, Communist governments were working to eradicate femininity on multiple levels. The problem was not merely that their economic plans did not allow for the production of enough lipstick and nail polish. The bigger issue for the report's authors was that they wanted to take women from their traditional roles as wives and mothers and move them into the labor force. The reason married women were no longer beautiful, claimed the report, was that they had to juggle paid work, standing in line for food, and all their usual domestic chores. They had no energy left for beauty.[35] For the interviewees and the RFE analysts, this was a tragedy that encapsulated the pernicious effects that Communism would have on gender roles and family life.

In contrast, the Communist press around the region touted women's entrance into the labor force and participation in new sectors of employment as an achievement. The ubiquitous image of a woman in a unisex work coverall driving a tractor, operating a machine in a factory, or toiling underground in a mine was presented as an emblem of women's new independence and equality.[36] However, despite the positive image in the media, attempts to bring women into previously male professions were actually quite contentious in Eastern Europe, often actively resisted within the region's Communist parties as well as outside them.[37] But this conflict went unnoticed in the West. There, the picture of a woman working in heavy industry symbolized everything that was wrong with the Communist system. In one of Leland Stowe's articles in the *Washington Post*, for example, he had only to list the number of women employed as machinists in Warsaw or as miners in Romania to make his point. No further commentary was necessary to suggest that Communist regimes intended to overthrow the social order and destroy the nuclear family.[38]

Refugee interviewees, who were mostly younger men, echoed this contention that Communist economic policy destroyed the family by driving women into the workforce. One RFE report from 1954 was tellingly titled "The Decline of Family Life." It told the story of a carpenter from the Czech town of Ústi nad Labem. For health reasons, his wife and young child had gone to live with her mother in the Slovak town of Nové Mesto nad Váhom. He stayed in Ústi nad Labem to keep his job and visited only on the weekends. Soon, he said, his wife complained to him that there was not enough money for her to buy a pair of stockings or go to the hairdresser. She wanted to get a job. He resisted, because marriage for him meant having a wife at home to take care of the children and do the housework. Rather than fight with him, the informant's wife got a position as a secretary without his knowledge. After he found out, he forgave her at first, but soon things became unbearable for him. Her new colleagues were Communists, who insisted that she send their son to the day care center, eat in the factory canteen, and send the laundry out to be done by the state laundry service. In day care, their son learned to curse, sang songs about Stalin, and came home scratched and dirty. Consumed with work, the informant's wife was rarely home, even on the weekends. When she was, she was always too tired to spend time with her

Communist women dressed to fight imperialism. This 1950 Czechoslovak poster reads, "Build the homeland, you will strengthen peace! Come with us to work in the factories for the happiness of your children." *Poster by Pekárek, All-Trade Union Archive of the Bohemian-Moravian Confederation of Trade Unions, poster collection*

husband. He agreed to move to Nové Mesto nad Váhom and for a while things improved, but then his own job became more demanding. Both he and his wife were exhausted all the time and too tired to even communicate. Eventually he started spending all his time at the pub, and she hardly seemed to notice he was gone. The carpenter began acting out at work and eventually fled over the border when he was told the police were looking for him.[39]

For the RFE interviewer who wrote the report, the carpenter's story was emblematic of Communism's "big lie." "Communist poison" had attacked this family, tearing it apart with its "mendacity." The RFE evaluator concurred, presenting the carpenter's story as evidence of a deliberate policy to destroy families. For his part, the carpenter had married in good faith, believing that his wife would fulfill her traditional roles as homemaker and mother. Communist propaganda gave her a new set of goals and expectations that did not match his. What started from her consumer dissatisfaction had turned into something much bigger and more fundamental. Yet the carpenter, the interviewer, and the RFE evaluator all placed the blame for the end of the marriage on Communism. The carpenter was simply the victim of a pernicious regime that crushed families economically and put false ideas into women's heads. They did not consider that some women, including perhaps the carpenter's wife, might have welcomed the opportunity to take on new roles in economic and public life.[40]

Most refugee reports about the impact of Communism on the family were written from a man's perspective. An exception is the story of Ilona, a young Hungarian mother of three children, ages two, five, and seven. Ilona was married to a laborer who earned little and who adhered to traditional beliefs about his rights and privileges in the family. Because food was so expensive, any meat was given to Ilona's husband, while she and her children made do with potato *paprikás*. The scarcity made for family quarrels; Ilona remembered that once her hungry oldest son ate his father's salami and was beaten for it. Finally, after a particularly bad fight, Ilona took the two youngest children to her sister's, grabbed the oldest boy, and fled across the border. According to the RFE report about her experience, Ilona's plight was an example of how Communist shortages destroyed the family, reducing the domestic hearth to a site of bitter struggle over scarce resources.[41] But Ilona's domestic situation, up to the moment of her flight, was not very different from that in poor working-class households all over the world, where husbands controlled the finances and demanded the recognition and privileges that went along with their role as the family's primary breadwinner.[42]

As Ilona's story suggests, women's equality was far from a reality in 1950s Eastern Europe. Despite the party's egalitarian rhetoric, even Communist officials resisted bringing women into public life on equal terms with men. Women brought into local village or town councils might be treated as mere figureheads, expected to ceremoniously occupy their positions while men made the decisions.[43] Even adult women's labor force participation did not increase as rapidly as many believed. In Poland, for example, it increased from 31 percent in 1950 to only 33 percent in 1954.[44] Yet refugees constantly asserted that Communist governments had pulled women into the workforce and harmed family life. The VOA interview project of 1951–1952 included a question about the effects that Communist rule had on family life; this was one of only two questions dealing directly with social conditions in the interviewees' home countries that were distinct from radio listening.[45] The responses to this question were remarkably uniform; regardless of differences in educational level, occupation, country of origin, or political orientation, the respondents generally said that Communism had a deleterious effect on families. This trend was broken only by respondents from villages where most residents continued to work on family farms.

For most of the respondents, the idea of a "normal" family life was tied to American abundance. It was capitalist prosperity that allowed men to fulfill their natural roles as breadwinners and enabled wives to devote themselves to homemaking and child care. According to them, it was not Communist ideology that pushed women into the workforce, but rather Communist poverty. Women did not, as they portrayed it, take new jobs to be independent or equal to men, but because high prices and low salaries made two-earner families a necessity. N.Z., a well-educated young Hungarian, son of an army officer and a sports enthusiast who practiced gymnastics and yoga, told VOA that Hungarian families suffered because wives were forced to work. He hypothesized that American workers, who, he assumed, were men, were happier than Hungarians because they could have "real homes," by which he meant ones with stay-at-home wives.[46]

The Czech Ladislav Novak, a student of physical education at the Charles University in Prague, was also convinced that family life had worsened under Communism. He remarked, "In Czechoslovakia nowadays family life is almost destroyed, as predominantly mothers and fathers are compelled to work in order to be able to subsist. For that reason children are abandoned during the day and compelled to be in Communist kindergartens." For Novak, it was Communism, not industrialization or modernization, that caused women to move into the paid workforce. He said, "These terrible things cannot happen in American families where the mother is not forced to go to work in factories or offices in general; the mother can devote herself to the education of her children."[47] Both men imagined that the United States offered male workers the chance to fulfill their masculine duties as breadwinners and heads of households, a dream they feared Communism would make impossible. Part of their idealization of the United States rested on their belief that it protected the traditional family and its strictly defined gender roles.[48]

A young, unskilled laborer from Slovakia, A.S., illuminated the crux of the issue: women's domestic labor. He claimed that "family life deteriorated a great deal owing to the fact that women must work and those that have children must send them to a day-nursery. The housewives must do domestic work, too, at home and if they fail to do so there are arguments in the family. The husband often comes home from work and his wife can give him nothing to eat; the children are hungry too."[49] Husbands, according to the unmarried A.S., had difficulty adjusting their expectations to the new economic realities their families faced. They wanted to come home to dinner on the table and resented the fact that their wives were unable to maintain the household in the manner they expected. A.S.'s comments echoed those of the carpenter from Ústi nad Labem, who saw his wife's desire to get a job as the end of his happiness.

Because most of those interviewed by VOA were men, they tended to focus on how Communism deprived husbands and children of a woman's presence at home. L.P., one of the few women to be interviewed by VOA, had a slightly different perspective. She was a Czech sculptor who fled the country because she hated socialist realism. Though childless herself, L.P. had observed the situation of the married mothers in her apartment building. These women were exhausted from trying to combine their paid work with the domestic labor they were still expected to do at home. Their situation was made worse by the shortage economy, which required them to wait in long lines to do the grocery shopping (probably not the case in America, noted L.P.). L.P. did not challenge the assumption that cleaning, child care, and cooking were women's work. Instead, she decried the Czechoslovak press for claiming that the Communist system made it easy for women to combine work and family responsibilities by offering day care facilities, laundries, and cafeterias. Her own observations, she said, showed this was mere propaganda.[50] If VOA wanted to prove that Communists lied, then it should broadcast programs that revealed how hollow their promises to women really were.[51]

All of these respondents to the VOA interviews gave the impression that their answers to this question stemmed primarily from their own experience, even though, aside from L.P., not one was actually married or had children. Their responses were stated as if they were readily apparent to any observer. The remarks of the Hungarian Janos Jasko, however, indicated that some of the respondents' statements about the impact of Communism on family life might have been shaped in various ways by the print media or radio broadcasts. When asked about family life, Jasko told the interviewer, "I read a Communist paper which said that Marxism, Leninism and Stalinism can't be realized as long as family and home exist; the father strives to get ahead and secure a better life for his family. This prevents him from thinking of the Communist community." Jasko may actually have read such an article or he may not have; regardless, he believed that the Communist media itself had declared its intention to destroy the family as a means of consolidating its power. His views on American family life were similarly shaped by his exposure to public media. He went on, "On the other hand, on VOA I heard someone tell what an American woman does during the day, how she started her work, what her home was like, what facilities she had for taking care of her children and husband."[52] Listening to VOA had confirmed his impression of America as a place where ordinary women could devote themselves to being housewives. Jasko's comment suggested that Western radio stations like VOA helped to sustain the conviction that Communist regimes wanted to attack traditional gender roles, whereas Americans tried to maintain them.

A tale like that of Mr. X, however, brought this easy dichotomy into question. Mr. X was a fisherman from Gdynia in Poland. Although he made only a modest income, he and his wife agreed that she would not work so that their three young children did not have to attend a state-run day care facility. According to his account, their life was very spare. Mrs. X did the best she could, allowing herself only a "tiny snack" for a midday meal, but still the family could afford meat only once a week and subsisted mostly on bread, butter, cheese, and tea. Even with this limited diet, Mrs. X was forced to get up at 4:00 a.m. and stand in line to buy food for her family. Despite these hardships, the X family supposedly remained strong. They had a "harmonious home-life" that "somewhat made up for all the outside annoyances."

Yet Mr. X nonetheless escaped to Sweden. The report, while not explicit on this point, strongly implied that Mr. X abandoned his family to move to the West. It is not clear why he left his dependent wife and children behind, expecting them to somehow get by without him, even though he was their only source of financial support. What is certain is that the RFE evaluators did not chide him for leaving his family in Communist Poland. They merely noted that his story "bore all the signs of authenticity." RFE analysts did not question why Mr. X wanted to leave Poland; his frugal life, as he described it, with a "shortage of even the most primitive and basic articles, such as buttons, sewing needles, threads, etc." was apparently reason enough, even though it was Mrs. X, of course, who had to figure out how to make do without needle and thread. For RFE, Mr. X was a victim, not a villain. Its report suggests that Mr. X's only alternative to his miserable economic situation was to flee to the prosperous West.[53] RFE's analysts could exonerate Mr. X of his decision to leave his family behind because they believed that fleeing the country was the only way he could regain control over his own life. As long as he remained in Poland, the state would control his standard of living. This was not, however, entirely true. The West might indeed have offered more economic opportunities to Mr. X, but East Europeans actually had many ways of trying to surmount Communism's ubiquitous shortages.

The Power of the Powerless?

When talking about the political sphere, many East European refugees characterized themselves as captive or enslaved peoples. They argued that they were incapable of opposing their Communist rulers, with their powerful security services and legions of informers on every corner. When talking about economic grievances, however, refugees used the language of powerlessness much less frequently. Speaking with interviewers from Western radio stations, they eagerly recounted the economic hardships they had experienced at home, recalling the frustration of empty store shelves and high prices for scarce goods and expressing disappointment with low pay, work quotas, and ever-increasing speeds of production. Rather than bemoan their inability to alter their material situation, they often bragged about the ways they found to improve their standard of living. Interviews with recent refugees highlighted a wide variety of activities intended to subvert Communist economic policies; ranging from the devious to the highly illegal, these activities included hoarding, black marketeering, theft, and denunciation. In their narratives, refugees presented themselves as resourceful and clever, or at least successful in their bid to fight what they depicted as Communist-mandated deprivation. Stories of this kind show that, although refugees consistently declared that they were helpless against Communist states and their repressive apparatus, they openly acknowledged their ability to undermine the strictures of the Communist planned economy.

One common response to shortages was panic buying and hoarding. The practice of hoarding scarce goods has been widely recognized as ubiquitous in the Soviet Bloc, although it is better documented for later decades of the Communist era.[54] In the years before 1956, all countries of the Soviet Bloc experienced currency reforms and changes in rationing and price systems that were often announced suddenly. Overnight, people found that their savings had plummeted in value or that the cost of bread or milk had changed significantly. These experiences helped to create fertile ground for rumors of sudden shortages or price hikes.[55] Rumors of a coming shortage sometimes triggered panic, and individuals raced to the store to purchase as much as they could of the item in question before it disappeared from the shelves. If widespread, such panic could potentially cause the very shortage that had been rumored.[56] The refugee Jan Kusis claimed that this kind of incident was a common occurrence in his native Poland. He remembered, "Sometimes people talked that . . . there would be a shortage of sugar; so people went buying sugar like madmen. Sometimes people were buying socks, or sausages, or lard."[57] These instances of panic buying represented the efforts of ordinary people to exert such control as they could over their material situation. Faced with the possibility of shortage, they acted, dramatically and immediately.

Rumors about coming shortages were fed by multiple sources, both local and international. In its interview project, VOA asked respondents about their memories of panic buying and how such incidents began. Many of the Czech respondents remembered a particular moment in the spring of 1950 when there was a run on bread and flour. These products had been taken off the rationing system, but rumors that they would again be rationed caused a panic that ended with new bread rationing, confirming the rumors. F.K., a clerk at a chemical company in Prague, said he had heard rumors about flour rationing and admitted to buying thirty kilos of flour as a precaution.[58] The worker J.K. said he had also done so. When asked what had motivated him to hoard flour, he said he had heard rumors about a shortage but did not remember the precise circumstances. As he explained it, such rumors could come from anywhere, and people often responded to them immediately and without reflection. He said, "People were most interested in such news and they acted accordingly without bothering much about who spread the news."[59] P., the former mining supervisor from Jachymov mentioned earlier, had also heard these rumors, but he said that what actually inspired him to hoard flour was an article in a Czech newspaper castigating farmers for buying up cheap, subsidized bread and feeding it to their livestock. P. reasoned that this diatribe against the farmers was the government's way of rationalizing the reintroduction of rationing. He got a wheelbarrow and purchased 150 kilograms of flour. When rationing was indeed reintroduced shortly thereafter, P. believed this vindicated the rumors.[60]

Both J.K. and P. specifically said that they had not heard rumors about the rationing of bread and flour on VOA; both thought the rumors came from domestic sources. J.K. remembered that after the panic the Czech press tried to blame VOA for spreading unfounded rumors that caused the scare and the resulting shortages, but he thought this story had no basis in fact.[61] Other respondents, however, contradicted this interpretation. K.S., a married farmer with three children and an active anti-Communist, said he had heard the rumors about coming bread rationing on VOA. A local publication tried to deny them, but K.S. distrusted everything in the Czech press. Everyone in his village similarly believed VOA and started hoarding grain. As K.S. recalled, "I remember that four days before rationing was re-introduced, Gottwald had a speech and said that only alarmists believed that there would be a shortage of bread in the CSR. Four days after this speech by the President the Minister of Internal Commerce announced that bread rationing would be re-introduced."[62] For K.S., the incident confirmed his belief that Western radio stations told the truth, whereas Communists only lied.

This incident undoubtedly interested VOA officials because the station had been regularly accused of spreading unfounded rumors about shortages and causing panic of this kind. In 1949, the American legation in Budapest reported that rumors had been circulating for months that there would be another currency reform that would significantly devalue the forint. The rumors reached a fever pitch at the end of October, resulting in widespread panic buying of all kinds of goods. According to the report, "The population of Budapest stampeded state stores and private shops and began buying everything in sight—radios, jewelry, fur coats, silver, chinaware, Oriental rugs and other luxury goods," all in a desperate attempt to spend their savings before the currency was devalued. The rumors, however, were unfounded; there was no pending currency reform.[63] After the panic ended, local newspapers like *Szabad Nép* (Free people) blamed VOA for starting the rumors, saying it had undertaken a "campaign of lies" that deluded gullible reactionaries.[64] According to the American Legation's report, VOA had in fact repeated the rumors on the air on October 27, but "there is no reason to believe that the panic was a direct result of VOA broadcasts." The report concluded that the incident was "nourished almost entirely by indigenous rumors." Indeed, some alleged that the rumors had been started by the Hungarian government itself as a means of flushing out hidden savings from under mattresses and diverting them into state coffers (most money was spent at state stores). Now, the report claimed, the Hungarian government was merely trying to capitalize on the situation further by blaming VOA for its own scheme.[65]

Both sides agreed the panic had occurred, but they gave the incident very different meanings. From the Hungarian perspective, this was an example of how the West attempted to sabotage socialism. *Szabad Nép* insisted VOA had broadcast lies in order to attack the Hungarian economy. The article also mentioned the panic buying of white bread, which, it claimed, was part of a fascist and imperialist plot to discredit Communist promises to provide cheap white bread—the symbol of a privileged, bourgeois diet—to the masses.[66] From the American perspective, the panic exemplified why centrally planned economies were doomed to failure. For VOA, the incident was evidence of how Communist economic policies bred fear and uncertainty, showing how much Hungarians distrusted their leaders.

Black markets were another venue in which individuals tried to overcome the shortcomings of the centrally planned economy. Black markets in consumer goods existed in all of the Soviet Bloc countries. Although networks for the illicit sale of rationed or scarce goods may have been inherited from wartime economies, they blossomed after governments across the region moved to establish centrally planned economies. Given the shortages in official stores, participation in this illicit economy was widespread, despite state attempts to crack down on such practices. Many refugees offered RFE information about black market operations and prices. A typical example concerned a former bricklayer and tractor driver from northern Moravia in Czechoslovakia. This man had a large family with four small children, which the report implied he had left behind when he illegally crossed the border to Austria in 1952. Because the family was so large, they could not survive on what they received via ration cards, and so before the man abandoned his family he turned to the black market. He told RFE that it was easy to find food in this way and described buying chickens, geese, smoked meat, lard, and speck (a cured meat) without much problem. Although the family was able to purchase some sugar via the ration system, when they ran out he was able to turn to employees from the nearby sugar plant who stole their product to sell on the black market. It was not even hard, he said, to find clothes for his large family. There were always elderly villagers who were willing to sell their old clothes. RFE evaluators called this report "in line with the general trend" and wondered only if the rather reasonable prices the source quoted for his black market purchases were low. They concluded that this was quite possible, given the source's extensive experience with black markets.[67] Throughout, the source was presented as a capable operator who provided for his family despite obstacles. He was resourceful, not helpless.

The drive for a better material existence could even trump fears of the police. A report from an Austrian citizen who had lived in Poland for twenty-five years made this point. The man, who had owned a fur-dyeing business, applied to leave Poland only in 1951, for economic rather than political reasons (it would take him a further two years to get his exit visa). When he spoke with RFE, the man claimed the inhabitants of Warsaw were so "terrorized by the police" that they refused to make any overt sign or gesture of happiness when they heard of Stalin's death on March 5, 1953, although many got drunk in celebration. Yet he also declared that anyone who wanted to have a decent standard of living was forced "to swindle right and left," so much so that, he said, "swindling is an integral part of the Communist system." People lived with the constant fear that the police would discover their illegal activities, yet they continued them. As this source presented it, Poles were afraid of the repressive power of the state, but when it was a matter of economic interest, they were able to act despite their fear. Political opposition, however, they saw as futile, given the extent of police terror.[68]

Another RFE report from Poland related a similar set of circumstances. A refugee from Poznań told RFE in 1952 that local officials had started a campaign to reduce the smuggling of food, especially meat. The police began to check passengers on trains and in railway stations for contraband. The source claimed that more than twenty-five people a day were being arrested for trying to bring meat into the city illegally from the countryside. Yet, the source said, despite the threat of "going to a labor camp for at least thirteen months," people continued to smuggle meat. The reason, according to the informant, was pure self-interest. Meat was very expensive in the city, and farmers would sell it for as little as a fifth of the regular price. Smugglers hoped that if they were searched it would be by a lone inspector, because then they could try to bribe him.[69] In both of these examples, people knew the risks of their illegal activities but continued them anyway. As smugglers, they were willing to confront the police in ways they claimed were impossible when asked about the possibility of political opposition.

Western analysts from RFE did not comment on this dichotomy. For the most part, they took smuggling or black market dealing as a natural and unavoidable consequence of planned economies, just as they accepted political passivity as the normal state of the captive and enslaved peoples of Eastern Europe. As an evaluator's comment on another report noted, that black marketeering and the transport of illicit goods occurred despite the known risks was simply a "well-known fact." The source for this report, a black market dealer from Poland, was particularly brazen, declaring to the interviewer, "Every law can be broken. The only question is how to go about it." But his claim that anyone who was even "a bit clever" could live well by illegal means did not spark the station's analysts to question their assumptions about East European powerlessness.[70]

The report about meat smuggling in Poznań does not make it clear if the pork that entrepreneurs acquired in the countryside was sold legally. In many instances, farmers slaughtered and sold animals that were technically state property.[71] Thefts from state enterprises were crucial to sustaining black market commerce. According to refugee reports, such thefts quickly became commonplace. One RFE report claimed that a remarkable number of cotton pullovers were seen on the streets of the Polish town of Chelmsko Slaskie. The sweaters were knitted by women weavers who worked at the Mieszko mill. The source alleged that these women routinely stole skeins of thread, somehow sneaking their contraband out under the eyes of the guards who regularly searched them as they were leaving the factory.[72] Another report described thefts from state forests in Czechoslovakia. According to the source, woodcutters were constantly stealing wood and trying to defraud their employers. Both the source and the RFE evaluators concurred that this kind of theft was required to maintain a decent standard of living under Communism. Faced with low wages and high quotas, workers had no choice but to steal or falsify their production records.[73]

A similar dynamic was described in a report about the Czechoslovak collective farm at Ruprechtice. The director of the collective was dismayed that women stopped work at 11:00 a.m. and then went home and spent several hours preparing lunch for their households. To better meet their production targets, he suggested that the collective establish a canteen where all the farmworkers could eat lunch during the harvest. They would even slaughter a pig to provide meat for the meals. An argument then ensued about who would be appointed as the cooks. According to the source, a young man who had worked at the collective before emigrating, each man wanted his own wife to work in the kitchen so that she could steal food. After a contentious debate, the farm director asked two women who did not work for the collective if they would take the jobs, since their time in the kitchen would not affect the progress of the harvest. Immediately, however, there were allegations of dishonesty and theft. On the first day, hungry workers expected plates of pork and dumplings but got only soup and offal. The next day, there was only sausage meat and soon only dry potatoes. Some alleged the cooks had been seen leaving the kitchen at night with bags of meat. The director decreed that the cooks write down everything edible that entered and left the kitchen. A new pig was slaughtered, but still no roast pork materialized at lunchtime. Shortly thereafter someone broke into the pantry and stole half of the remaining meat. The thief left the door open, and what was not stolen was destroyed or eaten by the dog that one of the cooks had left to guard the place. The director replaced the first cooks with two Communist women, but they also stole from the kitchen. Since it was impossible to control theft and no one was happy with the quality of the food, the canteen was eventually closed down.[74]

After this experience, the director of the collective farm at Ruprechtice became convinced that theft was inevitable. Rather quickly, it seemed, pilfering became so commonplace that everyone expected it. Few refugees condemned theft or other forms of illegal dealing. Rather than place the onus for these crimes on the individuals who did it, they blamed Communist governments for putting people into a position where they were ostensibly forced to steal in order to survive. A middle-class woman from the Polish city of Łódź told RFE in 1953 that the "enforced poverty" of Communism had made theft practically essential. "The one consolation," she said, was "that one is not usually robbing a friend or a fellow citizen, but the State, and that is a salve to most consciences."[75] A former merchant from Budapest told RFE that many Hungarians regarded theft with nonchalance. Their attitude, he said, was, "The State is exploiting me as much as it can. I should do exactly the same to the State. I am working just enough to avoid being charged with sabotage, and try by other means to get what I need."[76] According to the merchant, government officials knew very well that many people had this attitude and that was why the officials tried to control them so strictly. The merchant was unusual because he believed that such an attitude was immoral. But he still blamed Communism for creating the atmosphere in which this kind of disregard for others could flourish. Both respondents emphasized that their fellow citizens conceived of the "State" (which the reports capitalized) as an impersonal entity that deserved to be cheated for what it did to them.

In taking this position, these respondents proceeded from the notion that the capitalist concept of the individual—motivated by rational self-interest—was the natural state of humanity. Communism, they implied, had perverted this natural state of things by asking people to live for a greater good. They were therefore justified in engaging in economic activities that undermined the Communist system, even if such activities were against the law. Following similar reasoning, some historians have characterized practices like theft and black marketeering as a form of resistance.[77] These kinds of activities are indeed examples of how individuals could register disapproval of the Stalinist economic system, although the perpetrators themselves usually did not endow their activities with political meaning. Dissatisfied with their options in the stores, they took matters into their own hands. They explicitly went against the wishes of the state, which defined their actions as crimes. But it is difficult to neatly categorize such practices. Though they were against the law, activities like illegal trading could also be a means of folding people into the institutions of the Stalinist system, creating participation out of "resistance." One example of this comes from the Mieszko textile plant, where the workers allegedly stole yarn to knit sweaters. One of these enterprising knitters was caught by the UB (Urząd Bezpieczeństwa, or Office of State Security). She promptly denounced another young woman in an effort to save herself. This set off a chain reaction in which five women denounced each other.[78] Not wanting to go to jail, the women attempted to use the repressive capacity of the state to their own advantage. Their own fear pushed them to perpetuate and even extend the institutions that created so much fear. Their actions revealed that the boundary between the state and the people (or "us" and "them") was fluid. These women were persecuted by "the State" (police officers), but they also effectively became "the State" by participating in the process of repressing others.

This same dynamic came to the fore in an example of black market activity in Romania. This incident reveals how the pursuit of economic advantage led ordinary people to collaborate with a state they reviled. The story, which came from a Romanian who spoke to RFE in Trieste in July 1952, described incidents in the Hala Obor market in Bucharest. She claimed militia agents (the police in this period were called the militia) frequently patrolled the market to stop illegal or black market transactions. Peasants, however, still came to the market to illegally sell their wares and were sometimes arrested. In June 1952 the source went to the market to buy a black market chicken. She observed several people trying to surreptitiously sell chickens for three times the daily wage of an average worker (and more than twice the official price of a chicken). For each illicit chicken on offer, there were multiple housewives angling for the opportunity to buy, no matter the price. Faced with limited supply and excessive demand, the buyers began to threaten each other with arrest. When the source tried to buy a chicken from one of the peasants, she was told by two other people who were eyeing the chicken, "Don't buy it; if you do we will call a militia agent!" The source was frightened and retreated, but then saw one of the people who had threatened her move in to buy the chicken herself.

The source then tried the same tactic on her competition, claiming she would denounce the woman to the police if she came away with a chicken. Scared, the other woman also retreated. To break the impasse, the source whispered to the peasant seller (whom she knew) to follow her home and conduct the deal there. The source began to walk home, followed by the peasant with the chicken. The second woman and a man with her followed them, hoping to disrupt the sale and procure the chicken themselves. But the source happened to live opposite a militia office, and when the couple saw that she was heading there, they walked away, fearing she would report them to the militia, leaving the source free to buy (and presumably eat) the chicken. Like the tale of the weavers, this account shows that fear was not simply created by the regime, but mobilized by ordinary individuals. The participants in this transaction did not passively accept the repression of the regime; they used the institutions of state repression to try to achieve a better daily existence for themselves, at the expense of others. In the market, the practice of denunciation was no longer an issue of "them" trying to get "us" but a survival strategy that everyone, even the source, took part in.

We Are Hungry, Feed Us

In their book *Satellite Mentality*, Siegfried Kracauer and Paul L. Berkman noted that interview respondents from the working class often expressed intense feelings of disappointment and betrayal stemming from their experience with Communist rule. The reason, Kracauer and Berkman hypothesized, was that these workers had initially been supportive of their Communist governments. They had become emotionally invested in the Communist experiment and believed that they would soon see a marked improvement in their everyday lives. When they were instead asked to work more hours for less reward, they felt as if they had been tricked. In the book, the authors quoted a Czech worker, a Communist sympathizer until 1949, who explained, "We found that the Communists betrayed us ... They were exploiting us and lying to us."[79] But, although Kracauer and Berkman saw this emotional reaction as a significant trend in their survey sample, they did not imagine that these feelings of discontent and betrayal would fuel active opposition to Communist regimes. Instead, they reiterated the refugees' own contention that they were unable to resist their rulers. Though they did note that some interviewees mentioned instances of what they called active resistance, such as passing out opposition leaflets, go-slow actions at work, and organized resistance groups, they emphasized that the interviewees downplayed these activities as minor and largely ineffectual.[80]

This conviction that workers were unhappy but unwilling to openly express their discontent was belied by an RFE report of April 1953. In this report, a technical clerk from the Czech district of Uherské Hradiště discussed workers' discontent on a building site in Třnec. The report concentrated on dissatisfaction with the quality and price of food in the workers' canteen. The workers had few options other than the canteen, but their right to purchase subsidized meals there depended on their completing at least six shifts per week. If they could not prove they had worked the required amount, they were forced to pay more than twice as much per meal, which they considered unfair. Even more, they found the food scanty and dissatisfying. Lunch and dinner usually consisted of soup and some kind of meat with an accompanying sauce and starch. But the source complained that, even though the weekly menu announced different kinds of soup or different sauces each day, they all tasted exactly the same. Even more disappointing, the portions of meat or salami were only eight dekagrams (about one-eighth of a pound) per serving. Because the food was so poor, the workers felt compelled to buy snacks at the company store. Although they could buy plenty of rolls and salami there, the price of ten dekagrams (three and a half ounces) of salami and three white bread rolls was two to three times the cost of a regular meal. To top it off, canteen patrons had to wait in line for as long as an hour and provide their own cutlery. The fact that the canteen was also an instrument of propaganda deepened their annoyance. Workers ate surrounded by posters of Stalin and Gottwald, with slogans about the necessity of working harder and faster.[81]

The situation worsened in February 1952. Management attempted to increase the price workers paid for each meal, while serving them even more unpalatable food. The workers began to complain. When enterprise managers appeared in the cafeteria, the workers loudly demanded that they improve the quality of the food and lower the price. For days, the workers made demands, only to be met with speeches about the necessity of completing the Five-Year Plan. In the end, nothing happened. The workers were nervous about taking things further. This incident did not result in a full-blown strike, but it did show that the workers were not passive, either. They assertively confronted management with their demands. Although, at least as far as the source knew, they had not gotten results, they were still taken seriously by officials. Significantly, they were not imprisoned, fired, or docked pay for their insubordination.

These kinds of incidents were much more common, even during the height of Stalinism, than notions of captive societies and prisoner peoples could account for. In Poland, for example, there were 432 strikes between 1949 and 1952, and in Czechoslovakia, there were 218 strikes between 1948 and 1953.[82] Yet there was a marked disconnect between these kinds of protests and Western images of resistance. Most protests by workers, like the incident in Třinec, were local affairs that took place at the level of the plant or enterprise. They generally lasted for only a few hours, and the protesters presented specific demands, such as better food, higher pay, or an end to a particular labor policy. The attitudes of many workers involved in these protests were complicated; though they criticized existing policies and demanded change, they did not necessarily advocate a return to a capitalist system.[83] The protests did not fit easily into the analytical categories of Western observers. Kracauer and Berkman, for example, defined active resistance as "serious efforts to undermine, attack, and overthrow the regime."[84] In their interpretation, workers who fought within the system rather than destroy it were still operating under the influence of "Communist propaganda." This is perhaps why knowledge of these kinds of incidents could coexist perfectly well in the minds of both refugee interviewees and their Western interpreters with beliefs about the essential powerlessness of East Europeans.

Although Western analysts like Kracauer and Berkman were more interested in activities they recognized as political resistance to Communist rule, East European governments recognized the power and legitimacy of workers' anger over poor material conditions. After the death of Stalin in 1953, they began to systematically address issues of material scarcity. Their efforts were not always enough to appease consumption-starved citizens. In both instances of large-scale popular unrest that erupted in 1956, anger over material conditions played a fundamental role. The June protests in the city of Poznań that began the march toward the Polish October arose out of workers' frustrations with pay and a falling standard of living. The protests in Poznań centered on demands for bread and freedom, printed on signs that were posted on the local party headquarters. According to secret police reports, the protesters first shouted, "We want bread," adding, "Down with the Russkis" and "Freedom" as the demonstrations continued.[85]

In Hungary, where the unrest began with university students in Budapest, complaints about food supplies were less noticeable at first, although they certainly influenced the decisions of working people around the country who decided to join the growing revolt. In Hungary, the legacy of material scarcity was perhaps even more pronounced during the years after 1956, after the revolution had failed. In November 1956, few observers would have guessed that the Hungarian János Kádár, who came to power with the assistance of Soviet tanks, would become one of the most successful and popular leaders of the Soviet Bloc. It was the Kádár regime's ability to construct a "workerist" solution that took into account emotions over food and material scarcity that formed the basis of its astounding stability.[86] In the early 1950s, Hungarian workers could not imagine being able to buy salami on a daily basis. A decade later, they could count on "abundant, nutritious meals every day." By the 1970s, wages had doubled and per capita consumption had increased two and a half times. Televisions, refrigerators, and other consumer durables had become commonplace.[87] Under the Kádár regime, Hungary was transformed from a hotbed of revolution into the so-called happiest barracks in the Soviet camp, in large part because its citizens were able to achieve a measure of material comfort and ease.

The failed Hungarian revolution and its consumerist aftermath provide a vivid illustration of both the applicability and the limits of the totalitarian tropes that the West used to describe Eastern Europe's Soviet allies. As the march of Soviet tanks into Budapest in November 1956 showed, there was no leaving the Soviet Bloc. East Europeans could not choose another form of government. But within the Communist system, there was considerable room for maneuver. According to the totalitarian model, Communist citizens would always be ruled by fear. But in the years after 1956—in Hungary and elsewhere—fear would give way to a socialist brand of normality that, like its Western counterpart, rested on the ability of individuals to forget politics and simply concentrate on living their private lives.[88]

Living a Lie?

In 1978, more than two decades after the end of Stalinism, the Czech dissident playwright Václav Havel wrote an essay entitled "The Power of the Powerless." In this piece, Havel dissected the nature of power in 1970s Czechoslovakia. It was wrong, he wrote, to imagine a Communist dictatorship as a tiny minority of leaders oppressing the masses. Society was not divided into victims and oppressors. Instead, Havel suggested, everyone—from ordinary people to party leaders—participated in and sustained the very system that controlled them. This system compelled participation less with the threat of physical violence than with the fear of material deprivation. People agreed to play the parts the system required of them in order to have access to the benefits of the consumer society that had arisen after de-Stalinization. They quelled what Havel assumed were their true feelings in order to keep their jobs, to be allowed to take a vacation at a Bulgarian resort, or to purchase automobiles and washing machines. Havel called this state of affairs "living a lie," because, he claimed, people were forced to betray their true convictions in order to maintain their access to modern consumer goods and leisure time. He urged his fellow citizens to reject this consumerist bargain and act on the basis of their real beliefs, which he called "living in truth." Havel did not imagine that living in truth would end Communist rule in Eastern Europe (he believed the Soviet Union would never let that happen), but he did think it would be possible for individuals to create more authentic lives for themselves outside the confines of the system.[89]

Havel portrayed ordinary East Europeans as having a great deal of power, since the system could survive only with their consent. He urged them to use that power, set aside their fear, and take responsibility for their own lives. What he did not admit, however, was that people had been doing this for decades, but in the service of their economic interests. Havel defined acting ethically as openly refusing the regime's political demands; working in the shadows in defense of one's own material advantage, even if this went against state policies, was not the same thing as living in truth. Havel wanted people to risk material security to assert their intellectual freedom, not risk jail to acquire the goods they wanted. For Havel, much like Kracauer and Berkman before him, people who put themselves in conflict with Communist regimes only so they could satisfy their consumer desires were not challenging the system; they were only perpetuating it.

Refugees' stories from the 1950s about theft, black markets, denunciations, and strikes did, however, challenge the widely held notion that citizens of Communist societies were so paralyzed by fear they could not assert any control over their own lives. Despite the terror these regimes wielded, people often defied them in small yet significant ways. The power these men and women exerted did not threaten to overthrow Communist regimes, but it nonetheless showed the limits of the era's totalitarian thinking, which posited that East Europeans were no more than captive slaves, and revealed that everyday life even under Stalinism was much more complicated than writers like Leland Stowe imagined it. Crucially, however, few at the time recognized the import of such actions, including East Europeans themselves. Like the researchers who interviewed them or the broadcasters they listened to, they continued to interpret their actions through the lens of their own powerlessness.

CONCLUSION

Histories of the Cold War have often been preoccupied with issues of accountability and intent. Such histories have generally focused on leading political actors and concerned themselves with issues that implicitly or explicitly pitted one camp against another, asking questions such as: Who was responsible for starting the Cold War? Who made key decisions? Who won and who lost? This study has been motivated by a different set of concerns. Rather than setting one side against the other, it has examined the Cold War as a shared political environment and tried to illuminate some of the ways a political culture that relied on moral absolutes affected patterns of thought on both sides of the Iron Curtain. It has tried to expand the question of who knew what and when by shifting the focus to how knowledge about Eastern Europe was produced, showing how some experiences took on the weight of evidence, whereas others seemingly provoked little thought.

As it was popularly used in the 1950s, the idea of totalitarianism was itself an artifact of the Cold War insistence on absolutes. Totalitarianism—defined as the total control of the state over the individual— stood as the opposite of Western freedom. Many historians have asked whether totalitarianism is a useful concept for thinking about Communist Eastern Europe. I have tried to shift this conversation to a different question. Rather than asking if Stalinist Eastern Europe was totalitarian, I have examined why assumptions about the nature of totalitarian regimes were so persistent among anti-Communists on both sides of the Iron Curtain, despite the existence of evidence that suggested the need for a more nuanced picture of Communist societies. The records of interviews given by men and women who fled the Soviet Bloc in the early 1950s provided the means to investigate that question. My approach to those sources has not been to determine what in them was true or false, but to use them to complicate these very categories. I have tried to preserve the voices of interviewees and take their stories seriously, while at the same time critically analyzing how interviewees and their interlocutors assigned meaning to their experiences and used them to create knowledge about totalitarian regimes.

The case of Ladislav Novak illustrates the complexity of this process. Novak was a twenty-nine-year-old student of physical education at the Charles University in Prague when he decided to flee across the border to Austria. According to his own account, he had made no secret of his dislike of the Communist regime at school. When the security forces told him that he would be imprisoned if he did not change his attitude, he decided he had no choice but to leave Czechoslovakia. Voice of America interviewed him in September 1951 in Salzburg, about nine months after he had left his country. During that conversation, Novak spoke at length about how he obtained the news and his opinions of different news sources. "Most news," he said, "I got naturally by reading CS [Czechoslovak] newspapers." His method of extracting information from those sources, however, was complicated. Novak had a low opinion of his country's newspapers, which he said were infused with uncompromising Communist orthodoxy. Their coverage was neither "complete" nor "objective"; they emphasized the government's achievements and did not report on resistance to its policies. The only way to get real information from them was by "reading between the lines" in order to "imagine the real meaning of the news." Reading between the lines meant realizing that when the government claimed rationing had been reintroduced because of imperialist sabotage, it was more likely due to government incompetence or Soviet requisitions. "Experience," Novak said, showed that what people learned by reading between the lines was usually the truth. Novak's practice of reinterpreting local news by assuming it lied was the very method promoted by Radio Free Europe's regular program "Other Side of the Coin," although Novak did not mention being influenced by these broadcasts. Instead, he suggested his way of creatively reading local newspapers was a widespread practice that had arisen naturally after Czechoslovakia's mass media had become saturated with Communist ideology.[1]

The Czechoslovak newspapers were not, however, his only source of news. He also relied on "little groups formed by students who believed [each other] to be of the same opinion." He recalled that it had gradually become more dangerous for students, like Novak, who were seen as "reactionaries" to meet in groups, so they began to meet only in pairs and only with those they knew were staunch anti-Communists. "During these two-man conversations, news was discussed, getting at the root of affairs concerning us, in a frank democratic way," he claimed. These conversations were one of his key sources of information. In addition, Novak listened to foreign radio stations, including the BBC, VOA, RFE, Paris, and the Vatican station. He tried to listen every night, despite obstacles. Every apartment building, he said, had at least one person who tried to find out which residents were listening to foreign radio stations in order to denounce them. The seemingly unending evening political meetings in workplaces were also, according to Novak, designed to keep people from listening to Western radio stations. "But very often," he claimed, "people left such meetings before they were ended in order to be able to listen to the radio and get moral support. It was often simply the longing for the truth."[2]

Novak's comments do not tell a simple story. On the one hand, he described how people lived in a culture of censorship. As he noted, domestic newspapers and radio programs were forced to adopt the government's perspective. Unlike the media in the West, they could not publish opposing viewpoints or support investigative journalists who might dig up information that challenged an official story. Novak and his friends tried as best they could to work around this lack of press freedom, but in their attempts to acquire information beyond what was officially published, they were forced to rely at least in part on rumor and hearsay. As people who opposed the Communist regime, they worried about the possibility of informers denouncing them either for their opinions or for listening to foreign radio stations. They formed a tight-knit, closed community of like-minded individuals, all in pursuit of alternative sources of information. As the months went on, they began to see this alternative news as a source of comfort and solace. The search for accurate information merged with a search for emotional fulfillment, and in this environment, the project of finding the truth came to mean much more than just ferreting out the facts. It represented the confirmation of their ideological and political views as the right ones.

This community that Novak and his fellow "reactionaries" created included the foreign radio stations they listened to. These stations were popular because, as Novak noted, they answered an emotional need, a "longing," to hear anti-Communist beliefs confirmed as right and the policies of the Communists decried as wrong. Those like Novak who emigrated illegally to the West answered a similar need for foreign broadcasters: the need for information. In the early Cold War, when travel across borders was difficult and media within Eastern Europe was heavily censored, these radio stations did not have many alternatives to using refugees as information sources. This practice, however, had the effect of magnifying the insularity of the community of listeners and broadcasters. Refugees who had often looked to foreign radio stations to confirm their beliefs provided data that helped shape the convictions of those very broadcasters. The information that refugee listeners provided might be accurate, but it was also interpreted through a set of assumptions shared by the entire community and therefore tended to reinforce those assumptions. The commonality of belief among source, researcher, broadcaster, and listener made it easier to discount divergent bits of information that pushed uncomfortably against what had become established truths.

The "longing for the truth" that Novak described was not unique to the first years of the Cold War. Many of us want to feel confirmed in our convictions and to believe ourselves in possession of the truth. Today it has become even easier to experience that emotion. The proliferation of media outlets made possible by cable television, satellite radio, social media, and the Internet has made it possible for more and more people to get their news only from sources that share their basic assumptions. Research has shown that many people gravitate toward news sources that share their own political orientation and shun those that do not, believing them to be less reliable and objective.[3] A 2009 study about news preferences noted a cascading effect as consumers increasingly sought news sources that matched their views, leading news providers to increase partisan content and creating an "echo chamber effect" where "news serves to reinforce existing beliefs and attitudes."[4] It is not surprising that this tendency has been linked to increased political polarization. In this kind of polarized political climate, people are more likely not only to violently disagree, but, in an echo of the Cold War, to suspect that facts wielded by their ideological opponents are incontrovertibly biased. The danger in such a situation lies in the possibility that ideological certainty will imperil our ability to think critically about our opponents and about ourselves. We do not need to accept an opponent's beliefs. Yet we should beware the lure of a comfortable truth. If our goal is real understanding, when we are confronted with unpleasant facts we must be wary of simply dismissing them as lies.

NOTES

INTRODUCTION

1. On the history of totalitarianism, see Abbot Gleason, *Totalitarianism: The Inner History of the Cold War* (Oxford: Oxford University Press, 1997).
2. The text of the speech is printed in Denise M. Bostdorff, *Proclaiming the Truman Doctrine: The Cold War Call to Arms* (College Station, TX: Texas A&M University Press, 2008), 1–9. It is also available online from Yale University's Avalon Project: "The Truman Doctrine: President Harry S. Truman's Address Before a Joint Session of Congress, March 12, 1947," http://avalon.law.yale.edu/20th_century/trudoc.asp (accessed December 29, 2016).
3. A. Zhdanov, "The International Situation," *For a Lasting Peace, For a People's Democracy*, November 10, 1947, 1–2.
4. Ibid., 2.
5. This debate preceded the end of the Cold War. For example, Milan Kundera, "The Tragedy of Central Europe," trans. Edmund White, *New York Review of Books*, April 26, 1984, 33–38.
6. Most textbooks in English about the region in this period have come to a similar conclusion: Geoffrey Swain and Nigel Swain, *Eastern Europe Since 1945*, 4th ed. (London: Palgrave Macmillan, 2009); Gale Stokes, *The Walls Came Tumbling Down: Collapse and Rebirth in Eastern Europe*, 2d ed. (New York: Oxford University Press, 2011); Padraic Kenney, *The Burdens of Freedom: Eastern Europe since 1989* (New York: Zed Press, 2008); Mark Pittaway, *Eastern Europe, 1939–2000* (London: Bloomsbury Academic, 2004).
7. Mark Pittaway, *The Workers' State: Industrial Labor and the Making of Socialist Hungary, 1944–1958* (Pittsburgh: University of Pittsburgh Press, 2012).
8. Norman Naimark and Leonid Gibianskii, eds., *The Establishment of Communist Regimes in Eastern Europe, 1944–1949* (Boulder, CO: Westview Press, 1997).

9. Even in English alone, there is a large literature on this period in Eastern Europe. In these notes, I highlight only those works that have been particularly useful to me. For example, on social transformation in Eastern Europe under Stalinism, see John Connelly, *Captive University: The Sovietization of East German, Czech, and Polish Higher Education, 1945–1956* (Chapel Hill: University of North Carolina Press, 2000), and Katherine Lebow, *Unfinished Utopia: Nowa Huta, Stalinism, and Polish Society, 1949–56* (Ithaca, NY: Cornell University Press, 2013), or on the interactions between Eastern Europe and the Soviet Union, Patryk Babiracki, *Soviet Soft Power in Poland: Culture and the Making of Stalin's New Empire, 1943–1957* (Chapel Hill: University of North Carolina Press, 2015).

10. Outside of Czechoslovakia and Bulgaria, the parties that ruled the countries of the Soviet Bloc in this period had official names other than the "Communist party," although local people often referred to their members as Communists. For example, in Hungary, the ruling party was formally called the Hungarian Workers' Party. To avoid confusion, I have generally just referred to these parties as "Communist parties."

11. For a survey of recent scholarship on Stalinist terror, see Kevin McDermott and Matthew Stibbe, eds., *Stalinist Terror in Eastern Europe* (Manchester: Manchester University Press, 2010).

12. On workers in this period, see Pittaway, *The Workers' State*; Padraic Kenney, *Rebuilding Poland: Workers and Communists, 1945–1950* (Ithaca, NY: Cornell University Press, 1997); Malgorzata Fidelis, *Women, Communism, and Industrialization in Postwar Poland* (Cambridge: Cambridge University Press, 2010); Peter Heumos, "*Vyhrňme si rukávy, než se kola zastaví!*": *Dělníci a státní socialismus v Československu, 1945–1968* (Prague: Ústav pro soudobé dějiny, 2006).

13. Gail Kligman and Katherine Verdery, *Peasants under Siege: The Collectivization of Romanian Agriculture, 1949–1962* (Princeton, NJ: Princeton University Press, 2011).

14. For example, Anne Applebaum, *Iron Curtain: The Crushing of Eastern Europe, 1944–1956* (New York: Doubleday, 2012), or Vladimir Tismaneau, "Diabolical Pedagogy and the Il(logic) of Stalinism in Eastern Europe," in *Stalinism Revisited: The Establishment of Communist Regimes in Eastern Europe*, ed. Vladimir Tismaneau (Budapest: Central European University Press, 2009), 25–50.

15. Prominent examples that I have found particularly useful include Kligman and Verdery, *Peasants under Siege*; Pittaway, *The Workers' State*; Lebow, *Unfinished Utopia*; and Fidelis, *Women, Communism, and Industrialization*.

16. On the intersection between fear and politics, see Corey Robin, *Fear: The History of a Political Idea* (New York: Oxford University Press, 2004). For Eastern Europe, Mark D. Steinberg and Valeria Sobol, eds., *Interpreting Emotions in Russia and Eastern Europe* (De Kalb: Northern Illinois University Press, 2011).

17. Zhdanov, "The International Situation," 4.

18. For a fascinating look at how this border developed over time, see Edith Sheffer, *Burned Bridge: How East and West Germans Created the Iron Curtain* (New York: Oxford University Press, 2011).
19. Paweł Machcewicz, *Poland's War on Radio Free Europe, 1950–1989*, trans. Maya Latynski (Washington, DC: Woodrow Wilson Center Press, 2014).
20. On this kind of transfer, see Mark Pittaway, "The Education of Dissent: The Reception of the Voice of Free Hungary, 1951–1956," *Cold War History* 4, no.1 (2003): 97–116. Also Friederike Kind-Kovács, "Voices, Letters, and Literature through the Iron Curtain: Exiles and the (Trans)mission of Radio in the Cold War," *Cold War History* 13, no. 2 (2013): 193–219.
21. Interview 081, Norbert Rak, December 4, 1951, US National Archives and Records Administration, College Park, MD (henceforth, NARA), RG 59, Department of State, International Information Administration/International Evaluation Staff, Iron Curtain Interviews, 1951–1952 (Iron Curtain Interviews), box 3, 1–2. Only the Polish respondents to this interview project were given full names; except in rare cases, Czechoslovak and Hungarian respondents were referred to only by their initials. Diacritical marks are not used in the transcripts. I have kept all names as they appear in the original sources, even when they are common names that would normally take diacriticals (e.g., "Wladyslaw" and not "Władysław"). A full discussion of the background of the VOA interview project appears in chapter 3.
22. Ibid., 3. When quoting from any English-language archival source, I have kept the original spelling, grammar, capitalization, and punctuation, even if it is not standard English. Since mistakes were very common, I have not used "[sic]" to indicate this.
23. Ibid., 4.
24. Ibid.
25. Ibid., 5–6.
26. Ibid., 7.
27. Ibid., 9.
28. A more complete discussion of the background of each of these source collections appears in chapters 3 and 4.
29. For example, reports on the response of the population to rationing, the arrests of various KSČ officials, etc. in Archiv bezpečnostních složek, Prague (henceforth, ABS), fond Velitelství státní bezpečnosti (henceforth, VSB), folder 310-92-5.
30. This was particularly the case with RFE evaluators. There is a more detailed discussion of the RFE interviews in chapter 4.
31. For example, Karl Brown, "Regulating Bodies: Everyday Crime and Popular Resistance in Communist Hungary" (PhD diss., University of Texas at Austin, 2007), esp. 23–24.
32. Scholars with such views do not generally publish material that uses these sources, but several historians have personally communicated such opinions to me.
33. The debate on experience as historical evidence is long-standing indeed (at least among feminist scholars), but it crystalized around the article by Joan W. Scott,

"The Evidence of Experience," first published in *Critical Inquiry* 17, no. 4 (1991): 773–797.
34. I use the term "Western analysts" (or researchers or interlocutors) to refer to anyone located in the West who worked for a Western news organization. This includes émigrés from the region.
35. Interview 081, Norbert Rak, 11.

CHAPTER I

1. *László Rajk and His Accomplices before the People's Court* (Budapest: n.p., 1949), 8–16 (for the testimony itself, 33–81).
2. Ibid., 254.
3. Ibid., 255.
4. Arthur Koestler, *Darkness at Noon*, trans. Daphne Hardy (New York: Scribner, 2006). A 1951 play based on the novel was broadcast on Voice of America. See script in NARA, RG 59, Department of State, US International Information Administration/International Broadcasting, Voice of America Historical Files, 1946–1953, box 1.
5. "Americans Deny Charges by Rajk," *New York Times*, September 16, 1949.
6. On the influence of *Darkness at Noon*, see Anna Krylova, "The Tenacious Liberal Subject in Soviet Studies," *Kritika* 1, no. 1 (2000): 119–146.
7. This is, for example, the approach of the many works of the Czech historian Karel Kaplan, such as *Report on the Murder of the General Secretary*, trans. Karel Kovanda (Columbus: Ohio State University Press, 1990), or the more recent work of Igor Lukes, *Rudolf Slánský: His Trials and Trial*, Cold War International History Project Working Paper 50 (Washington DC: Woodrow Wilson International Center for Scholars, 2008). An exception to this trend is István Rév, "In Mendacio Veritas (In Lies There Lies the Truth)," *Representations* 35 (Summer 1991), 1–20.
8. Igal Halfin has published several books on this topic: *Terror in My Soul: Communist Autobiographies on Trial* (Cambridge, MA: Harvard University Press, 2003); *Intimate Enemies: Demonizing the Bolshevik Opposition, 1918–1928* (Pittsburgh: University of Pittsburgh Press, 2007); *Stalinist Confessions: Messianism and Terror at the Leningrad Communist University* (Pittsburgh: Pittsburgh University Press, 2009).
9. George H. Hodos, *Show Trials: Stalinist Purges in Eastern Europe, 1948–1954* (New York: Praeger, 1987).
10. Stalin himself, for example, carefully monitored the case developing against Rudolf Slánský. Lukes, *Rudolf Slánský*, 28–32, 43–47, 52.
11. For the number of political prisoners, see data in McDermott and Stibbe, eds., *Stalinist Terror*.
12. In Romania, Ana Pauker was jailed in preparation for a potential trial but later released. Lucrețiu Pătrășcanu was eventually put on trial in 1954 after five years in jail, but in

a closed proceeding and without a confession. Dennis Deletant, "Political Purges and Mass Repression in Romania, 1948–1955," in *Stalinist Terror*, ed. McDermott and Stibbe, 141–159. Gomułka was imprisoned in 1951 but eventually released without trial in 1954. On why there was no Gomułka trial, see Łukasz Kamiński, "Proč se Gomułka nestal polským Slánským?" in *Politické procesy v Československu po roce 1945 a 'případ Slánský,'* ed. Jiří Pernes and Jan Foitzik (Brno: Prius, 2005), 33–37.
13. This vocabulary came from Soviet sources. Sheila Fitzpatrick, *Tear Off the Masks! Identity and Imposture in Twentieth Century Russia* (Princeton, NJ: Princeton University Press, 2005).
14. Lukes, *Rudolf Slánský*, 32–33.
15. *Proces s vedením protistátního spikleneckého centra v čele Rudolfem Slánským* (Prague: Ministerstvo Spravedlnosti, 1953), 48.
16. Quoted in Josefa Slánská, *Report on My Husband*, trans. Edith Pargeter (London: Hutchinson, 1969), 27.
17. *Proces s vedením protistátního spikleneckého centra*, 44–45. In a critical letter at the time, a KSČ member, Karel Kreibich, claimed that this phrase was used in Czech courts only one other time: in the 1899 Hilsner blood-libel case. Cited in Lukes, *Rudolf Slánský*, 54, n. 196.
18. *Proces s vedením protistátního spikleneckého centra*, 67.
19. I have left the spelling of Yugoslav names as they were in the original. *László Rajk and His Accomplices*, 264.
20. *Proces s vedením protistátního spikleneckého centra*, 8, 62.
21. *László Rajk and His Accomplices*, 253.
22. Ciobanu was sentenced to death despite this argument. *Trial of the Group of Spies and Traitors in the Service of Imperialist Espionage* (Bucharest: n.p., 1950), 40.
23. *The Trial of Traïcho Kostov and His Group* (Sofia: n.p., 1949), 507.
24. *How Foreign Intelligence Operates in Poland: The Turner Trial* (Warsaw: Książka I Wiezda, 1951), 44–45. Turner gave his own version of the story in his *International Incident* (London: Wingate, 1957).
25. *How Foreign Intelligence Operates in Poland*, 205.
26. Rawicz's article is quoted at length in Edward A. Morrow, "New Polish Curbs on Envoys Likely," *New York Times*, December 13, 1950.
27. *Trial of Traïcho Kostov*, 523.
28. *Proces s vedením protistátního spikleneckého centra*, 495 (also 63). On Gomułka and Pătrășcanu, see note 12.
29. Lukes, *Rudolf Slánský*, 22–27; Tony Sharp, *Stalin's American Spy: Noel Field, Allen Dulles and the East European Show Trials* (London: Hurst, 2014), 2–7.
30. *Trial of Traïcho Kostov*, 564.
31. *How Foreign Intelligence Operates in Poland*, 136.
32. *R. Vogeler, E. Sanders and Their Accomplices before the Criminal Court* (Budapest: Hungarian State Publishing House, 1950), 227–228.

33. *How Foreign Intelligence Operates in Poland*, 124.
34. *Trial of Traicho Kostov*, 83–84.
35. *László Rajk and His Accomplices*, 270.
36. *How Foreign Intelligence Operates in Poland*, 137.
37. *László Rajk and His Accomplices*, 15.
38. *Proces s vedením protistátního spikleneckého centra*, 275–276.
39. Ibid., 428. According to Igor Lukes, three Soviet advisers wrote most of the trial script; they perhaps did not consider that the Czechoslovak audience might not see the sacrifice of Russian prisoners in the same light that they did. Lukes, *Rudolf Slánský*, 52.
40. *Proces s vedením protistátního spikleneckého centra*, 456–459.
41. Similar allegations of collaboration with the occupying Germans would have been familiar to audiences from previous trials of wartime collaborators. See Benjamin Frommer, *National Cleansing: Retribution against Nazi Collaborators in Postwar Czechoslovakia* (Cambridge: Cambridge University Press, 2004).
42. *Proces s vedením protistátního spikleneckého centra*, 8.
43. *Trial of the Group of Spies and Traitors*, 9, 25.
44. There is indeed film footage of the atomic tests conducted by the United States at Bikini Atoll in 1946. Some if it is now available on the Internet: https://archive.org/details/CEP00110 (accessed December 29, 2016).
45. *How Foreign Intelligence Operates in Poland*, 205.
46. There is a large Czech-language literature on the Horáková trial. The first, and still standard, work is Karel Kaplan, *Největší politický proces: Milada Horáková a spol* (Prague: Doplněk, 1995). In English, see Melissa Feinberg, *Elusive Equality: Gender, Citizenship and the Limits of Democracy in Czechoslovakia, 1918–1950* (Pittsburgh: University of Pittsburgh Press, 2006), 211–222.
47. *War Conspirators before the Court of the Czechoslovak People* (Prague: Orbis, 1950), 49–50. Testimony in the published transcripts was doctored and misrepresented what was actually said in the courtroom. However, the Czech public was not aware of that at the time. A ten-part documentary broadcast on Czech Television in 2009 re-created the trial from more than six hours of once lost film footage, audiotapes, and transcripts. The whole series is available online (only in Czech) at http://www.ceskatelevize.cz/porady/10153697395-proces-h/ (accessed December 29, 2016). The actual last speeches of the accused were published in Karel Kaplan and Marek Janáč, "Poslední slova obžalovaných v procesu s Miladou Horákovou 'a spol,'" *Soudobé dějiny* 13, nos.1–2 (2006): 197–238.
48. Pavlina Formánková and Petr Koura, *Žádáme trest smrti! Propagandistická kampaň provázející proces s Milada Horákovou a spol* (Prague: Ústav pro studium totalitních režimů, 2008), 388.
49. Feinberg, *Elusive Equality*, 216–217.
50. Formánková and Koura, *Žádáme trest smrti!*, 84–85.
51. Ibid., 407.

52. Ibid., 434.
53. Hungary had quite a few similar trials, including the MAORT (Hungarian-American Oil Company) case. The Vogeler trial was atypical in that an American was present among the accused. On the American reaction to the trial, see Susan Carruthers, *Cold War Captives: Imprisonment, Escape, and Brainwashing* (Berkeley: University of California Press, 2009), 136–173.
54. *R. Vogeler, E. Sanders and Their Accomplices*, 10–20.
55. For example, Katherine Verdery, *What Was Socialism and What Comes Next?* (Princeton, NJ: Princeton University Press, 1996), 19–38.
56. *R. Vogeler, E. Sanders and Their Accomplices*, 60–63.
57. Ibid., 52–57.
58. *Trial of the Group of Spies and Traitors*, 145–147.
59. The published transcript, however, *includes* Kostov's outburst. *Trial of Traïcho Kostov*, 66–73.
60. Ibid., 209.
61. Ibid., 119–164.
62. For a detailed analysis of the reaction of workers to new production rules, see Pittaway, *The Workers' State*, 114–143.
63. Bela Szász, *Volunteers for the Gallows: Anatomy of a Show Trial*, trans. Kathleen Szász (New York: Norton, 1972), 81–83.
64. Artur London, *On Trial*, trans. Alastair Hamilton (London: MacDonald, 1970), 110–114. His codefendant Eugen Loebl was told the same thing. Eugen Loebl, *My Mind on Trial* (New York: Harcourt Brace Jovanovich, 1976), 46–48. See also Jana Kopelentova Rehak, *Czech Political Prisoners, Recovering Face* (Lanham, MD: Lexington Books, 2012), 35–62.
65. London, *On Trial*, 47–94; Loebl, *My Mind on Trial*, 74–90; Szász, *Volunteers for the Gallows*, 18–66; Robert Vogeler, *I Was Stalin's Prisoner* (New York: Harcourt, 1952), 136–152; Hodos, *Show Trials*, 67–72; George Paloczi-Horvath, *The Undefeated* (Boston: Little, Brown, 1959), 139–158.
66. Szász, *Volunteers for the Gallows*, 12–17, 108–109; Paloczi-Horvath, *The Undefeated*, 149–150; Hodos, *Show Trials*, 58, 67. On torture in Czech prisons, see Kopelentova Rehak, *Czech Political Prisoners*, 35–63, and Tomáš Bouška and Klára Pinerová, *Czechoslovak Political Prisoners: Life Stories of 5 Male and 5 Female Victims of Stalinism*, trans. Kamila Nováková and Justin A. Osswald (Prague: Europe for Citizens Programme, 2009).
67. Krylova, "The Tenacious Liberal Subject," 125, and Gleason, *Totalitarianism*, 55–63.
68. Koestler, *Darkness at Noon*, 257–266.
69. Associated Press, "Rajk Avidly Admits to Plot in Hungary with United States and Tito," *New York Times*, September 17, 1949; Endre Marton, "Hungary's Former #2 Red Admits Helping 'Plot Revolt,'" *Washington Post*, September 17, 1949; "Hungarians Doom Rajk in Spy Trial," *New York Times*, September 24, 1949.

70. "The Pattern of Justice," *New York Times*, September 21, 1949.
71. "Prague and the West," *New York Times*, June 1, 1950.
72. John MacCormac, "Purge of Czechs Serves Several Communist Ends," *New York Times*, November 30, 1952.
73. Anne Applebaum, for example, makes reference to Koestler several times in her discussion of show trial victims. Applebaum, *Iron Curtain*, 275–299.
74. Jochen Hellbeck, "With Hegel to Salvation: Bukharin's Other Trial," *Representations* 107, no. 1 (2009) : 56–59.
75. Ibid., 78.
76. The memoir literature from Eastern Europe that I have used was largely written by emigres and published in the West, giving it a particular perspective.
77. This was also true of the way show trials were reported on Western radio stations that broadcast to Eastern Europe. See Melissa Feinberg, "Fantastic Truths, Compelling Lies: Radio Free Europe and the Response to the Slánský Trial in Czechoslovakia," *Contemporary European History* 22, no. 1 (2013): 107–125.
78. London, *On Trial*, 340–342; Marian Šlingová, *Truth Will Prevail* (London: Merlin, 1968), 70–75; Paloczi-Horvath, *The Undefeated*, 144.
79. Cited in Slánská, *Report on My Husband*, 40. Also Kaplan, *Report on the Murder of the General Secretary*, 140.
80. Szász, *Volunteers for the Gallows*, 165.
81. Formánková and Koura, *Žádáme trest smrti!*, 43.
82. Ibid., 40–47 (quote on 47).
83. Ibid., 57.
84. A few also wrote to ask for mercy, but they were in the minority. Ibid., 61.
85. Ibid., 316.
86. Ibid., 340.
87. Ibid., 348.
88. Ibid., 331.
89. Serhy Yekelchyk, "The Civic Duty to Hate: Stalinist Citizenship as Political Practice and Civic Emotion (Kiev, 1943–1953)," *Kritika* 7, no. 3 (2006): 529–556.
90. Formánková and Koura, *Žádáme trest smrti!*, 64.
91. Heda Margolius Kovaly, *Under a Cruel Star: A Life in Prague, 1941–1968*, trans. Helen Epstein (Teaneck, NJ: Holmes and Meier, 1997), 140–142.
92. London, *On Trial*, 332–351.
93. Slánská, *Report on My Husband*, 130.
94. At this point, Slánský had already been demoted and forced to undergo self-criticism. "Záznam z mimořádné schůze předsednictva ÚV-KSČ, která se konala dne 24.XI.1951 v 16 hodin na Hradě," Národní Archiv, Prague (henceforth, NA), fond Předsednictvo ÚV-KSČ 1945–1951, folder 29, aj. 287.
95. For example, London, *On Trial*, 108.
96. Paloczi-Horvath, *The Undefeated*, 265–266.

97. London, *On Trial*, and Paloczi-Horvath, *The Undefeated*, include examples of both kinds of reaction.
98. Paul Corner, "Introduction," in Paul Corner, ed., *Popular Opinion in Totalitarian Regimes: Fascism, Nazism, Communism* (Oxford: Oxford University Press, 2008), 6. See also, in the same volume, Jan Plamper, "Beyond Binaries: Popular Opinion in Stalinism," 64–80.
99. "Referat 2021," ABS, VSB, 310-114-6; "Ohlas procesu se Slánským" (November 24, 1952), ABS, VSB, aj. 310-114-6; "Dílčí zprávy veřejného mínění k procesu s protistántím centrem" (from Prague regional StB office to VStB, November 24, 1952), ABS, VSB, aj. 310-114-6.
100. "Předmět: veřejné mínění k procesu—zpráva" (from Prague region StB office to Ministry of National Security and StB main administration, November 26, 1952), ABS, VSB, aj. 310-114-6.
101. Yet the same report also showed the hotel staff members, who otherwise evinced doubt about the trial, giving vent to antisemitic feelings. They mentioned that Geminder (one of the defendants) had been to the hotel frequently to visit a Jewish family who "lolled about and ate" there for months, with the bill paid by the KSČ Central Committee. "We are working ourselves to the bone and the Jews have it good here!" they griped. "Předmět: veřejné mínění k procesu—zpráva" (from Prague region StB office to Ministry of National Security and StB main administration, November 29, 1952), ABS, VSB, aj. 310-114-6.
102. Information Bulletin 70 (December 12, 1952), NA, fond 1261/0/2 (ÚV-KSČ-014), sv. 14/12/7-9, aj. 71. On this subject, also see Kevin McDermott, "'A Polyphony of Voices': Czech Popular Opinion and the Slánský Affair," *Slavic Review* 67, no. 4 (2008), 855.
103. Many such denunciations were reported in the Information Bulletins from December 23, 1952, and December 31, 1952, NA, fond 1261/0/2 (ÚV-KSČ-014), sv. 14/12/7-9, aj. 81 and aj. 84.
104. "Předmět: veřejné mínění k procesu—zpráva" (from Prague region StB office to Ministry of National Security and StB main administration, November 26, 1952,), ABS, VSB, aj. 310-114-6.
105. "Ohlas procesu s protistátním centrem na závodech Pražského kraje ku dni 26. listopadu 1952" (November 27, 1952), NA, fond 1261/2/1 (KSČ-ÚV-05/1) sv. 370, aj, 2327.
106. "Ohlas procesu s protistátním centrem na závodech Pražského kraje ku dni 26. listopadu 1952" (November 29, 1952), NA, fond 1261/2/1 (KSČ-ÚV-05/1) sv. 370, aj, 2327.
107. "Předmět: veřejné mínění k procesu—zpráva" (from Prague region StB office to Ministry of National Security and StB main administration, November 26, 1952), ABS, VSB, aj. 310-114-6; Information Bulletin 60 (November 26, 1952), NA, fond 1261/0/2 (ÚV-KSČ-014), sv. 14/12/7-9, aj. 61.

108. See, for example, the folders of regional StB telexes on the response to the trial. ABS, fond VSB, aj. 310-114-8 (Ústí nad Labem), 310-114-9 aj. (Plzeň), aj. 310-114-10 (Karlovy Vary), aj. 310-114-11 (České Budějovice), etc.
109. McDermott, '"A Polyphony,'" 850–855.
110. "Ohlas procesu s protistátním spikleneckým centrem Slánský a spol.," (November 22, 1952), ABS, VSB, aj. 310-314-6,
111. "Předmět: veřejné mínění k procesu a rozsudkům—zpráva" (from Prague region StB office to Ministry of National Security and StB main administration, November 29, 1952,), ABS, VSB, aj. 310-114-6
112. "Průzkum veřejného mínění k probíhajícímu procesu," ABS, VSB, aj. 310-111-3.
113. "Ohlas procesu s protistátním spikleneckým centrem," ABS, VSB, aj. 310-314-6.
114. "Referát 2043 (dne 2 prosince 1952)—Věc: Ohlas procesu se Slánským a spol.," ABS, VSB, aj. 310-314-6.
115. Ibid. Also, Report from regional StB office Prague to Ministry of National Security, November 24, 1952, "Dílčí zprávy veřejného mínění k procesu s protistántím centrem," ABS, VSB, aj. 310-114-6.
116. Hillel Kieval makes a similar argument about how ritual murder charges in the 1890s seemed plausible, despite the lack of objective evidence. Hillel Kieval, *Languages of Community: The Jewish Experience in the Czech Lands* (Berkeley: University of California Press, 2000), 188–189.
117. "Spořitelny a založny v Praze II Václavské nám. 42.— Zjištění jak komunisté a všichni pracující reagují na process s bandou Slánského," NA, fond 1261/2/1 (KSČ-ÚV-05/1), sv. 370, aj, 2327.

CHAPTER 2

1. Mikhail Suslov, "Defence of Peace and the Fight against the Warmongers," in *Meeting of the Information Bureau of the Communist Parties in Hungary in the Latter Half of November, 1949* (New York: For a Lasting Peace, For a People's Democracy, 1950), 37.
2. Ibid., 40–41.
3. Lawrence S. Wittner, *The Struggle against the Bomb: One World or None—A History of the World Nuclear Disarmament Movement through 1953* (Stanford, CA: Stanford University Press, 1995), 177–186; Lawrence S. Wittner, *Confronting the Bomb: A Short History of the World Nuclear Disarmament Movement* (Stanford, CA: Stanford University Press, 2009), 26.
4. For this perspective, see US House of Representatives Committee on Un-American Activities, *Report on the Communist "Peace" Offensive: A Campaign to Disarm and Defeat the United States* (Washington, DC: HUAC, 1951). Richard Felix Staar claims that the WPC indeed received directives (as well as most of its funding) directly from the Communist Party of the Soviet Union. Richard Felix Staar, *Foreign Policies of the Soviet Union* (Stanford, CA: Hoover Institution Press, 1991), 84.

5. Wittner, *One World*, 180.
6. Francisca de Haan, "Continuing Cold War Paradigms in Western Historiography of Transnational Women's Organizations: The Case of the Women's International Democratic Federation (WIDF)," *Women's History Review* 19, no. 4 (2010): 547–573.
7. Günter Wernicke, "The Communist-Led World Peace Council and the Western Peace Movements: The Fetters of Bipolarity and Some Attempts to Break Them in the Fifties and Early Sixties," *Peace and Change* 23, no. 3 (1998): 265–311.
8. As one example in the Czechoslovak context, see Olga Hillová, ed., *Buduj vlast—posílíš mír: Z první celostátní konference údernic a vzorných zemědělek v Praze v březnu, 1949* (Prague: Ministerstvo informací a osvěty, 1949). Or, on Poland, see Marian Turski and Henryk Zdanowski, *The Peace Movement: People and Facts*, trans. Magdalena Mierowska (Bydgoszcz: Interpress, 1976).
9. Jan C. Behrends, "Von Panslavismus zum 'Friedenskampf' Außenpolitik, Herrschaftslegitimation und Massenmobilisierung im sowjetischen Nachkriegsimperium (1948–1953)," *Jahrbücher für Geschichte Osteuropas* 56 (2008): 27–53.
10. Turski and Zdanowski, *The Peace Movement*, 38.
11. Wrocław was located in the territory ceded to Poland from Germany at the end of the Second World War. Much of the American coverage of the congress referred to the city by its German name: Breslau.
12. On the organization of the conference, see Zygmunt Woźniczka, "Wrocławski kongres intelektualistów w obronie pokoju," *Kwartalnik Historyczny* 94, no. 2 (1987): 131–157.
13. Ivor Montagu, *What Happened at Wrocław* (London: British Cultural Committee for Peace, 1949), 4. Although he presented himself as an impartial observer, Montagu was a member of the Communist party and, apparently, at one time a Soviet spy. See Ben Mcintyre, *Operation Mincemeat: How a Dead Man and a Bizarre Plan Fooled the Nazis and Assured an Allied Victory* (New York: Crown, 2010), 87–92.
14. "Einstein Clears Up 'Message' Mystery," *New York Times*, August 30, 1948.
15. Katarzyna Murawska-Muthesius, "Modernism between Peace and Freedom: Picasso and Others at the Congress of Intellectuals in Wrocław, 1948," in *Cold War Modern: Design, 1945–1970*, ed. David Crowley and Jane Pavitt (London: V & A Publishing, 2008), 33–42.
16. Sydney Gruson, "Tarle and Vavilov Will Lead Russians Attending World Congress of Intellectuals," *New York Times*, August 18, 1948.
17. "Times Writer Barred from Breslau Talks," *New York Times*, August 24, 1948.
18. All quotes in this paragraph and in the next from A. Fadeyev, "Science and Culture in the Struggle for Peace, Progress and Democracy," *Soviet Literature*, no. 11 (1948): 142–152. On the speech, see also Montagu, *What Happened at Wrocław*, 11–12.
19. Kingsley Martin, "Hyenas and Reptiles," *New Statesman and Nation*, September 4, 1948; Montagu, *What Happened at Wrocław*, 12; Woźniczka, "Wrocławski kongres," 147–148.

20. Wittner, *One World*, 175–176.
21. Sydney Gruson, "Briton Assails Intellectual Parley for 'Preaching War,' Not Peace," *New York Times*, August 27, 1948; "Huxley Denounces Breslau Congress," *New York Times*, September 1, 1948.
22. US House of Representatives Committee on Un-American Activities, *Report on the Communist "Peace" Offensive*, 8.
23. Martin, "Hyenas and Reptiles."
24. Ibid.; Montagu, *What Happened at Wrocław*, 13; Wittner, *One World*, 176. According to Ivor Montagu, Taylor's defense of the West was most forcefully challenged by some of the nonwhite delegates from the still extant British Empire, who charged that Western imperialism was most definitely more than a slogan.
25. Martin, "Hyenas and Reptiles."
26. A. J. P. Taylor, J. Bernal, R. Hughes, et al., "Congress of the Intellectuals, Wrocław, August 1948: A Forum," *Our Time* 7, no. 13 (1948): 336–341 (quote on 336).
27. Martin, "Hyenas and Reptiles."
28. Feliks Topolski, *Confessions of a Conference Delegate* (London: n.p., 1948), 21–31. Part of the British resolution was printed in Sydney Gruson, "Manifesto Adopted: 'Handful' in America and Europe Charged with Seeking War," *New York Times*, August 29, 1948.
29. Taylor et al., "Congress of Intellectuals," 337.
30. Ibid., 340.
31. Topolski, *Confessions*, 14–18 (quote on 14).
32. Ibid., 44.
33. Taylor et al., "Congress of Intellectuals," 336.
34. For example, Sydney Gruson, "Soviet Scores U.S. at Breslau Parley," *New York Times*, August 28, 1948; "Red Novelist Assails U.S.," *Washington Post*, August 26, 1948; Martin, "Hyenas and Reptiles."
35. Gruson, "Soviet Scores U.S.," and Sydney Gruson, "Breslau Speakers Score Communists," *New York Times*, August 28, 1948. In similar fashion, "Rogge Hits Soviet Attacks against U.S.," *Washington Post*, August 27, 1948.
36. "Savants sans Savvy," *Washington Post*, August 30, 1948.
37. Gruson, "Manifesto Adopted."
38. There was no mention of his "hyenas and jackals" comment. "Vratislavský sjezd splní své poslání vysloví-li se proti imperialismu,' *Rudé právo*, August 26, 1948.
39. "V otázce míru není kompromisů," *Rudé právo*, August 28, 1948.
40. "Zrod lidových demokracií je velké mírové dílo," *Rudé právo*, August 29, 1948.
41. "Lidstvo má dost síly, aby ochránilo mír a kulturu" and "Kulturní pravovníci v boji za mír," *Rudé právo*, August 31, 1948.
42. The Czech rendition, "skupina kořistníků," is translated more accurately into English as "group of exploiters" and not "a handful of self-interested men," as in the English version of the resolution.

43. Jiří Hronek, "Dvě pravdy z Vratislavi," *Rudé právo*, September 2, 1948.
44. Ibid.
45. Turski and Zdanowski, *The Peace Movement*, 25.
46. *Second World Peace Congress, Warsaw, November 16–22, 1950*, Supplement to *Voks Bulletin*, no. 66 (1951), 5–7.
47. Fadeyev, "Science and Culture in the Struggle for Peace."
48. Suslov, "Defence of Peace."
49. *Congress of the Peoples for Peace, Vienna, December 12th–19th, 1952* (World Council of Peace, 1952), 514.
50. This language did not change substantially from 1953 to 1956, but this chapter concentrates on examples from the earlier, formative period.
51. Turski and Zdanowski, *The Peace Movement*, 38.
52. Behrends, "Von Panslavismus zum 'Friedenskampf,'" 49.
53. Suslov, "Defence of Peace," 35–36.
54. *Congress of the Peoples for Peace, Vienna*, 102–103.
55. Ibid., 146.
56. *Second World Peace Congress, Warsaw*, 29.
57. Ibid., 31. Ehrenburg referred to Nance as the president of the University of Florida, but he was actually at the University of Tampa. Several other speakers at the Congress also cited Dr. Nance's remarks.
58. Jan C. Behrends and Árpád von Klimó, "'Friedenskampf' und Kriegsangst: Auswirkungen des Koreakriegs auf Polen und Ungarn, in *Der Koreakrieg. Wahrnehmung, Wirkung, Erinnerung*, ed. Christoph Kleßmann and Bernd Stöver (Cologne: Böhlau, 2008): 55–74.
59. *Second World Peace Congress, Warsaw*, 17.
60. Women's International Democratic Federation, *We Accuse!* Report of the Commission of the Women's International Democratic Forum in Korea, May 16–27, 1951 (Berlin: Women's International Democratic Forum, 1951), 23.
61. Ibid., 33. My goal here is not to evaluate the accuracy of the WIDF report. However, we should not automatically assume that because these incidents were used for propaganda purposes they did not have some basis in fact. For an overview of Korean War atrocities on both sides, see Bruce Cummings, *The Korean War: A History* (New York: Modern Library, 2010).
62. Women's International Democratic Federation, *We Accuse!*, 6.
63. Ibid., 2. The WIDF report was printed in many languages and provided the basis for peace activities in countries around the Soviet Bloc. On this, see papers from meeting of the Executive Committee of WIDF, NA, fond Ústřední komise žen—KSČ, a.j. 98.
64. David S. Foglesong, "Roots of 'Liberation': American Images of the Future of Russia in the Early Cold War, 1948–1953," *International History Review* 21, no. 1 (1999): 57–79; Chris Tudda, "'Reenacting the Story of Tantalus': Eisenhower,

Dulles, and the Failed Rhetoric of Liberation," *Journal of Cold War Studies* 7, no. 4 (2005): 3–35.
65. *Congress of the Peoples for Peace, Vienna*, 187–188.
66. Ibid., 188.
67. *Second World Peace Congress, Warsaw*, 17.
68. Ibid., 29.
69. *Congress of the Peoples for Peace, Vienna*, 433.
70. Ilya Ehrenbourg [sic], *This Can't Go On: An Address to the People of the United States* (Chicago: Chicago Council of Soviet–American Friendship, 1952), 6.
71. *Congress of the Peoples for Peace, Vienna*, , 433.
72. Ehrenbourg, *This Can't Go On*, 7.
73. Ibid., 6.
74. *Congress of the Peoples for Peace, Vienna*, 428.
75. *Second World Peace Congress, Warsaw*, 56.
76. Ibid.
77. *Congress of the Peoples for Peace, Vienna*, 157.
78. *Second World Peace Congress, Warsaw*, 29. The historian Timothy Johnston argues that for this reason the peace campaign was actually quite popular with many Soviet citizens, in "Peace or Pacifism? The Soviet 'Struggle for Peace in All the World,' 1948–54," *Slavonic & East European Review* 86, no. 2 (2008): 259–282.
79. *Congress of the Peoples for Peace, Vienna*, 514.
80. *Second World Peace Congress, Warsaw*, 29.
81. Ibid., 88.
82. Ibid., 89.
83. Ibid., 24.
84. Ibid., 25.
85. *Congress of the Peoples for Peace, Vienna*, 182–183.
86. Behrends, "Von Panslavismus zum 'Friedenskampf,'" 45–47.
87. *Congress of the Peoples for Peace, Vienna*, 156.
88. Ibid., 542.
89. Turski and Zdanowski, *The Peace Movement*, 38; Wernicke, "Communist-Led World Peace Council," 273.
90. Suslov, "Defence of Peace," 53.
91. Ibid., 55.
92. "News from Other Lands—Bulgaria," *In Defence of Peace* 2, no. 3 (March 1950): 75; "News from Other Lands—Hungary," *In Defence of Peace* 2, no. 6 (June 1950): 73–74; "News from Other Lands—Romania," *In Defence of Peace* 2, no. 4 (April 1950): 94 and no. 4 (May 1950): 79.
93. Turski and Zdanowski, *The Peace Movement*, 42.
94. "News from Other Lands—Romania," *In Defence of Peace* 2, no. 7 (July 1950): 72–73.
95. Behrends, "Von Panslavismus zum 'Friedenskampf,'" 45–49.

96. Roman Krakovsky, "The Representation of the Cold War: The Peace and War Camps in Czechoslovakia, 1948-1960," *Journal of Transatlantic Studies* 6, no. 2 (2008): 158-167. This same kind of imagery is present in the fake 1950s propaganda film embedded in Andzrej Wajda's film, *Man of Marble* (Poland, 1977).
97. "News from Other Lands—Czechoslovakia," *In Defence of Peace* 2, no. 8 (September 1950): 72-73.
98. "News from Other Lands—Czechoslovakia," *In Defence of Peace* 2, no.7 (July 1950): 57.
99. "News from Other Lands—Poland," *In Defence of Peace* 2, no. 7 (July 1950): 71-72.
100. "News from Other Lands—Poland," *In Defence of Peace* 2, no. 6 (June 1950): 77.
101. "News from Other Lands—Poland," *In Defence of Peace* 2, no. 5 (May 1950): 70-71.
102. Turski and Zdanowski, *The Peace Movement*, 40.
103. "News from Other Lands—Poland," *In Defence of Peace* 2, no. 7 (July 1950): 71-72.
104. "Všem krajským, okresním a mistním akčním výborům Národní Fronty!" NA, fond ÚAV-NF, box 12.
105. "News from Other Lands—Hungary," *In Defence of Peace* 2, no. 6 (June 1950): 73-74.
106. "News from Other Lands—Romania," *In Defence of Peace* 2, no. 6 (June 1950): 78.
107. Ibid.; "News from Other Lands—Romania," *In Defence of Peace* 2, no. 7 (July 1950): 72-73.
108. "News from Other Lands—Hungary," *In Defence of Peace* 2, no. 7 (July 1950); "News from Other Lands—Hungary," *In Defence of Peace* 2, no. 8 (September 1950): 56. On Protestant and Catholic clergy and the Stockholm Appeal, see Wittner, *One World or None*, 241-242.
109. See US House of Representatives Committee on Un-American Activities, *Report on the Communist "Peace" Offensive*, 34; Wittner, *One World or None*, 183, 235, 237.
110. "Zpráva o průběhu mírové podpisové akce, Hlášení za dny 27.-29.1950," NA, fond ÚAV-NF, box 12.
111. "Zpráva o výsledcích mírové podpisové akce, Hlášení za den 16.5.1950," NA, fond ÚAV-NF, box 12, 1-2.
112. "Zpráva o průběhu mírové podpisové akce, Hlášení za dny 27.-29.1950," NA, fond ÚAV-NF, box 12, 4.
113. Dariusz Jarosz, "Polish Peasants under Stalinism," in *Stalinism in Poland, 1944-1956*, ed. Anthony Kamp-Welch (London: Macmillan, 1999), 67.
114. Turski and Zdanowski, *The Peace Movement*, 41-42.
115. Johnston, "Peace or Pacifism?"
116. "Zpráva o průběhu mírové podpisové akce, Hlášení za dny 27.-29.1950," 1.
117. Turski and Zdanowski, *The Peace Movement*, 58.

118. "Zpráva o výsledku mírové podpisové akce, Hlášení za den 24.5.1950," NA, fond ÚAV-NF, box 12.
119. For example, "Zpráva o výsledcích mírové podpisové akce, Hlášení za den 16.5.1950," NA, fond ÚAV-NF, box 12.
120. Hillová, ed., *Buduj vlast—posílíš mír*, and also Vlastimila Drozdová, ed., *Buduj vlast—posílíš mír* (Prague: Ústředí lidové tvořivosti a Rada žen, 1950). For a detailed history of the Czech women's movement in this era, see Denisa Nečasová, *Buduj vlast—posílíš mír! Ženské hnutí v českých zemích, 1944–1955* (Brno: Matice Moravská, 2011).
121. "Zápis z porady poslankyň KSČ konané dne 19.12.1950 o MDŽ 1951," NA, ÚKŽ-KSČ, aj. 20; Nečasová, *Buduj vlast—posílíš mír!*, 242–243.
122. "Zápis z porady poslankyň KSČ konané dne 19.12.1950 o MDŽ 1951."
123. "Zprávy o výsledek MDŽ 1950," NA, fond ÚKŽ-KSČ, aj. 19; untitled report (in English) about Women's Day 1950, NA, fond ÚKŽ-KSČ, aj. 95.
124. "Celkové výsledky oslav MDŽ 1951 podle hlášení na předsednictvu ÚV ČSŽ," NA, fond ÚKŽ-KSČ, aj. 20.
125. For example, efforts in Czechoslovakia to bring housewives into the workforce were not very successful. Nečasová, *Buduj vlast—posílíš mír!*, 314.
126. Taylor et al., "Congress of Intellectuals," 337.
127. US House of Representatives Committee on Un-American Activities, *Report on the Communist "Peace" Offensive*, 1–3, 24, 32.
128. Phillip Deery, "The Dove Flies East: Whitehall, Warsaw and the 1950 World Peace Congress," *Australian Journal of Politics & History* 48, no. 4, (2002): 449–468.
129. Germ metaphors were common in American rhetoric about Communists. Ellen Schrecker, *Many Are the Crimes: McCarthyism in America* (New York: Little, Brown, 1998), 144.
130. US House of Representatives Committee on Un-American Activities, *Report on the Communist "Peace" Offensive*, 24–27. On Rogge, see Phillip Deery, "'A Divided Soul'? The Cold War Odyssey of O. John Rogge," *Cold War History* 6, no. 2 (2006): 177–204.
131. US House of Representatives Committee on Un-American Activities, *Report on the Communist "Peace" Offensive*, 42–46; Schrecker, *Many Are the Crimes*, 373–379.
132. US House of Representatives Committee on Un-American Activities, *Report on the Communist "Peace" Offensive*, 71–76.
133. Helen Laville, "The Memorial Day Statement: Women's Organizations in the 'Peace Offensive,'" *Intelligence and National Security* 18, no. 2 (2003): 203.
134. de Haan, "Continuing Cold War Paradigms," 548–49; Wittner, *The Struggle against the Bomb*, 218–224; Jolyon Howorth, *France: The Politics of Peace* (London: Merlin, 1984), 26–27.

CHAPTER 3

1. John Foster Dulles, "A Policy for Boldness," *Life*, May 19, 1952, Truman Library Online Collection. http://www.trumanlibrary.org/whistlestop/study_collections/achesonmemos/view.php?pagenumber=13&documentid=70-5_30&pagination=&documentVersion=both&documentYear=1952 (accessed March 17, 2016).
2. Walter L. Hixson, *Parting the Curtain: Propaganda, Culture, and the Cold War, 1945–1961* (New York: St. Martin's, 1997), 12.
3. For an overview of such activities, see ibid.; Laura Belmonte, *Selling the American Way: U.S. Propaganda and the Cold War* (Philadelphia: University of Pennsylvania Press, 2008); Kenneth Osgood, *Total Cold War: Eisenhower's Secret Propaganda Battle at Home and Abroad* (Lawrence: University of Kansas Press, 2006); Frances Stonor Saunders, *The Cultural Cold War: The CIA and the World of Arts and Letters*, 2d ed. (New York: New Press, 2013); Giles Scott-Smith, *The Politics of Apolitical Culture: The Congress for Cultural Freedom, the CIA and Postwar American Hegemony* (London: Routledge, 2002).
4. Quoted in Hixson, *Parting the Curtain*, 15.
5. Harry S. Truman, Speech to American Society of Newspaper Editors, April 20, 1950, Truman Library Online Collection http://www.trumanlibrary.org/public-papers/index.php?pid=715 (accessed March 17, 2016).
6. The organization's name was initially the National Committee for a Free Europe, but it was soon changed to the Free Europe Committee. For the sake of simplicity, I will refer to it only as the Free Europe Committee or FEC.
7. A. Ross Johnson, *Radio Free Europe and Radio Liberty: The CIA Years and Beyond* (Washington, DC: Woodrow Wilson Center Press, 2010), 15.
8. The idea of a crusade had been part of the US approach to Russia since even before the 1917 Revolution. See David S. Foglesong, *The American Mission and the "Evil Empire": The Crusade for a Free Russia since 1881* (New York: Cambridge University Press, 2007).
9. For a comparison of CIA funding versus donations, see Richard H. Cummings, *Radio Free Europe's "Crusade for Freedom": Rallying Americans behind Cold War Broadcasting, 1950–1960* (Jefferson, NC: McFarland, 2010), 217–218.
10. Wendy D. Wall, *Inventing the American Way: The Politics of Consensus from the New Deal to the Civil Rights Movement* (Oxford: Oxford University Press, 2008), 272; Wendy Melillo, *How McGruff and the Crying Indian Changed America: A History of Iconic Ad Council Campaigns* (Washington, DC: Smithsonian Books, 2013), 87–102.
11. For an overview, see Cummings, *Radio Free Europe's "Crusade for Freedom."*
12. Arch Puddington, *Broadcasting Freedom: The Cold War Triumph of Radio Free Europe and Radio Liberty* (Lexington: University of Kentucky Press, 2000), 22. Also quoted in Wall, *Inventing the American Way*, 272.

13. All quotes from the speech are in Dwight D. Eisenhower, "The Crusade for Freedom: Truth, Our Most Formidable Weapon," *Vital Speeches of the Day* 16, no. 24 (1950): 746–747. For an analysis of the speech, see Martin J. Medhurst, "Eisenhower and the Crusade for Freedom: The Rhetorical Origins of a Cold War Campaign," *Presidential Studies Quarterly* 27, no. 4 (Fall 1997): 646–661.
14. Cummings, *Radio Free Europe's "Crusade for Freedom,"* 30.
15. Thomas Winship, "'Crusade for Freedom' Petitions Draw Area Signatures," *Washington Post*, October 3, 1950.
16. Cummings, *Radio Free Europe's "Crusade for Freedom,"* 46 (amount raised), 114 (quote).
17. Free Europe Committee, *The Story of the World Freedom Bell* (Minneapolis: NL Crabtree: 1952).
18. Drew Middleton, "Berlin Dedicates the Freedom Bell," *New York Times*, October 25, 1950.
19. Advertising Council, *Help Truth Fight Communism: Radio Free Europe, Radio Free Asia* (New York: n.p., 1951).
20. Wall, *Inventing the American Way*, 275. Ad pictured in Cummings, *Radio Free Europe's "Crusade for Freedom,"* 93. Among its placements, the ad was published in the business section of the *New York Times* on December 5, 1952 (it takes up about one-third of a page).
21. Wall, *Inventing the American Way*, 275.
22. On Iron Curtain "escapes" in the American media, see Carruthers, *Cold War Captives*, 59–97.
23. "Czechs Tell Story of Flight by Train," *New York Times*, September 16, 1951; "A Red Train Jumps Off Party Line," *Life*, September 24, 1951, 39–41; Tara Zahra, *The Great Departure: Mass Migration from Eastern Europe and the Making of the Free World* (New York: Norton, 2016), 217–219.
24. "Czechs Tell Story of Flight by Train."
25. Cummings, *Radio Free Europe's "Crusade for Freedom,"* 69.
26. American immigration policies made it very difficult for East European refugees to obtain US visas. Carruthers, *Cold War Captives*, 79–81.
27. "Czech Casey Jones Here to Be Citizen," *New York Times*, November 20, 1951.
28. Victor Salvatore, "Freedom Train Plot of Czechs Took 6 Months," *Washington Post*, November 26, 1951.
29. Konvalinka took the train in part so that he could leave with his wife and two young children, who would have had a more difficult time sneaking over the border than three teenagers. "A Pact with Pavel," *Time*, October 22, 1951, 38.
30. Cummings, *Radio Free Europe's "Crusade for Freedom,"* 64.
31. Ibid., 110.
32. Ibid., 124–128.
33. Anna Mazurkiewicz, "'Join or Die': The Road to Cooperation among East European Exiled Political Leaders in the United States," *Polish American Studies* 69, no. 2 (2012): 5–43.

34. Leland Stowe, *Conquest by Terror: The Story of Satellite Europe* (New York: Random House, 1952), x.
35. Ironically, given the content of *Conquest by Terror*, Stowe's career at RFE was cut short when he was unable to get a routine security clearance. More than twenty-five years later, after obtaining his own FBI file via a Freedom of Information Act request, Stowe realized his failure to obtain security clearance was likely due to the fact that he had been investigated by the FBI as a Communist sympathizer, charges Stowe claimed were false and could have easily been disproved. James Gregory Bradsher, "Privacy Act Expungements: A Reconsideration," *Provenance: The Journal of the Society of Georgia Archivists* 6, no. 1 (1988): 12–15.
36. Stowe, *Conquest by Terror*, xiii.
37. Ibid., xiii–xiv.
38. Ibid., 4.
39. Ibid., 48.
40. Ibid., 75.
41. Ibid., 9–10. Later chapters occasionally mentioned attempts to confiscate the property of the bourgeoisie, but this was not a theme of the book. Wendy Wall notes that the Advertising Council campaigns for the Crusade for Freedom also rarely talked about Communism as a set of economic ideas. Wall, *Inventing the American Way*, 276.
42. Stowe, *Conquest by Terror*, 92–93.
43. Leland Stowe, "Russians Rule Satellites by Murder, Terror Methods," *Washington Post*, July 28, 1952; "Russian System of Control Rests on Vast Spy Network," *Washington Post*, July 29, 1952; "Fifteen Million Workers in Shackles," *Washington Post*, August 2, 1952; and "Eastern Europe Slaves Exceed One Million," *Washington Post*, August 4, 1952.
44. Stowe, "Russians Rule Satellites by Murder."
45. Leland Stowe, "Conquerors Have Nightmares," *Washington Post*, August 8, 1952.
46. Stowe, *Conquest by Terror*, 284–293.
47. Leland Stowe, "Russian Lead in Cold War Explained," *Washington Post*, August 9, 1952.
48. Johnson, *Radio Free Europe*, 17–22.
49. On the relationship between RFE and exiles, see Kind-Kovács, "Voices, Letters, and Literature through the Iron Curtain."
50. Puddington, *Broadcasting Freedom*, 24–30.
51. For most of the period considered here, these reports came out biweekly or monthly. Program planning reviews from 1951 to 1956 in Hoover Institution Archives (henceforth HIA), Stanford, CA (HIA), RFE-corporate, box 194.
52. RFE handbook (undated, probably 1951), HIA, Arch Puddington Collection, box 2.
53. On cultivating objectivity as a form of propaganda, see Nicholas J. Schlosser, "Creating an 'Atmosphere of Objectivity': Radio in the American Sector, Objectivity and the United States' Propaganda Campaign against the German Democratic Republic, 1945–1961," *German History* 29, no. 4 (2011): 610–627.

54. On how VOA tried to present the truth of America to its global audience, see Belmonte, *Selling the American Way*.
55. Review of Hungarian programs from June 22, 1951, HIA, RFE-corporate, box 194, 3.
56. Quote from a review of RFE production for July 15–July 31, 1953, C5, H6. See also the review of Hungarian desk production for the week ending June 8, 1951, the review of RFE production from March 27 to April 9, 1952, and other reports in HIA, RFE-corporate, box 194.
57. Script from "Other Side of the Coin (Czech/Slovak Version)," August 18, 1953, HIA, RFE-broadcast, reel 46a.
58. Script from "Other Side of the Coin (Czech/Slovak Version)," May 29, 1951, HIA, RFE-broadcast, reel 46a.
59. Script of Special Commentary by Paul Tigrid, February 25, 1952, HIA, RFE-corporate, box 276.
60. At the Hoover Institution Archives, I was able to read scripts from programs broadcast by the Czechoslovak, Polish, and Romanian services and internal policy documents that additionally covered Hungarian- and Bulgarian-language broadcasts.
61. Script of "Inside Romania #23," October 9, 1952, HIA, RFE-corporate, box 180, 1.
62. Script from "Other Side of the Coin (Polish Version)," July 16, 1952, HIA, RFE-broadcast, reel 8b.
63. Review of RFE production for the period March 27, 1952–April 9, 1952, HIA, REF-corporate, box 194.
64. Script for "Romanian Independence Day," by L. Romanos, May 10, 1952, HIA, RFE-corporate, box 180.
65. Script from "Other Side of the Coin (Polish Version)," May 18, 1952, HIA, RFE-broadcast, reel 8b.
66. Script from "Communist Police #2," February 6, 1951, HIA, RFE-corporate, box 180, 2.
67. Review of Hungarian desk for the week ending August 17, 1951, HIA, RFE-corporate, box 194, 5.
68. This did not prevent some McCarthyites from suspecting some RFE staffers (like Ferdinand Peroutka and Hubert Ripka) of being "crypto-Communists." Puddington, *Broadcasting Freedom*, 82–88.
69. Review of Hungarian desk for the week ending August 17, 1951.
70. Radio Free Europe Policies, 1950–1956, HIA, RFE-corporate, box 288, 1.
71. Review of RFE production for the period January 31, 1952–February 13, 1952, HIA, RFE-corporate, box 288, 2.
72. Review of RFE production for the period January 4–January 18, 1952, HIA, RFE-corporate, box 288, 2.
73. Czechoslovak guidance of February 14, 1952, HIA, RFE-corporate, microprint box 2.

74. Czechoslovak guidance of May 17, 1951, HIA, RFE-corporate, microprint box 2.
75. Script from "Communist Police #2," 4.
76. Memo from Lewis Galantiere to Mihai Farcasanu, June 13, 1952, HIA, RFE-corporate, box 180, 2.
77. Radio Free Europe Policies, 1950–1956, 2.
78. Czechoslovak guidance of June 23, 1953, HIA, RFE-corporate, microprint box 2.
79. RFE's Hungarian desk was roundly criticized for irresponsible coverage in 1956 that might have given false hope to the revolutionaries. While historians have debated whether it really did so, the fiasco was a turning point for RFE. Johanna Granville, "'Caught with Jam on Our Fingers': Radio Free Europe and the Hungarian Revolution of 1956," *Diplomatic History* 29, no. 5 (2005): 811–839; Johnson, *Radio Free Europe*, 91–118.
80. "Text of Truman's Speech at Arlington," *Washington Post*, December 22, 1949.
81. Later, the term would also be used in connection with Asia.
82. On "gulag consciousness" in 1950s American culture, see Carruthers, *Cold War Captives*, 98–135.
83. Charles King, "Happy Captive Nations Week!," *Slate*, July 24, 2014 http://www.slate.com/articles/news_and_politics/history/2014/07/captive_nations_week_an_annual_commemoration_of_a_weird_cold_war_artifact.single.html (accessed March 16, 2016).
84. Script from "Other Side of the Coin (Polish Version), April 11, 1952, HIA, RFE-corporate, reel 8b.
85. Dulles, "A Policy for Boldness."
86. "Freeing the Satellites," *Washington Post*, August 28, 1952.
87. On the limits of this policy, see Tudda, "'Reenacting the Story of Tantalus,'" and Foglesong, *The American Mission*, 108–127.
88. "Goal of Freeing Satellite Lands Restated by U.S.," *New York Times*, December 31, 1955.
89. King, "Happy Captive Nations Week!"
90. "Exiles from Soviet Bloc Proclaim Principles for a Liberated Europe," *New York Times*, February 12, 1951.
91. The ACEN existed until 1989. On its founding, see Mazurkiewicz, "'Join or Die.'"
92. Letter from Philip Vaudrin to Czesław Miłosz, March 14, 1952, Yale University Beinecke Library, Czesław Miłosz Collection, box 5.
93. Letter from Philip Vaudrin to Czesław Miłosz, June 2, 1952, Yale University Beinecke Library, Czesław Miłosz Collection, box 5. A short essay from the book was published in French, German, and Italian in 1952 as *The Great Temptation: The Tragedy of Intellectuals in the People's Democracies*: Czesław Miłosz, *La grande tentation: Le drame des intellectuels dans les démocraties populaires* (Paris: Societé des éditions des Amis de la liberté, 1952); Czesław Miłosz, *Die grosse Versuchung die Tragödie der Intellektuellen in den Volksdemokratien* (Berlin: Kongreß f. kulturelle

Freiheit, 1952); Czesław Miłosz, *La grande tentazione: Il dramma degli intellettuali nelle democrazie popolari* (Rome: Associazione italiana per la libertà della cultura, 1952). All of these editions were sponsored by the anti-Communist Congress for Cultural Freedom, a CIA-funded organization.

94. Letter from Philip Vaudrin to Czesław Miłosz, July 16, 1952, Yale University Beinecke Library, Czesław Miłosz Collection, box 5.
95. Leonard Nathan and Arthur Quinn, *The Poet's Work: An Introduction to Czesław Miłosz* (Cambridge, MA: Harvard University Press, 1991), 38–40.
96. Letter from Philip Vaudrin to Czesław Miłosz, October 5, 1954, Yale University Beinecke Library, Czesław Miłosz Collection, box 5.
97. Miłosz implied that Beta's suicide was the result of his disillusionment with the regime, but this was only speculation. Czesław Miłosz, *The Captive Mind*, trans. Jane Zielonko (New York: Vintage, 1990), 134.
98. Ibid., 80.
99. Ibid., 61–64.
100. Ibid., 55.
101. Ibid., 80.
102. Peter Viereck, "Red Roots for the Uprooted," *New York Times Book Review*, June 7, 1953, 6.
103. Edwin D. Gritz, "The Perversion of Men's Minds," *Washington Post*, June 7, 1953.
104. Letter from Philip Vaudrin to Czesław Miłosz, June 12, 1953, Yale University Beinecke Library, Czesław Miłosz Collection, box 5.
105. William P. Clancy, "The Fatal Payment," *Commonweal* 13 (1953): 328–330.
106. Dwight MacDonald, "In the Land of Diamat," *New Yorker*, November 9, 1953, 173–182.
107. Ewa Czarnecka and Alexander Fiut, *Conversations with Czesław Miłosz*, trans. Richard Lourie (New York: Harcourt Brace, 1987), 144–147; Robert Faggen, Andrzej Walicki, Irena Grudzinska-Gross, Adam Michnik, and Edith Kurzweil, "The Captive Mind," *Partisan Review* 66, no. 1 (1999): 49–69.
108. Daniel Bell, "Paper Curtain," *Saturday Review*, July 11, 1953, 33; Czesław Miłosz, *A Year of the Hunter*, trans. Madeline G. Levine (New York: Farrar, Strauss and Giroux, 1995), 147.
109. Letter from Miłosz to Radio Free Europe, December 14, 1953, Yale University Beinecke Library, Czesław Miłosz Collection, box 52.
110. Faggen et al., "The Captive Mind."
111. Item 4863/54, "The Dilemma of Polish Engineers: For or Against the West?" June 11, 1954, Open Society Archives, Budapest, Hungary (henceforth OSA), fond 3-1-2, reel 39.
112. Grabowski also spent much of his time in Berlin and Munich consulting with RFE researchers and reading their materials. Dr. Z. Grabowski, "Report on a Visit to Poland," November 9, 1954, BBC Written Archives Centre, Caversham Park, Reading, UK (henceforth, BBC WAC), E3/84/7 OS Audience Research, Poland, File 7, 1954.

113. Miłosz, *Captive Mind*, 16–18, passim.
114. Siegfried Kracauer and Paul L. Berkman, *Satellite Mentality: Political Attitudes and Propaganda Susceptibilities of Non-Communists in Hungary, Poland and Czechoslovakia* (New York: Praeger, 1956), 4, also front matter (unpaginated).
115. A summary report from 1953 ("Political Attitudes and Propaganda Susceptibilities of non-Communists in Hungary, Poland and Czechoslovakia") is in NARA, RG 59, Department of State, US International Information Administration/International Broadcasting, Voice of America Historical Files, 1946–1953, box 18.
116. István Rév, "The Unnoticed Continuity: The Prehistory of the Hungarian Refugee Interview Project," Open Society Archive website, http://w3.osaarchivum.org/digitalarchive/blinken/The_Unnoticed_Continuity.pdf (accessed June 28, 2016).
117. Kracauer and Berkman, *Satellite Mentality*, 6–7.
118. István Rév, "Just Noise? The Impact of RFE in Hungary," in *Cold War Broadcasting: Impact on the Soviet Union and Eastern Europe*, ed. A. Ross Johnson and R. Eugene Parta (Budapest: Central European University Press, 2010), 240–243; and István Rév, *Retroactive Justice: A Prehistory of Post-Communism* (Stanford, CA: Stanford University Press, 2005), 266.
119. Kracauer and Berkman, *Satellite Mentality*, 6.
120. "Selected Hypotheses Bearing on the Situation in Poland, Czechoslovakia, and Hungary," Records of the Columbia Bureau of Applied Social Research, Columbia University Special Collections, box 32, 6.
121. Kracauer and Berkman, *Satellite Mentality*, 35. Terms like "thought control" do not appear in the interview transcripts. On American fascination with Communist "brainwashing," see Rév, "The Unnoticed Continuity," and Carruthers, *Cold War Captives*, 174–216.
122. Kracauer and Berkman, *Satellite Mentality*, 37.
123. Ibid., 90.
124. Ibid., 102.
125. Ibid., 10–11.
126. Ibid., 13–14.
127. Ibid., 142. Kracauer and Berkman do not cite Arendt, but the influence is patent in this characterization (the book has few citations in any event).
128. Ibid., 125–143.
129. Ibid., 15.

CHAPTER 4

1. Item 1078, "Persecution and Police," June 23, 1951, OSA, fond 300-1-2, reel 1. When I first took notes on the collection of RFE items, they existed only on microfilm or, occasionally, on paper. Since then, the collection has been put online on the Open Society Archive website (www.osaarchivum.org). When giving citations for the materials I consulted on microfilm, I note the archive as

"OSA" and give the fond and reel or box number. For Items I consulted online, I note the archive as "OSA online" and give the online document number.
2. As an additional complication, researchers were sometimes paid by the Item and some apparently submitted completely false reports in order to receive a check. Rév, *Retroactive Justice*, 265–266.
3. Some of these translations were sent to RFE's New York office or to other news or intelligence agencies. Some RFE items, for example, were shared with the BBC and remain in its archives. See items in BBC WAC, E3/130, Overseas Audience Research, Eastern Europe, Romania, 1952–1954.
4. Rév, *Retroactive Justice*, 255–266.
5. Item 1078, "Persecution and Police."
6. Although it is not possible to tie individual research reports to particular scripts, the report about the bell fear and the uniform fear, despite being labeled unverifiable and old news, was nonetheless translated into English for use by all of RFE's language services.
7. Selected quotations from this letter (including the ones used here) appeared in Special Report 53, Letters from Czechoslovakia, December 1, 1952, OSA, fond 300-7-7, box 24.
8. Item 4607/54, "Some Comments on Political Mood and Morale in CSR," June 8, 1954, OSA, fond 300-1-2, reel 38; Item 05941/53, "Life and Morale of Czechoslovak People," June 12, 1953, OSA, fond 300-30-2, reel 136.
9. Item 4813, "Secret Police Methods," April 11, 1952, OSA online, 300-1-2-18176.
10. Item 1205, "The Polish Secret Police or so-called Public Security," January 25, 1952, OSA online, 300-1-2-14540.
11. Item 5140/51, August 22, 1951, OSA, fond 300-30-2, reel 136.
12. Item 1273/55, "An Electrician's Political Attitude," February 21, 1955, OSA, fond 300-1-2, reel 50.
13. Item 105036/52, "Secret Police Agents in Sofia," December 6, 1951, OSA online, 300-1-2-28491.
14. "Bulgarian Police System," October 16, 1951, OSA, fond 300-7-4, box 6.
15. Item 01118/53, "Notes on Conditions in Czechoslovakia," February 4, 1953, OSA, fond 300-1-2, reel 19, 5–6.
16. Ibid., 2.
17. Item 06695/53, "Budapest Viewed by a Housewife," June 27, 1953, OSA, fond 300-1-2, reel 25.
18. Item 01116/53, "Odds and Ends from Prague," February 3 1953, OSA, fond 300-1-2, reel 19.
19. Item 1346/55, "Communist Regime in Czechoslovakia Will Fall within Three Years . . . Opinion of a Widow from Prague," February 24, 1955, OSA, fond 300-1-2, reel 50.

20. For a detailed overview, see Krysztof Persak and Łukasz Kamiński, eds., *A Handbook of the Communist Security Apparatus in East Central Europe, 1944–1989* (Warsaw: Institute of National Remembrance, 2005).
21. Antoni Dudek and Andrzej Paczkowski, "Poland," in *Communist Security Apparatus*, ed. Persak and Kamiński, 255.
22. In the case of the East German Stasi in the 1980s (which had the largest network of secret collaborators in the bloc), the number was approximately 1 informer for every 95 inhabitants. Jens Gieseke, "German Democratic Republic," in *Communist Security Apparatus*, ed. Persak and Kamiński, 198–199.
23. Persak and Kamiński, eds., *Communist Security Apparatus*, passim. Lavinia Stan also makes this argument in "Reckoning with the Communist Past in Romania: A Scorecard," *Europe–Asia Studies* 65, no. 1 (2013): 130–131.
24. For example, the range of numbers discussed by Dennis Deletant, "Romania," in *Communist Security Apparatus*, ed. Persak and Kamiński, 316–317.
25. On the interaction between RFE and the listening population, see Pittaway, "The Education of Dissent."
26. Review of Hungarian programs. August 17–25, 1951, HIA, RFE-corporate, box 194, 4. There are many other examples, such as Romania policy guidance 12 (August 14, 1951) about starting a weekly program dedicated to revealing informers. HIA, RFE-corporate, microprint box 2.
27. "Western Broadcasts to Poland: Report on Interrogation of Recent Refugees from Poland," BBC WAC, E3/129 OS Audience Research, Eastern Europe, Poland, 1952–1956.
28. Interview 001, Ryszard Rekowski, August 18, 1951, NARA, Iron Curtain Interviews, box 5, 3.
29. Interview 039, K.A., November 19, 1951, NARA, Iron Curtain Interviews, box 1, 5–6.
30. Given that they were telling VOA that they liked one of its competitors, it is unlikely these comments were made to curry favor with the interviewers.
31. Interview 039, K.A, 1–5.
32. Dudek and Paczkowski, "Poland," 254.
33. Item 02169/53, "Experiences in Budapest," March 5, 1953, OSA, fond 300-1-2, reel 20.
34. Dudek and Paczkowski, "Poland," 254.
35. Katherine Verdery, *Secrets and Truths: Ethnography in the Archive of Romania's Secret Police* (Budapest: CEU Press, 2014), 178–179.
36. Item 00039/53, January 3, 1953, OSA, fond 300-30-2, reel 136.
37. "How People in Poland Spend Their Leisure Time," March 3, 1954, OSA, fond 300-7-2, box 16.
38. Item 15335/52, "Wroclaw Atmosphere," December 13, 1952, OSA, 300-1-2, reel 17.

39. Item 03939/53, "The Present Internal Situation in Bulgaria," April 11, 1953, OSA, fond 300-1-2, reel 22.
40. Item 00951/53, "Scenes from Life in Warsaw," January 30, 1953, OSA, fond 300-1-2, reel 18.
41. Item 7490/53, "Prison for Decent Dress," July 18, 1953, OSA, fond 300-1-2, reel 26; also see Item 1706/53, "Polish Women and Their Wardrobe Worries," February 20, 1953, OSA, fond 300-1-2, reel 19.
42. Item 841/54, "Political Propaganda for the Housewife," January 27, 1954, OSA, fond 300-1-2, reel 33.
43. Item 13494, "A Visit with a People's Educator," November 21, 1952, OSA, fond 300-7-1-3, box 3.
44. Item 6995/54, "General Mood in Czechoslovakia," August 13, 1954, OSA, fond 300-30-2, reel 136.
45. Item 5406/52, "The New Type of Spectators in Polish Theatre," April 28, 1952, OSA, fond 300-1-2, reel 9. This woman's remarks echo the disparaging comments Krakovians made about the muddy boots of workers from Nowa Huta in Lebow, *Unfinished Utopia*, 60.
46. Item 6320/52, "Pity the Old," May 15, 1952, OSA, fond 300-1-2, reel 10.
47. Item 03074/53,"Parents and Children," March 25, 1953, OSA, fond 300-1-2, reel 21.
48. Item 8118/53, "Private Life of a Polish Prep School Boy," August 10, 1953, OSA, fond 300-1-2, reel 27.
49. These fears were also exploited in Voice of America broadcasts. See Belmonte, *Selling the American Way*, 144–147.
50. Item 15298/52, "Living Conditions of a Journalist's Family from Brno," December 12, 1952, OSA, fond 300-1-2, reel 17.
51. Item 3132/52, "Educational Problems of a Non-Communist Father," March 23, 1953, OSA, fond 300-1-2, reel 21.
52. Item 4026/53, "Denmark," April 14, 1953, OSA, fond 300-1-2, reel 22.
53. Item 01567/53, ". . . We Criticized Our Professors," February 17, 1953, OSA online 300-1-2-30957.
54. Bradley F. Abrams, "The Second World War and the East European Revolution," *East European Politics and Societies* 16, no. 3 (2002): 556–559.
55. Connelly, *Captive University*, 126–127, 143–144.
56. Pittaway, *Eastern Europe, 1939–2000*, 92–93. Also Mark Pittaway, "The Reproduction of Hierarchy: Skill, Working-Class Culture, and the State in Early Socialist Hungary," *Journal of Modern History* 74, no. 4 (2002): 737–769.
57. Item 5105/53, "Polish Youth," May 13, 1953, OSA, fond 300-1-2, reel 23.
58. "Czechoslovak Guidance 7," May 3, 1951, HIA, RFE-corporate, box 180.
59. Item 1383/55, "A Communist View of Poland Today," February 24, 1955, OSA, fond 300-1-2, reel 50. Some RFE analysts did talk about the need to take young

people seriously and not treat them like confused children, but they did so as a strategy for converting them to anti-Communism.
60. Item 6738/53, "The Daily Life in Zabrze," July 2 1953, OSA, fond 300-1-2, reel 25.
61. The historian Padraic Kenney makes similar observations about the city of Wrocław, in *Rebuilding Poland*.
62. Interview 033, Jerzy Wierzbowski, October 15, 1951, NARA, Iron Curtain Interviews, box 5, 4.
63. Item 1957/53, "A Young Hairdresser Tells about Life and Work in Vansdorf [sic]," February 26, 1953, OSA, fond 300-1-2, reel 19.
64. Interview 094, Wladyslaw Tomczynski, December 12, 1951, NARA, Iron Curtain Interviews, box 3, 1–4.
65. Questionnaire: IPOR Survey Study (Polish version), Columbia University Special Collections, Bureau of Applied Social Research Collection, box 32, 9. This Polish version was the only copy of the interview questionnaire I found, but it is clear from the interview transcripts that similar questions were asked of Czech, Slovak, and Hungarian respondents as well.
66. Interview 032, B.T., November 7, 1951, NARA, Iron Curtain Interviews, box 1, 10.
67. Interview 036, Mrs. I.K., November 19, 1951, NARA, Iron Curtain Interviews, box 1, 14.
68. Interview 042, J.R., November 19, 1951, NARA, Iron Curtain Interviews, box 4, 20.
69. Interview 043, J.M., November 21, 1951, NARA, Iron Curtain Interviews, box 4, 21.
70. Interview 044, J.D., November 23, 1951, NARA, Iron Curtain Interviews, box 4, 1 and 20–21.
71. Interview 029, J.Z., November 6, 1951, NARA, Iron Curtain Interviews, box 2, 26.
72. Interview 069, V.K, January 7, 1952, NARA, Iron Curtain Interviews, box 2, 17.
73. Interview 049, S.L., December 11, 1951, NARA, Iron Curtain Interviews, box 1, 25.
74. It was much more likely for there to be no answer to this question at all than for the respondent to say friendship had not changed. A few respondents from small villages remarked that in their insulated communities people treated each other as before, but this was a rare response.
75. Interview 038, I.V., November 15, 1951, NARA, Iron Curtain Interviews, box 1, 15.
76. Ibid., 5–6.
77. Columbia University Bureau of Applied Social Research, *Listening to the Voice of America and Other Foreign Broadcasts in Czechoslovakia* (New York: Bureau of Applied Social Research, 1954), 5.
78. Ibid., 4. The bureau's other reports noted similar tactics elsewhere. For Poland, see also Machcewicz, *Poland's War on Radio Free Europe*, 45–81.
79. Columbia University Bureau of Applied Social Research, *Listening to the Voice of America and Other Foreign Broadcasts in Romania* (New York: Bureau of Applied Social Research, 1954), 3.

80. Columbia University Bureau of Applied Social Research, *Listening to the Voice of America and Other Foreign Broadcasts in Poland* (New York: Bureau of Applied Social Research, 1954), 6.

81. Columbia University Bureau of Applied Social Research, *Listening to the Voice of America and Other Foreign Broadcasts in the Soviet Satellites* (New York: Bureau of Applied Social Research, 1954), 10–11. Unlike the later analysis in Kracauer and Berkman, *Satellite Mentality*, this first set of reports included data from Romania and Bulgaria. The transcripts from those Romanian and Bulgarian interviews, however, were not preserved with the others in the US National Archives and Records Administration.

82. Columbia University Bureau of Applied Social Research, *Listening to the Voice of America and Other Foreign Broadcasts in Poland*, 17.

83. Columbia University Bureau of Applied Social Research, *Listening to the Voice of America and Other Foreign Broadcasts in the Soviet Satellites*, 6.

84. Interview 049, S.L., 9.

85. Plamper, "Beyond Binaries."

86. Interview 031, Jerzy Szopa, October 11, 1951, NARA, Iron Curtain Interviews, box 5, 3.

87. Interview 049, S.L., 24–25.

88. Interview 041, Zygmunt Machinowski, October 20, 1951, NARA, Iron Curtain Interviews, box 5, 9.

89. Interview 029, Jezef Wrobel, October 10, 1951, NARA, Iron Curtain Interviews, box 5, 7.

90. Item 4530/52, "Old Tunes and Vodka—to Remember the Past," April 2, 1952, OSA, fond 300-1-2, reel 7. Similar comments about Bulgaria appear in Item 3050/53, "They Speak," March 26, 1953, OSA, fond 300-1-2, reel 21.

91. Item 9574/56, "What People Talk about in Czechoslovakia," October 15, 1956, OSA fond 300-30-2, reel 46.

92. Item 93/54, "Lowering of Moral Standards in Poland," January 10, 1954, OSA, fond 300-1-2, reel 32. A similar example for Czechoslovakia is Item 2765/54, "Life in Košice Today," April 3, 1954, OSA, fond 300-1-2, reel 26.

93. Item 174, February 7, 1952 OSA, fond 300-30-2, reel 136.

94. Report for the Deputy of the Minister of National Security Col. Prcha, March 7, 1953, ABS, fond VSB, aj. 310-113-1.

95. A number of historians have written about drinking as a form of leisure during the Stalinist period. For example, Lebow, *Unfinished Utopia*, 139–142, and Sándor Horvath, "Alltag in Sztálinvaros: Die 'Zivilisierten' und die 'Wilden' in der ersten Stadt Ungarns," in *Sozialgeschichtliche Kommunismusforschung: Tschechoslowakei, Polen, Ungarn und DDR, 1948–1968*, ed. Christiane Brenner and Peter Heumos (Munich: R. Oldenbourg, 2005), 505–526.

96. Interview 036, Zygmunt Ostrowski, October 17, 1951, NARA, Iron Curtain Interviews, box 5, 2 and 9.
97. Item 11479/53, "Spying for the ZMP," November 13, 1953, OSA, fond 300-1-2, reel 30.
98. Item 00930/53, "The Queue," January 28, 1953, OSA, fond 300-1-2, reel 18.
99. Item 03939/53, "The Present Internal Situation in Bulgaria," April 11, 1953, OSA, fond 300-1-2, reel 22.

CHAPTER 5

1. Interview 032, B.T., November 7, 1951, NARA, Iron Curtain Interviews, box 1, 4.
2. Kracauer and Berkman, *Satellite Mentality*, 158.
3. Ibid.
4. "Refugees Give Assorted Interpretations of Life in Communist Bulgaria," February 10, 1953, OSA, fond 300-7-4, box 7.
5. Item 6014/56, "Terror in Bucharest," June 14, 1956, OSA, fond 300-1-2, reel 70.
6. Radio Free Europe Policies, 1950–1956, HIA, RFE-corporate, box 288, 1. For a more detailed exposition of this argument, see chapter 3.
7. Item 2451/54, "How Gottwaldov's Population Is Waiting for Liberation," April 3, 1954, OSA, fond 300-30-2, reel 136, 3.
8. Ibid., 2.
9. He claimed the police had tried to confiscate his father's grain. Interview 016, Janos (Tokar) Jasko, September 17–18, 1951, NARA, Iron Curtain Interviews, box 1, 2.
10. Ibid., 11.
11. Ibid., 15.
12. Ibid., 16. The interviewers specifically asked about the respondent's views of the United Nations.
13. Interview 010, L.J., November 12, 1951, 11.
14. Interview 024, X.Y., October 20, 1951, NARA, Iron Curtain Interviews, box 1, 14.
15. Kracauer and Berkman, *Satellite Mentality*, 13–14.
16. Item 1531/55, "Attitude and Research Interview," February 28, 1955, OSA, fond 300-1-2, reel 50.
17. Interview 007, Stanislaw Mitkowski, August 25–26, 1951, NARA, Iron Curtain Interviews, box 5.
18. Interview 060, P.H., December 28, 1951, NARA, Iron Curtain Interviews, box 1, 22.
19. Interview 038, I.V., November 15, 1951, NARA, Iron Curtain Interviews, box 1, 15.
20. Interview with 050, D.Sz., December 14, 1951, box 1, 2.
21. Interview 043, I.H., December 3, 1951, NARA, Iron Curtain Interviews, box 1, 3.
22. Interview 055, O.P., December 21–22, 1951, NARA, Iron Curtain Interviews, box 2.

23. Interview 083, Jan Osiewicz, December 6, 1951, Berlin, NARA, Iron Curtain Interviews, box 3, 12.
24. Abrams, "The Second World War and the East European Revolutions," 623–664; Jan T. Gross, "The Social Consequences of War: Preliminaries of the Study of the Imposition of Communist Regimes in East-Central Europe," *East European Politics and Societies* 3, no. 2 (1989): 198–214.
25. Interview 086, Stefan Birlet, December 7, 1951, NARA, Iron Curtain Interviews, box 3, 17.
26. I did not read another interview that specifically mentioned the number of Polish deaths from the Second World War.
27. Interview 002, Z.H., September 18, 1951, NARA, Iron Curtain Interviews, box 1, 8.
28. Item 2516/54, "Opinions on the International Political Situation," April 3, 1954, OSA, fond 300-1-2, reel 36, 1.
29. Interview 022, Jaroslav Salivar, NARA, Iron Curtain Interviews, box 4, 49.
30. Item 3484/51, "Czechoslovakia: Morals and General Mood," July 20, 1951, OSA, fond 300-30-2, reel 141.
31. Joanna Bourke, *Fear: A Cultural History* (Emeryville, CA: Shoemaker and Hoard, 2006), 255–285. American reactions to the atomic bomb were not always consistent during this period: there was a complicated mix of fear and nonchalance, so that fear rarely translated into political action. See Paul Boyer, *By the Bomb's Early Light: American Thought and Culture at the Dawn of the Atomic Age* (Chapel Hill: University of North Carolina Press, 1994); and Laura McEnaney, *Civil Defense Begins at Home* (Princeton, NJ: Princeton University Press, 2000).
32. Item 2734/52, February 1952, OSA, fond 300-1-2, reel 7.
33. Item 2472/52, "Bulgaria: Communist Propaganda," February 22, 1952, OSA, fond 300-1-2, reel 7.
34. For example, Interview 065, K.J, January 2, 1952, NARA, Iron Curtain Interviews, box 2, or Interview 082, Mieczyslaw Surowiecki, December 4, 1951, or Interview 030, Marian Stefanski, October 10, 1951, NARA, Iron Curtain Interviews, box 3.
35. Item 5782/54, "A Czech Discusses Present Day Political Problems," July 7, 1954, OSA, fond 300-30-2, reel 141.
36. Item 4677/56, "A British Woman's Experiences as Housewife in Prague," May 5, 1956, OSA, fond 300-30-2, reel 136.
37. Interview 084, Boguslawa Smolka-Bauer, December 5–6, 1951, 14; Kracauer and Berkman, *Satellite Mentality*, 164–166, also note this trend.
38. Item 2865/54, "Popular Opinion as Learned from Conversations with Polish Sailors," April 3, 1954, OSA, fond 300-1-2, reel 36. Numerous interviewees made similar claims. For example, from Czechoslovakia: Item 7085/52, "A Common Laborer's Opinion on World and Home Problems," May 29, 1952, OSA, fond 300-1-2, reel 10.
39. Item 5603/56, "A Young Rumanian Views His Country and the West," June 1, 1956, OSA, fond 300-1-2, reel 69. Another example of this attitude is Item 1459/

54, "A Polish Refugee Eyes the World Around Him," February 17, 1954, OSA, fond 300-1-2, reel 34.
40. Interview 023, N.Z., October 10, 1951, NARA, Iron Curtain Interviews, box 1, 19.
41. Interview 064, M.V, January 2–3, 1952, NARA, Iron Curtain Interviews, box 2, 20.
42. Interview 053, P., December 14, 1951, NARA, Iron Curtain Interviews, box 2, 27.
43. Interview 039, K.A., November 19, 1951, NARA, Iron Curtain Interviews, box 1, 13.
44. Item 1110/55, "Source's Attitude to Various Problems," March 10, 1955, OSA, fond 300-1-2, reel 49.
45. Item 6431/56, "Audience Analysis Interview with a Sculptor," June 26, 1956, OSA, fond 300-1-2, reel 70, 16.
46. Item 15580/52, December 20, 1952, OSA, fond 300-30-2, reel 136,
47. Item 6995/54, "General Mood in Czechoslovakia," August 13, 1954, OSA, fond 300-30-2, reel 136.
48. Interview 049, S.L., December 11, 1951, NARA, Iron Curtain Interviews, box 1, 9–10.
49. Interview 001, Hungarian, September 14–15, 1951, NARA, Iron Curtain Interviews, box 1, 9.
50. Item 4160/53, "People Believe in American Flying Discs," April 17, 1953, OSA, fond 300-1-2, reel 22.
51. Item 3982/54, "Life in the Kilian György Apprentices Home," April 10, 1954, OSA, fond 300-1-2, reel 36.
52. Interview 022, S.M., October 8, 1951, NARA, Iron Curtain Interviews, box 1, 12.
53. Interview 082, Mieczyslaw Surowiecki, 16.
54. John Grenville and Bernard Wasserstein, eds., *The Major International Treaties of the Twentieth Century* (London: Routledge, 2013), 514–515.
55. Ilya Ehrenburg, *Speech Delivered to the World Council of Peace, Vienna Session, November 23–28th, 1953* (World Council of Peace, 1953), 12–13, 19.
56. Item 6755/52, "Bulgarian Opinion about the Armament of the Germans," May 24, 1952, OSA, fond 300-1-2, reel 10.
57. German troops also occupied Hungary in March 1944, when the Hungarian government threatened to switch sides and join the Allies. But although a pro-German prime minister was installed, the Germans did not set up their own occupation administration in Hungary.
58. Slovakia became an independent country allied with Germany for the duration of the war.
59. On the Czech borderlands, see Eagle Glassheim, *Cleansing the Czechoslovak Borderlands: Migration, Environment, and Health in the Former Sudetenland* (Pittsburgh: Pittsburgh University Press, 2016).
60. Item 3640/54, "Mood and Morale in Slovakia," May 6, 1954, OSA, fond 300-1-2, reel 37.
61. Item 4262/1952, "Public Opinion in Prague about Rearmament of Western Germany," March 31, 1952, OSA, fond 300-1-2, reel 8.

62. The source did not elaborate, but was probably referring to farms collectivized or property nationalized. Item 10117/52, "Public Opinion in Czechoslovakia Described by a Refugee," August 7, 1952, OSA, fond 300-1-2, reel 8.
63. Items 4260, 4261, 4262, 4263, 4264, 4265, 4266 (all March 1952), OSA, fond 300-1-2, reel 8.
64. Item 7085/52, "A Common Laborer's Opinion on World and Home Problems," May 29, 1952, OSA, fond 300-1-2, reel 10.
65. Item 5781/52, "Public Opinion about Rearmament of Western Germany," May 3, 1952, OSA online, 300-1-2-19146.
66. For example, Item 2865/54, "Popular Opinion as Learned from Conversations with Polish Sailors," April 3, 1954, OSA, fond 300-1-2, reel 36.
67. Item 326/56, "Small Town in the Poznan Voivodship," January 12, 1956, OSA online, 300-1-2-66308.
68. In several interviews, refugees mentioned they had planned to join the "Polish army in the West": Interview 001, Ryszard Rekowski, August 18, 1951, NARA, Iron Curtain Interviews, box 5, 9, Interview 002, Tadeusz Zielinski, August 22, 1951; and Interview 004, Wlodimierz Malekowicz, August 20, 1952. Also in NARA, Iron Curtain Interviews, box 5.
69. On life for Polish refugees see, in addition to the preceding note, Interview 080, Mieczyslaw Ghylinski, December 4, 1951; Interview 086, Stefan Birlet, December 7, 1951; and Interview 087, Antoni Twardzik, December 7, 1951, NARA, Iron Curtain Interviews, box 3. Also Zahra, *The Great Departure*, 236–240.
70. Interview 008, K.J., October 31, 1951, NARA, Iron Curtain Interviews, box 1, 2.
71. Interview 024, X.Y., 2.
72. Interview 088, Bogumil Bryda, December 7-9, 1951, NARA, Iron Curtain Interview, box 3, 3–5.
73. Kracauer and Berkman, *Satellite Mentality*, 111–115.
74. Interview 094, Wladyslaw Tomczynski, December 12, 1951, NARA, Iron Curtain Interviews, box 3, 17.
75. Kracauer and Berkman, *Satellite Mentality*, 155–156.
76. Interview 036, Mrs. I.K., November 19, 1951, NARA, Iron Curtain Interviews, box 1, 15.
77. Interview 029, J.Z, November 6, 1951, NARA, Iron Curtain Interviews, box 4, 28.
78. Interview 007, L.P., October 8, 1951, NARA, Iron Curtain Interviews, box 2, 21. Also cited in Kracauer and Berkman, *Satellite Mentality*, 156.
79. Interview 002, Tadeusz Zielinski, August 22, 1951, NARA, Iron Curtain Interviews, box 5, 10.
80. This was clear to VOA's own analysts at the time. See Columbia University Bureau of Applied Social Research, *Listening to the Voice of America and Other Foreign Broadcasts in the Soviet Satellites*, 14.

81. Interview 033, T.B., November 8, 1951, NARA, Iron Curtain Interviews, box 1, 1–8.
82. Interview 036, Zygmunt Ostrowski, October 17, 1951, NARA, Iron Curtain Interviews, box 3, 3–6.
83. Item 4219/54, "Current Topics and How the Czechs Feel about Them, According to a KNV Official," June 2, 1954, OSA, fond 300-1-2, reel 38.
84. Item 1531/55, "Attitude and Research Interview," 9.
85. Item 3882/56, "A Bulgarian Physician Answers the Audience Analysis Schedule," April 14, 1956, OSA, fond 300-1-2, reel 67.
86. Item 5684/56, "Audience Analysis Interview with a Mechanic," June 4, 1956, OSA, fond 300-1-2, reel 69, 12.
87. Item 6570/56, "Audience Analysis Interview with a Peasant Lad," June 28, 1956, OSA, fond 300-1-2, reel 70, 5.
88. "A Polish Refugee Eyes the World Around Him."
89. She was not an émigré, but a traveler who would return to Poland. Item 3913/56, "Poland after Bierut's Death," April 16, 1956, OSA, fond 300-1-2, reel 67. This respondent was quite critical of Polish émigré leaders in London.
90. De-Stalinization began in Poland before 1956, but that year was nevertheless a turning point. On the events of 1956 in Poland, see Paweł Machcewicz, *Rebellious Satellite: Poland, 1956*, trans. Maya Latynski, (Washington, DC: Woodrow Wilson Center Press, 2009).
91. Item 11364/56, "An Optimist's View of Poland's Future," December 20, 1956, OSA, fond 300-1-2, reel 76.
92. László Borhi, *Hungary in the Cold War, 1945–1956: Between the United States and the Soviet Union* (Budapest: Central European University Press, 2004), 243–268.
93. Ibid., 281.
94. Johanna Granville presents compelling evidence for RFE's influence, in "'Caught with Jam on Our Fingers.'"
95. "Policy Review of Voice for Free Hungary Programming, October 23–November 23, 1956," December 5, 1956, National Security Archive website, "The 1956 Hungarian Revolution: A History in Documents," http://www2.gwu.edu/~nsarchiv/NSAEBB/NSAEBB76/doc10.pdf (accessed December 29, 2016) (quote on 22).
96. "Radio Listening and Related Topics (Hungary): L & R Unit Report #245/B-1775," January 19, 1960, NARA, RG 306, US Information Agency, entry A1 1047, Foreign Service Dispatches, compiled 1954–1965, box 6, 2.
97. Item 11068/56, "We Shall Be Liberated Only When Communism Disappears in Russia," December 18, 1956, OSA, fond 300-1-2, reel 76.
98. "Refugees Give Assorted Interpretations of Life in Communist Bulgaria."
99. This is true even in Hungary, despite the failed revolution of 1956. It could easily be argued that by the 1970s, the Kádár regime had created the most livable form of socialism in the region.

CHAPTER 6

1. Interview 002, Z.H., September 15, 1951, NARA, Iron Curtain Interviews, box 1, 4.
2. Ibid.
3. Ibid., 7.
4. These stories did coexist with tales of exploitation and poverty awaiting migrants to the United States. Zahra, *The Great Departure*, 32–34.
5. Belmonte, *Selling the American Way*, 116–135.
6. For an insightful analysis of the effects of this economic disparity, see Kate Brown, *Plutopia: Nuclear Families, Atomic Cities, and the Great Soviet and American Plutonium Disasters* (New York: Oxford University Press, 2013).
7. All quotations in this paragraph are from Leland Stowe, "Conquest by Terror: Hunger Is a Political Weapon," *Washington Post*, July 31, 1952.
8. Item 10478/52, "Everyday Life of a Middle-Class Family in Budapest," August 16, 1952, OSA online, 300-1-2-23898.
9. Item 12152/52, "Standard of Living in the R.P.R.," September 19, 1952, OSA online, 300-1-2-25584.
10. "Everyday Life of a Middle-Class Family in Budapest."
11. "Standard of Living in the R.P.R."
12. For example, Item 5996/53, "The Food Situation Before the Currency Reform," June 11, 1953, OSA online, 300-1-2-35429.
13. Item 02762/53, "The Life of a Worker in Poland," March 17, 1953, OSA, fond 300-1-2, reel 21.
14. The Voice of America emphasized American prosperity in its broadcasts around the world. Belmonte, *Selling the American Way*, 116–135.
15. Interview 016, Janos (Tokar) Jasko, September 17–18, 1951, NARA, Iron Curtain Interviews, box 1, 3.
16. Ibid.
17. Scholars like Kracauer and Berkman acknowledged the problems of taking the refugee experience to represent the whole, but then they did it anyway. Kracauer and Berkman, *Satellite Mentality*, 6.
18. Lebow, *Unfinished Utopia*, 44–55 (quote on 55).
19. Leland Stowe, "Conquest by Terror: Fifteen Million Workers in Shackles," *Washington Post*, August 2, 1952.
20. Interview 094, Wladyslaw Tomczynski, December 12, 1951, NARA, Iron Curtain Interviews, box 3, 3.
21. Script from "Other Side of the Coin (Czech/Slovak Version)," May 29, 1951, HIA, RFE broadcast collection, reel 46a.
22. Interview 094, Wladyslaw Tomczynski, 6.
23. Interview 053, P., December 14, 1951, NARA, Iron Curtain Interviews, box 2, 5.
24. Kracauer and Berkman also noted this phenomenon, in *Satellite Mentality*, 38.
25. Interview 008, K.J., October 31, 1951, NARA, Iron Curtain Interviews, box 1, 1.

26. Ibid., 8.
27. Ibid., 7.
28. Ibid., 2.
29. All quotations and references to this interview are from Interview 033, F.P., November 8–9, 1951, NARA, Iron Curtain Interviews, box 4.
30. Interview 084, Boguslawa Smolka-Bauer, December 5–6, 1951, NARA, Iron Curtain Interviews, box 3, 10–11.
31. Item 12217/52, "The Polish Woman," September 19, 1952, OSA, fond 300-7-2, box 17, 1–3.
32. Ibid.
33. Ibid., 4.
34. Helen Laville, "'Our Country Endangered by Underwear': Fashion, Femininity and the Seduction Narrative in *Ninotchka* and *Silk Stockings*," *Diplomatic History* 30, no. 4 (2006): 623–644; Rhiannon Dowling, "Communism, Consumerism and Gender in Early Cold War Film: The Case of *Ninotchka* and *Ruskii vopros*," *Aspasia* 8 (2014): 26–44.
35. "The Polish Woman," 1.
36. As just one example, Eva Maříková, "Zvítězili na časem," *Vlasta* 6, no. 52 (1952): 2.
37. Fidelis, *Women, Communism, and Industrialization*; Lebow, *Unfinished Utopia*, 97–123; Pittaway, *The Workers' State*, esp. 144–173; Nečasová, *Buduj vlast—posíliš mír!*; Donna Harsch, *Revenge of the Domestic: Women, the Family, and Communism in the German Democratic Republic* (Princeton, NJ: Princeton University Press, 2006).
38. Stowe, "Conquest by Terror: Fifteen Million Workers in Shackles."
39. Item 687/54, "Decline of Family Life," January 29, 1954, OSA, fond 300-1-2, reel 33. For a translation of this document, see Melissa Feinberg, "The Source: Radio Free Europe Information Item #687/54 (29 January 1954)—The Decline of Family Life," *Aspasia* 10 (2016): 89–101.
40. Item 687/54, "Decline of Family Life."
41. Item 4413/54, "The Life of a Laborer's Wife with Three Children in Sopron," May 29, 1954, OSA, fond 300-1-2, reel 38.
42. See, for example, the many stories of husbands jealously guarding their right to the meat in the household in Ellen Ross, *Love and Toil: Motherhood in Outcast London, 1870–1918* (Oxford: Oxford University Press, 1993).
43. Nečasová, *Buduj vlast—posíliš mír!*, 305–308.
44. Lebow, *Unfinished Utopia*, 98.
45. Voice of America frequently cited Communism's pernicious effects on gender relations and family life in its broadcasts. Belmonte, *Selling the American Way*, 137–158.
46. Interview 023, N.Z., October 10, 1951, NARA, Iron Curtain Interviews, box 1, 12 and 17.
47. Interview 001, Ladislav Novak, September 6, 1951, NARA, Iron Curtain Interviews, box 2, 11.

48. Many Americans themselves clung to these family structures as a way of containing Cold War–inspired fears of Communist gender disorder. Elaine Tyler May, *Homeward Bound: American Families in the Cold War Era* (New York: Basic Books, 1990).
49. Interview 030, A.S., November 6, 1951, NARA, Iron Curtain Interviews, box 4, 9.
50. These promised services were indeed often very slow to materialize. Éva Fodor, *Working Difference: Women's Working Lives in Hungary and Austria, 1945–1995* (Durham, NC: Duke University Press, 2003), 122–124; Nečasová, *Buduj vlast—posílíš mír!*, 314–315.
51. Interview 007, L.P., October 8, 1951, NARA, Iron Curtain Interviews, box 2, 8. The US Information Agency did indeed incorporate such concerns into its propaganda. See Belmonte, *Selling the American Way*, 151–152.
52. Interview 016, Janos (Tokar) Jasko, 11.
53. Item 6303/53, "Everyday Life of the X Family," June 18, 1953, OSA, fond 300-1-2, reel 25. Mr. X was one of a group of only four to flee, yet his family numbered five. Given that the children were all too young to be left alone, it is strongly implied that Mr. X left on his own.
54. Bren and Neuburger, eds. *Communism Unwrapped*.
55. There were currency reforms in Hungary in 1946, Poland in 1950, Romania and Bulgaria in 1952, and Czechoslovakia in 1953. On the experience of the currency reform in Czechoslovakia, see Jiří Pernes, *Krize komunistického režimu v Československu v 50. letech 20. století* (Brno: Centrum pro stadium demokracie a kultury, 2008), 86–94; Dana Musilová, *Měnová reforma 1953 a její sociální důsledky. Studie a dokumenty* (Prague: Ústav pro soudobé dějiny, 1994).
56. Mark Pittaway details such an incident in Hungary's Zala County, in *The Workers' State*, 149.
57. Interview 027, Jan Kusis, 5.
58. Interview 068, F.K., January 5, 1952, NARA, Iron Curtain Interviews, box 2, 6.
59. Interview 058 J.K., December 27, 1951, NARA, Iron Curtain Interviews, box 2, 4–7.
60. Interview 053, P., December 14, 1951, NARA, Iron Curtain Interviews, box 2, 8–9.
61. Interview 058, J.K, 7.
62. Interview 054, K.S., December 18, 1951, NARA, Iron Curtain Interviews, box 2, 7.
63. Dispatch 974 from American Legation in Budapest. Confidential: Panic Buying in Hungary, November 17, 1949, NARA, RG 59, Department of State, US International Information Administration/International Broadcasting, Voice of America Historical Files, 1946-1953, box 1.
64. Ibid., appendix, English translation of "More Vigilance," *Szabad Nép*, November 5, 1949, 1–2.
65. "Confidential: Panic Buying in Hungary," 3.
66. "More Vigilance," 2.

67. Item 6648/52, "Black Market Prices of Food in Northern Moravia," May 22, 1952, OSA, fond 300-1-2, reel 10.
68. Item 5526/53, "The Atmosphere in Present-Day Poland," July 1, 1953, OSA, fond 300-1-2, reel 24.
69. Item 3939/52, "Poland: Standard of Living," March 22, 1952, OSA, fond 300-1-2, reel 8.
70. Item 1510/52, "How One Can Earn Money without Having a Job," December 9, 1952, OSA, fond 300-1-2, reel 17.
71. On the practice of illegal animal slaughtering and meat smuggling in this period, see Karl Brown, "The Extraordinary Career of *Feketevágó Úr*: Wood-Theft, Pig-Killing and Entrepreneurship in Communist Hungary, 1948–1956," in *Communism Unwrapped*, ed. Bren and Neuburger, 277–297.
72. Item 12680/53, "Chelmsko Slaskie: A Small Border Town," December 22, 1953, OSA, fond 300-1-2, reel 32.
73. Item 00744/53, "Morale at the Forest State Enterprise," January 23, 1953, OSA, fond 300-1-2, reel 18.
74. This story has obvious echoes in Miloš Forman's 1967 film *The Fireman's Ball*. Item 791/54, "Workers' Kitchen of the Farmers' Collective in Ruprechtice," January 26, 1954, OSA, fond 300-1-2, reel 33.
75. Item 7495/53, "Conditions in Lodz," July 18, 1953, OSA, fond 300-1-2, reel 26.
76. Item 1110/55, "Source's Attitude to Various Problems," February 15, 1955, OSA, fond 300-1-2, reel 49, 9.
77. For example, Brown, "The Extraordinary Career of *Feketevágó Úr*."
78. "Chelmsko Slaskie: A Small Border Town."
79. Kracauer and Berkman, *Satellite Mentality*, 30. This analysis fits with the general argument of Mark Pittaway about Hungarian workers, in *The Workers' State*.
80. Kracauer and Berkman, *Satellite Mentality*, 143–145.
81. Item 04627/53, "Construction Workers' Living Conditions and Board in Třnec," April 20, 1953, OSA online, 300-1-2-34046.
82. Fidelis, *Women, Communism, and Industrialization*, 83; Kevin McDermott, "Popular Resistance in Communist Czechoslovakia: The Plzeň Uprising, June 1953," *Contemporary European History* 19, no. 4 (2010): 291.
83. Peter Heumos, "State Socialism, Egalitarianism, Collectivism: On the Social Context of Socialist Work Movements in Czechoslovak Industrial and Mining Enterprises, 1945–1965," *International Labor and Working Class History* 68 (2005): 54. Other examples can be found in Fidelis, *Women, Communism, and Industrialization*, 84–96, and Pittaway, *The Workers' State*, 176–178.
84. Kracauer and Berkman, *Satellite Mentality*, 124.
85. Machcewicz, *Rebellious Satellite*, 100–102.
86. Pittaway, *The Workers' State*, 265.

87. Tamas Dombos and Lena Pellandini-Simanyi, "Kids, Cars, or Cashews? Debating and Remembering Consumption in Socialist Hungary," in *Communism Unwrapped*, ed. Bren and Neuburger, ,326.
88. Paulina Bren, *The Greengrocer and His TV: The Culture of Communism after the 1968 Prague Spring* (Ithaca, NY: Cornell University Press, 2010). Though in some ways an exception to this, even Romania had a brief period of increased consumerism after 1956. See Jill Massino, "From Black Caviar to Blackouts: Gender, Consumption and Lifestyle in Ceauşescu's Romania," in *Communism Unwrapped*, ed. Bren and Neuburger, 226–253.
89. Václav Havel, "The Power of the Powerless," in *Open Letters, Selected Writings, 1965–1990*, trans. Paul Wilson (New York: Vintage, 1992), 125–214.

CONCLUSION

1. Interview 001, Ladislav Novak, September 8, 1951, NARA, Iron Curtain Interviews, box 2, 1–5.
2. Ibid.
3. For an overview, see Tilo Hartmann and Martin Hanis, "Examining the Hostile Media Effect as an Intergroup Phenomenon: The Role of Ingroup Identification and Status," *Journal of Communication Studies* 63 (2013): 535–537. This study found that those with a high level of self-investment in a political cause are more likely than others to see neutral media as hostile to that cause, particularly if they believe that society as a whole is against their position (the study examined pro-life and pro-choice groups).
4. Shanto Iyengar and Kyu S. Hahn, "Red Media, Blue Media: Evidence of Ideological Selectivity in Media Use," *Journal of Communication Studies* 59 (2009): 34.

SELECTED BIBLIOGRAPHY

ARCHIVAL SOURCES

Archiv Bezpečnostních Složech, Prague, Czech Republic (ABS)
    Historický fond
    Studijní ústav Ministerstva vnitra
    Velitelství státní bezpečnosti (VSB)
BBC Written Archives Centre, Caversham Park, Reading, UK (BBC WAC), Overseas Audience Research (Central Europe, Eastern Europe)
Columbia University Special Collections, New York, Records of the Columbia Bureau of Applied Social Research
Hoover Institution Archives, Stanford, CA (HIA)
    Arch Puddington Collection
    Radio Free Europe Broadcast Collection (RFE-Broadcast)
    Radio Free Europe Corporate Collection (RFE-Corporate)
Národní Archiv, Prague, Czech Republic (NA)
    Ústřední akční výbor národní fronty (ÚAV-NF)
    Ústřední komise žen KSČ (ÚKŽ-KSČ)
    Ústřední výbor KSČ (ÚV-KSČ)
National Archives and Records Administration, College Park, MD (NARA)
    Record Group 59, General Records of the Department of State
        International Information Administration/International Evaluation Staff, Iron Curtain Interviews, 1951–1952 (Iron Curtain Interviews)
        Office of the Special Assistant to the Secretary for Intelligence, Office of Intelligence Research, Psychological Intelligence and Research Staff, Coordinator for Psychological Intelligence, Subject Files
        Office of the Special Assistant to the Secretary for Intelligence, Office of Intelligence Research, Psychological Intelligence and Research Staff, Coordinator for Psychological Intelligence, Special Papers

US International Information Administration/International Broadcasting, Voice of America Historical Files, 1946–1953
Record Group 306, US Information Agency
  Foreign Service Dispatches, compiled 1954–1965
  Special Reports
Open Society Archives, Budapest, Hungary (OSA), HU OSA 300 Records of Radio Free Europe/Radio Liberty Research Institute, 1949–1994
Yale University Beinecke Library, New Haven, CT, Czesław Miłosz Papers

PUBLISHED PRIMARY SOURCES

Advertising Council. *Help Truth Fight Communism: Radio Free Europe, Radio Free Asia*. New York: n.p., 1951.
Columbia University Bureau of Applied Social Research. *Listening to the Voice of America and Other Foreign Broadcasts in Czechoslovakia*. New York: Bureau of Applied Social Research, 1954.
Columbia University Bureau of Applied Social Research. *Listening to the Voice of America and Other Foreign Broadcasts in Poland*. New York: Bureau of Applied Social Research, 1954.
Columbia University Bureau of Applied Social Research. *Listening to the Voice of America and Other Foreign Broadcasts in Romania*. New York: Bureau of Applied Social Research, 1954.
Columbia University Bureau of Applied Social Research. *Listening to the Voice of America and Other Foreign Broadcasts in the Soviet Satellites*. New York: Bureau of Applied Social Research, 1954.
Congress of the Peoples for Peace, Vienna, December 12th–19th, 1952. World Council of Peace, 1952.
Drozdová, Vlastimila, ed., *Buduj vlast—posílíš mír*. Prague: Ústředí lidové tvořivosti a Rada žen, 1950.
Ehrenbourg [sic], Ilya. *This Can't Go On: An Address to the People of the United States*. Chicago: Chicago Council of Soviet–American Friendship, 1952.
Ehrenburg, Ilya. *Speech Delivered to the World Council of Peace, Vienna Session, November 23–28th, 1953*. World Council of Peace, 1953.
Formánková, Pavlína, and Petr Koura. *Žádáme trest smrti! Propagandistická kampaň provázející proces s Miladou Horákovou a spol*. Prague: Ústav pro studium totalitních režimů, 2008.
Free Europe Committee. *The Story of the World Freedom Bell*. Minneapolis: NL: Crab Tree, 1952.
Hillová, Olga, ed. *Buduj vlast—posílíš mír. Z první celostátní konference údernic a vzorných zemědělek v Praze v březnu, 1949*. Prague: Ministerstvo informací a osvěty, 1949.

How Foreign Intelligence Operates in Poland: The Turner Trial. Warsaw: Książka I Wiezda, 1951.

Kovaly, Heda Margolius. *Under a Cruel Star: A Life in Prague, 1941–1968.* Translated by Helen Epstein. Teaneck, NJ: Holmes and Meier, 1997.

Kracauer, Siegfried, and Paul L. Berkman. *Satellite Mentality: Political Attitudes and Propaganda Susceptibilities of Non-Communists in Hungary, Poland and Czechoslovakia.* New York: Praeger, 1956.

László Rajk and His Accomplices before the People's Court. Budapest, n.p: 1949.

Loebl, Eugen. *My Mind on Trial.* New York: Harcourt Brace Jovanovich, 1976.

London, Artur. *On Trial.* Translated by Alastair Hamilton. London: MacDonald, 1970.

Meeting of the Information Bureau of the Communist Parties in Hungary in the Latter Half of November, 1949. New York: For a Lasting Peace, For a People's Democracy, 1950.

Miłosz, Czesław. *The Captive Mind.* Translated by Jane Zielonko. New York: Vintage, 1990.

Montagu, Ivor. *What Happened at Wrocław.* London: British Cultural Committee for Peace, 1949.

Paloczi-Horvath, George. *The Undefeated.* Boston: Little, Brown, 1959.

Proces s vedením protistátního spikleneckého centra v čele Rudolfem Slánským. Prague: Ministerstvo Spravedlnosti, 1953.

R. Vogeler, E. Sanders and Their Accomplices before the Criminal Court. Budapest: Hungarian State Publishing House, 1950.

Second World Peace Congress, Warsaw, November 16–22, 1950. Supplement to *Voks Bulletin*, no. 66 (1951).

Slánská, Josefa. *Report on My Husband.* Translated by Edith Pargeter. London: Hutchinson, 1969.

Šlingová, Marian. *Truth Will Prevail.* London: Merlin, 1968.

Stowe, Leland. *Conquest by Terror: The Story of Satellite Europe.* New York: Random House, 1952.

Szász, Bela. *Volunteers for the Gallows: Anatomy of a Show Trial.* Translated by Kathleen Szász. New York: Norton, 1972.

The Trial of Traïcho Kostov and His Group. Sofia: n.p., 1949.

Topolski, Feliks. *Confessions of a Conference Delegate.* London: n.p., 1948.

Trial of the Group of Spies and Traitors in the Service of Imperialist Espionage. Bucharest: n.p., 1950.

Turner, Claude Henry. *International Incident.* London: Wingate, 1957.

US House of Representatives Committee on Un-American Activities. *Report on the Communist "Peace" Offensive: A Campaign to Disarm and Defeat the United States.* Washington, DC: HUAC, 1951.

Vogeler, Robert. *I Was Stalin's Prisoner.* New York: Harcourt, 1952.

War Conspirators before the Court of the Czechoslovak People. Prague: Orbis, 1950.

Women's International Democratic Federation. *We Accuse! Report of the Commission of the Women's International Democratic Forum in Korea, May 16–27, 1951.* Berlin: Women's International Democratic Forum, 1951.

SECONDARY SOURCES

Abrams, Bradley F. "The Second World War and the East European Revolution." *East European Politics and Societies* 16, no. 3 (2002): 556–559.

Apor, Balász, Péter Apor, and E. A. Rees. *The Sovietization of Eastern Europe: New Perspectives on the Postwar Period.* Washington, DC: New Academia, 2008.

Applebaum, Anne. *Iron Curtain: The Crushing of Eastern Europe, 1944–1956.* New York: Doubleday, 2012.

Babiracki, Patryk. *Soviet Soft Power in Poland: Culture and the Making of Stalin's New Empire, 1943–1957.* Chapel Hill: University of North Carolina Press, 2015.

Behrends, Jan C. "Von Panslavismus zum 'Friedenskampf' Außenpolitik, Herrschaftslegitimation und Massenmobilisierung im sowjetischen Nachkriegsimperium (1948–1953)." *Jahrbücher für Geschichte Osteuropas* 56 (2008): 27–53.

Behrends, Jan C., and Árpád von Klimó. "'Friedenskampf' und Kriegsangst: Auswirkungen des Koreakriegs auf Polen und Ungarn." In *Der Koreakrieg: Wahrnehmung, Wirkung, Erinnerung*, edited by Christoph Kleßmann and Bernd Stöver, 55–74. Cologne: Böhlau, 2008.

Belmonte, Laura. *Selling the American Way: U.S. Propaganda and the Cold War.* Philadelphia: University of Pennsylvania Press, 2008.

Betts, Paul. *Within Walls: Private Life in the German Democratic Republic.* Oxford: Oxford University Press, 2010.

Borhi, László. *Hungary in the Cold War, 1945–1956: Between the United States and the Soviet Union.* Budapest: Central European University Press, 2004.

Bourke, Joanna. *Fear: A Cultural History.* Emeryville, CA: Shoemaker and Hoard, 2006.

Bouška, Tomáš, and Klára Pinerová. *Czechoslovak Political Prisoners: Life Stories of 5 Male and 5 Female Victims of Stalinism.* Translated by Kamila Nováková and Justin A. Osswald. Prague: Europe for Citizens Programme, 2009.

Boyer, Paul. *By the Bomb's Early Light: American Thought and Culture at the Dawn of the Atomic Age.* Chapel Hill: University of North Carolina Press, 1994.

Bren, Paulina. *The Greengrocer and His TV: The Culture of Communism after the 1968 Prague Spring.* Ithaca, NY: Cornell University Press, 2010.

Bren, Paulina, and Mary Neuburger, eds. *Communism Unwrapped: Consumption in Cold War Eastern Europe.* Ithaca, NY: Cornell University Press, 2012.

Brenner, Christiane, and Peter Heumos, eds. *Sozialgeschichtliche Kommunismusforschung: Tschechoslowakei, Polen, Ungarn und DDR, 1948–1968.* Munich: R. Oldenbourg, 2005.

Brown, Karl. "Regulating Bodies: Everyday Crime and Popular Resistance in Communist Hungary." PhD diss, University of Texas at Austin, 2007.
Brown, Kate. *Plutopia: Nuclear Families, Atomic Cities, and the Great Soviet and American Plutonium Disasters.* New York: Oxford University Press, 2013.
Carruthers, Susan. *Cold War Captives: Imprisonment, Escape, and Brainwashing.* Berkeley: University of California Press, 2009.
Castillo, Greg. *Cold War on the Home Front: The Soft Power of Midcentury Design.* Minneapolis: University of Minnesota Press, 2010.
Connelly, John. *Captive University: The Sovietization of East German, Czech, and Polish Higher Education, 1945–1956.* Chapel Hill: University of North Carolina Press, 2000.
Corner, Paul, ed. *Popular Opinion in Totalitarian Regimes: Fascism, Nazism, Communism.* Oxford: Oxford University Press, 2008.
Cummings, Richard H. *Radio Free Europe's "Crusade for Freedom": Rallying Americans behind Cold War Broadcasting, 1950–1960.* Jefferson, NC: McFarland, 2010.
Czarnecka, Ewa, and Alexander Fiut. *Conversations with Czesław Miłosz.* Translated by Richard Lourie. New York: Harcourt Brace, 1987.
Deery, Philip. "'A Divided Soul'? The Cold War Odyssey of O. John Rogge." *Cold War History* 6, no. 2 (2006): 177–204.
Deery, Phillip. "The Dove Flies East: Whitehall, Warsaw and the 1950 World Peace Congress." *Australian Journal of Politics & History* 48, no. 4 (2002): 449–468.
de Haan, Francisca. "Continuing Cold War Paradigms in Western Historiography of Transnational Women's Organizations: The Case of the Women's International Democratic Federation (WIDF)." *Women's History Review* 19, no. 4 (2010): 547–573.
Dowling, Rhiannon. "Communism, Consumerism and Gender in Early Cold War Film: The Case of *Ninotchka* and *Ruskii vopros*." *Aspasia* 8 (2014): 26–44.
Engerman, David C. *Know Your Enemy: The Rise and Fall of America's Soviet Experts.* New York: Oxford University Press, 2009.
Faggen, Robert, Andrzej Walicki, Irena Grudzinska-Gross, Adam Michnik, and Edith Kurzweil. "The Captive Mind." *Partisan Review* 66, no. 1 (1999): 49–69.
Feinberg, Melissa. *Elusive Equality: Gender, Citizenship and the Limits of Democracy in Czechoslovakia, 1918–1950.* Pittsburgh: University of Pittsburgh Press, 2006.
Feinberg, Melissa. "Fantastic Truths, Compelling Lies: Radio Free Europe and the Response to the Slánský Trial in Czechoslovakia." *Journal of Contemporary European History* 22, no. 1 (2013): 107–125.
Feinberg, Melissa. "Soporific Bombs and American Flying Discs: War Fantasies in East-Central Europe, 1948–1956." *Zeitschrift für Ostmitteleuropa-Forschung* 6, no. 3 (2013): 450–471.
Fidelis, Malgorzata. *Women, Communism, and Industrialization in Postwar Poland.* Cambridge: Cambridge University Press, 2010.

Fitzpatrick, Sheila. *Tear Off the Masks! Identity and Imposture in Twentieth Century Russia*. Princeton, NJ: Princeton University Press, 2005.

Fodor, Éva. *Working Difference: Women's Working Lives in Hungary and Austria, 1945–1995*. Durham, NC: Duke University Press, 2003.

Foglesong, David S. "Roots of 'Liberation': American Images of the Future of Russia in the Early Cold War, 1948–1953." *International History Review* 21, no. 1 (1999): 57–79.

Foglesong, David S. *The American Mission and the "Evil Empire": The Crusade for a Free Russia since 1881*. Cambridge: Cambridge University Press, 2007.

Frommer, Benjamin. *National Cleansing: Retribution against Nazi Collaborators in Postwar Czechoslovakia*. Cambridge: Cambridge University Press, 2004.

Gleason, Abbott. *Totalitarianism: The Inner History of the Cold War*. New York: Oxford University Press, 1995.

Granville, Johanna. "'Caught with Jam on Our Fingers': Radio Free Europe and the Hungarian Revolution of 1956." *Diplomatic History* 29, no. 5 (2005): 811–838.

Gross, Jan T. "The Social Consequences of War: Preliminaries of the Study of the Imposition of Communist Regimes in East-Central Europe." *East European Politics and Societies* 3, no. 2 (1989): 198–214.

Halfin, Igal. *Intimate Enemies: Demonizing the Bolshevik Opposition, 1918–1928*. Pittsburgh: University of Pittsburgh Press, 2007.

Halfin, Igal. *Stalinist Confessions: Messianism and Terror at the Leningrad Communist University*. Pittsburgh: University of Pittsburgh Press, 2009.

Halfin, Igal. *Terror in My Soul: Communist Autobiographies on Trial*. Cambridge, MA: Harvard University Press, 2003.

Harsch, Donna. *Revenge of the Domestic: Women, the Family, and Communism in the German Democratic Republic*. Princeton, NJ: Princeton University Press, 2006.

Havel, Václav. *Open Letters, Selected Writings, 1965–1990*. Translated by Paul Wilson. New York: Vintage, 1992.

Hellbeck, Jochen. "With Hegel to Salvation: Bukharin's Other Trial." *Representations* 107, no. 1 (Summer 2009): 56–90.

Heumos, Peter. "State Socialism, Egalitarianism, Collectivism: On the Social Context of Socialist Work Movements in Czechoslovak Industrial and Mining Enterprises, 1945–1965." *International Labor and Working Class History* 68 (2005): 47–74.

Heumos, Peter. *"Vyhrňme si rukávy, než se kola zastaví!": Dělníci a státní socialismus v Československu, 1945–1968*. Prague: Ústav pro soudobé dějiny, 2006.

Hixson, Walter L. *Parting the Curtain: Propaganda, Culture, and the Cold War, 1945–1961*. New York: St. Martin's, 1997.

Hodos, George H. *Show Trials: Stalinist Purges in Eastern Europe, 1948–1954*. New York: Praeger, 1987.

Jarosz, Dariusz. "Polish Peasants under Stalinism." In *Stalinism in Poland, 1944–1956*, edited by Anthony Kemp-Welch, 60–75. London: Macmillan, 1999.

Johnson, A. Ross. *Radio Free Europe and Radio Liberty: The CIA Years and Beyond.* Washington, DC: Woodrow Wilson Center Press, 2010.

Johnson, A. Ross, and R. Eugene Parta, eds., *Cold War Broadcasting: Impact on the Soviet Union and Eastern Europe.* Budapest: Central European University Press, 2010.

Johnston, Timothy. "Peace or Pacifism? The Soviet 'Struggle for Peace in All the World,' 1948–54." *Slavonic & East European Review* 86, no. 2 (2008): 259–282.

Kaplan, Karel. *Největší politicky proces: Milada Horáková a spol.* Prague: Doplněk, 1995.

Kaplan, Karel. *Report on the Murder of the General Secretary.* Translated by Karel Kovanda. Columbus: Ohio State University Press, 1990.

Kaplan, Karel, and Marek Janáč. "Poslední slova obžalovaných v procesu s Miladou Horákovou 'a spol.'" *Soudobé Dějiny* 13, nos.1–2 (2006): 197–238.

Kenney, Padraic. *Rebuilding Poland: Workers and Communists, 1945–1950.* Ithaca, NY: Cornell University Press, 1997.

Kieval, Hillel. *Languages of Community: The Jewish Experience in the Czech Lands.* Berkeley: University of California Press, 2000.

Kind-Kovács, Friederike. "Voices, Letters, and Literature through the Iron Curtain: Exiles and the (Trans)mission of Radio in the Cold War." *Cold War History* 13, no. 2 (2013): 193–219.

Kligman, Gail, and Katherine Verdery. *Peasants under Siege: The Collectivization of Romanian Agriculture, 1949–1962.* Princeton, NJ: Princeton University Press, 2011.

Krakovsky, Roman. "The Representation of the Cold War: The Peace and War Camps in Czechoslovakia, 1948–1960." *Journal of Transatlantic Studies* 6, no. 2 (2008): 158–167.

Krylova, Anna. "The Tenacious Liberal Subject in Soviet Studies." *Kritika* 1, no. 1 (2000): 119–146.

Laville, Helen. "'Our Country Endangered by Underwear': Fashion, Femininity and the Seduction Narrative in *Ninotchka* and *Silk Stockings*." *Diplomatic History* 30, no. 4 (2006): 623–644.

Laville, Helen. "The Memorial Day Statement: Women's Organizations in the 'Peace Offensive.'" *Intelligence and National Security* 18, no. 2 (2003): 192–210.

Lebow, Katherine. *Unfinished Utopia: Nowa Huta, Stalinism, and Polish Society, 1949–56.* Ithaca, NY: Cornell University Press, 2013.

Lukes, Igor. *On the Edge of the Cold War: American Diplomats and Spies in Postwar Prague.* New York: Oxford University Press, 2012.

Lukes, Igor. *Rudolf Slánský: His Trials and Trial.* Cold War International History Project Working Paper 50 (Washington DC: Woodrow Wilson International Center for Scholars, 2008).

Machcewicz, Paweł. *Poland's War on Radio Free Europe, 1950–1989.* Translated by Maya Latynski. Washington, DC: Woodrow Wilson Center Press, 2014.

Machcewicz, Paweł. *Rebellious Satellite: Poland, 1956.* Translated by Maya Latynski. Washington, DC: Woodrow Wilson Center Press, 2009.

May, Elaine Tyler. *Homeward Bound: American Families in the Cold War Era.* New York: Basic Books, 1990.

Mazurkiewicz, Anna. "'Join or Die': The Road to Cooperation among East European Exiled Political Leaders in the United States." *Polish American Studies* 69, no. 2 (2012): 5–43.

McDermott, Kevin. "'A Polyphony of Voices': Czech Popular Opinion and the Slánský Affair." *Slavic Review* 67, no. 4 (2008): 840–865.

McDermott, Kevin. "Popular Resistance in Communist Czechoslovakia: The Plzeň Uprising, June 1953." *Contemporary European History* 19, no. 4 (2010): 287–307.

McDermott, Kevin, and Matthew Stibbe, eds. *Stalinist Terror in Eastern Europe.* Manchester: Manchester University Press, 2010.

McEnaney, Laura. *Civil Defense Begins at Home.* Princeton, NJ: Princeton University Press, 2000.

Medhurst, Martin J. "Eisenhower and the Crusade for Freedom: The Rhetorical Origins of a Cold War Campaign." *Presidential Studies Quarterly* 27, no. 4 (Fall 1997): 646–661.

Melillo, Wendy. *How McGruff and the Crying Indian Changed America: A History of Iconic Ad Council Campaigns.* Washington, DC: Smithsonian Books, 2013.

Murawska-Muthesius, Katarzyna. "Modernism between Peace and Freedom: Picasso and Others at the Congress of Intellectuals in Wrocław, 1948." In *Cold War Modern: Design, 1945–1970,* edited by David Crowley and Jane Pavitt, 33–42. London: V & A Publishing, 2008.

Musilová, Dana. *Měnová reforma 1953 a její sociální důsledky: Studie a dokumenty.* Prague: Ústav pro soudobé dějiny, 1994.

Naimark, Norman, and Leonid Gibianskii, eds. *The Establishment of Communist Regimes in Eastern Europe, 1944–1949.* Boulder, CO: Westview Press, 1997.

Nathan, Leonard, and Arthur Quinn. *The Poet's Work: An Introduction to Czesław Miłosz.* Cambridge, MA: Harvard University Press, 1991.

Nečasová, Denisa. *Buduj vlast—posílíš mír! Ženské hnutí v českých zemích, 1944–1955.* Brno: Matice Moravská, 2011.

Osgood, Kenneth. *Total Cold War: Eisenhower's Secret Propaganda Battle at Home and Abroad.* Lawrence: University of Kansas Press, 2006.

Pernes, Jiří. *Krize komunistického režimu v Československu v 50. letech 20. století.* Brno: Centrum pro stadium demokracie a kultury, 2008.

Pernes, Jiří, and Jan Foitzik, eds. *Politické procesy v Československu po roce 1945 a 'případ Slánský.'* Brno: Prius, 2005.

Persak, Krysztof, and Łukasz Kamiński, eds. *A Handbook of the Communist Security Apparatus in East Central Europe, 1944–1989.* Warsaw: Institute of National Remembrance, 2005.

Pittaway, Mark. *Eastern Europe, 1939—2000.* London: Bloomsbury Academic, 2004.

Pittaway, Mark. "The Education of Dissent: The Reception of the Voice of Free Hungary, 1951–1956." *Cold War History* 4, no.1 (2003): 97–116.

Pittaway, Mark. "The Reproduction of Hierarchy: Skill, Working-Class Culture, and the State in Early Socialist Hungary." *Journal of Modern History* 74, no. 4 (2002): 737–769.

Pittaway, Mark. *The Workers' State: Industrial Labor and the Making of Socialist Hungary, 1944–1948*. Pittsburgh: University of Pittsburgh Press, 2012.

Plamper, Jan. *The History of Emotions: An Introduction*. Translated by Keith Tribe. New York: Oxford University Press, 2015.

Puddington, Arch. *Broadcasting Freedom: The Cold War Triumph of Radio Free Europe and Radio Liberty*. Lexington: University of Kentucky Press, 2000.

Rehak, Jana Kopelentova. *Czech Political Prisoners, Recovering Face*. Lanham, MD: Lexington Books, 2012.

Rév, István. "In Mendacio Veritas (In Lies There Lies the Truth)." *Representations* 35 (Summer 1991): 1–20.

Rév, István. *Retroactive Justice: A Prehistory of Post-Communism*. Stanford, CA: Stanford University Press, 2005.

Robin, Corey. *Fear: The History of a Political Idea*. New York: Oxford University Press, 2004.

Saunders, Frances Stonor. *The Cultural Cold War: The CIA and the World of Arts and Letters*. 2d ed. New York: New Press, 2013.

Schlosser, Nicholas J. "Creating an 'Atmosphere of Objectivity': Radio in the American Sector, Objectivity and the United States' Propaganda Campaign against the German Democratic Republic, 1945–1961." *German History* 29, no. 4 (2011): 610–627.

Schrecker, Ellen. *Many Are the Crimes: McCarthyism in America*. New York: Little, Brown, 1998.

Scott, Joan W. "The Evidence of Experience." *Critical Inquiry* 17, no. 4 (1991): 773–797.

Scott-Smith, Giles. *The Politics of Apolitical Culture: The Congress for Cultural Freedom, the CIA and Postwar American Hegemony*. London: Routledge, 2002.

Sharp, Tony. *Stalin's American Spy: Noel Field, Allen Dulles and the East European Show Trials*. London: Hurst, 2014.

Sheffer, Edith. *Burned Bridge: How East and West Germans Created the Iron Curtain*. New York: Oxford University Press, 2011.

Staar, Richard Felix. *Foreign Policies of the Soviet Union*. Stanford, CA: Hoover Institution Press, 1991.

Stan, Lavinia. "Reckoning with the Communist Past in Romania: A Scorecard." *Europe–Asia Studies* 65, no. 1 (2013): 130–131.

Steinberg, Mark D., and Valeria Sobol, eds. *Interpreting Emotions in Russia and Eastern Europe*. De Kalb: Northern Illinois University Press, 2011.

Tismaneau, Vladimir, ed. *Stalinism Revisited: The Establishment of Communist Regimes in Eastern Europe*. Budapest: Central European University Press, 2009.

Tudda, Chris. " 'Reenacting the Story of Tantalus': Eisenhower, Dulles, and the Failed Rhetoric of Liberation." *Journal of Cold War Studies* 7, no. 4 (2005): 3–35.

Turski, Marian, and Henryk Zdanowski, *The Peace Movement: People and Facts*. Translated by Magdalena Mierowska. Bydgoszcz: Interpress, 1976.

Verdery, Katherine. *Secrets and Truths: Ethnography in the Archive of Romania's Secret Police*. Budapest: CEU Press, 2014.

Verdery, Katherine. *What Was Socialism and What Comes Next?* Princeton, NJ: Princeton University Press, 1996.

Wall, Wendy D. *Inventing the American Way: The Politics of Consensus from the New Deal to the Civil Rights Movement*. New York: Oxford University Press, 2008.

Wernicke, Günter. "The Communist-Led World Peace Council and the Western Peace Movements: The Fetters of Bipolarity and Some Attempts to Break Them in the Fifties and Early Sixties." *Peace and Change* 23, no. 3 (1998): 265–311.

Wittner, Lawrence S. *Confronting the Bomb: A Short History of the World Nuclear Disarmament Movement*. Stanford, CA: Stanford University Press, 2009.

Wittner, Lawrence S. *The Struggle against the Bomb: One World or None—A History of the World Nuclear Disarmament Movement through 1953*. Stanford, CA: Stanford University Press, 1995.

Woźniczka, Zygmunt. "Wrocławski kongres intelektualistów w obronie pokoju." *Kwartalnik Historyczny* 94, no. 2 (1987): 131–157.

Yekelchyk, Serhy. "The Civic Duty to Hate: Stalinist Citizenship as Political Practice and Civic Emotion (Kiev, 1943–1953)." *Kritika* 7, no. 3 (2006): 529–556.

Zahra, Tara. *The Great Departure: Mass Migration from Eastern Europe and the Making of the Free World*. New York: Norton, 2016.

INDEX

abundance under Communism, 150
agency, xiv–xv
    of Eastern Europeans as perceived in East, 118–123
    of Eastern European as perceived in West, 77–83
    hopes for in emigration, 135
alcohol, 113–114,
Államvédelmi Hatóság (ÁVH), 19, 89, 96
antisemitism, 6, 27, 29–30, 187n101
Andics, Erzsébet, 47
anti-Communism
    among Eastern European émigrés, 79, 85, 101, 112
    in Eastern Europe, xi, xv, 4–5, 126, 133, 141, 164, 176–177
    in Eastern European media, 15
    in Western media, xix, 20, 73, 81, 89, 101, 106, 120, 149–150
    use of in US, x, 60
Arendt, Hannah, 80, 82, 86
atomization of society. *See* friendship under Communism
Auschnitt, Max, 17

battle for hearts and minds. *See* psychological warfare
Berkman, Paul L. *See* Kracauer, Siegfried
Bierut, Bolesław, 54, 140, 150

black market, 143, 146, 163, 165–67, 169–170, 174
    See also pilfering
Bonn-Paris Convention of 1952, 131–132
British Broadcasting Corporation (BBC),
    broadcasting practices of, xvii, 73
    reception of, xix, 137, 176–177
    See also Western media

Captive Mind, 79–83, 119, 174
Chapin, Selden, 2
Ciobanu, Vasile, 7, 14, 183n22
Cominform. *See* Communist Information Agency
Communism
    belief in, xvi–xvii, xix, 3, 24, 26–30, 106–107, 120
    East European liberation from, 117, 133
    human agency under, 77–83, 118–123
    opposition to in Eastern Europe, 125
Communist Information Agency (Cominform), 31–32, 39–40, 50, 58
    creation of, ix–x
    expulsion of Yugoslavia from, 6
Communist media, xvi, 128–129, 135–136, 138, 153
    consumption of in Eastern Europe, xviii, 153

228 • Index

Communist media (*Cont.*)
  methods of reading in Eastern Europe, xvii, xix
  reportage on West in, xi, 117
  Western views of, ix
Communist youth, 102–107, 130–131
Congress of American Women (CAW), 57, 58
Conquest by Terror, 70–72, 146, 197n41
Crusade for Freedom, 62–70, 72
currency reform, 163–165

Darkness at Noon. *See* Koestler, Arthur
de-Stalinization, xiii, xv, 140–142
Du Bois, W.E.B., 57
Dulles, John Foster, 6, 10, 60, 78

Eastern Europe
  definition of, xii
Ehrenburg, Ilya, 37, 40–41, 43–46, 131
Eisenhower, Dwight D., 43, 60–61, 63–65, 79
espionage, 7, 10
  on trial for, 1–2, 11, 19–20, 95
  See also spies

Fadeyev, Alexander, 34
  August 1948 speech of, 34–35, 37–38
  remarks on Korean War of, 42–43
family under Communism
  background of, 97, 100, 103
  effect of Communism on, 145, 149, 157–163, 166
  emigration with, 100, 166
  fear of, 93, 103–106
  love for, 49
  protection of, 119, 127
fear, vii, xv–xviii, xxi–xxii, 33, 58, 71, 87–90, 116, 126, 141–142, 173–174
  and friendship, 107–116
  and Western media, 61, 66, 77, 81, 83, 86–87, 89–90, 95–97, 105, 146, 165
  as a political tool, 26, 30, 32, 45, 58, 66, 72, 130
  in the West, 126, 208n31
  of acting, 118–119, 142
  of change, 145
  of children, 90, 103–106
  of class enemies, 30
  of family members, 93
  of German rearmament, 134
  of German retribution, 132
  of illegal émigrés, 100
  of imprisonment, xviii
  of informers, xvii, 76, 88, 90–97, 107–116, 177
  of return of Nazis, 131
  of neighbors, 90, 93
  of nuclear war, 14, 126–128, 136, 139, 208n31
  of peace, 124
  of police, xxi, 88, 91, 107, 111, 166–170
  of saboteurs, 30, 88
  of scarcity, xvii, 146, 166, 173
  of social change, 102
  of spies, xvii, 88–90
  of surveillance, 101–102, 107–108
  of United States, 40, 44
  of war, xvii, 12, 117, 126
  of West, 58
  of Western imperialism, 30
  of Western inaction, 122
femininity in Eastern Europe, 15, 155–163
Findeisen, Irene, 11, 14
Free Europe Committee (FEC), 62, 65, 69, 70, 72, 79, 147, 195n6
friendship under Communism, 87, 107–116, 205n74
  See also totalitarianism

gender,
    and relationships, 108
    East European perceptions of in West, 160–162
    persistence of hierarchies of, 105
    upheaval, 145, 156–157, 161–162
    See also femininity in Eastern Europe
Gerő, Ernő, 140
Gomulka, Władisław, xv, 140, 183n12
    trial preparations for, 4, 9
Gottwald, Clement, 5, 23, 25, 28, 51, 54, 106, 109, 164, 171

Havel, Václav, 173–174
Hodinová-Spurná, Anežka, 47
Horáková, Milada, 22, 24
    trial of, 14–16, 21, 26, 93, 184n46
    popular participation in trial of, 22–24
House of Representatives Committee on Un-American Activities (HUAC), 56–58
Hovde, Bryn J., 35
Hungarian state security. *See* Államvédelmi Hatóság
Huxley, Julian, 35

informers, 26–27, 75, 91–97
    children as, 103–106
    fear of, xvii, 76, 92–97, 107–116, 177
    ubiquity of, 94, 125, 163
    Western media reports on, 90, 95–97
interrogation
    as political discourse, 2–3
    interpretation of, 2–3, 21
    methods for conducting, 19–20, 25, 88, 92
Iwaszkiewicz, Jaroslav, 41

Joliot-Curie, Frédéric, 38

Kádár, János, 172–173, 211n99

Khrushchev, Nikita, xv
Klosiewicz, Viktor, 39–40, 46
Koestler, Arthur, 2, 20–21
Konvalinka, Jaroslav, 68–69, 196n29
Korean War
    Cold War Western reportage about, 138
    discussion of among East European peace activists, 41–44
    Eastern European reportage of, xvi, 138, 191n61
    Eisenhower's remarks on, 64
Korneichuk, Alexander, 43–45
Kostov, Traïcho, 4–5, 7–9, 11, 12, 17–18
Kracauer, Siegfried, 84–87, 111, 117–118, 122, 170–172, 174, 212n17

London, Artur, 19
London, Lise, 25
Lowenthal, Leo, 84

Martin, Kingsley, 35–36
Metropolitan Nikolai, 46
Miłosz, Czesław, 79–83, 119, 174
Ministerium für Staatsicherheit (MfS), 203n22

Nagy, Imre, xv, 140
Nance, Ellwood, 41, 191n57
New York Times,
    and peace movement, 34, 37, 65
    and show trials, 20–21
    interviews with, 2
Notes from Behind the Curtain, 62
nuclear disarmament, 32
nuclear weapons, 13
    Eastern European perceptions of, 128–129, 139
    Soviet possession of, 13, 128

230 • Index

Office of State Security. *See* Urząd Bezpieczeństwa
Origins of Totalitarianism, 82, 86

Paloczi-Horvath, George, 25–26
Pătrășcanu, Lucrețiu, 4, 9, 182n12
Pavlov, Todor Dimitrov, 46, 49–50
peace movement, xii, 31–33, 58–59, 117–118, 131
    Communist participants in, 32–35, 36–41, 42–56
    Roosevelt, Eleanor, 58
    Stockholm Appeal, 50–54, 59
    Western participants in, 35–36, 56, 58
    Western perceptions of, 56–58, 65, 77, 117–118, 134
    women and, 32–33, 42, 50, 52, 57–58
    Women's International Democratic Federation (WIDF), 32, 42, 57–58
    Wrocław World Congress, 34, 39, 40, 43, 56
    See also World Congress of Intellectuals *and* World Peace Council
pilfering, 167–168
police brutality. *See* torture
Polish October, xv, 140, 172
propaganda (American), x–xi, 60–62, 69, 72
    Communist views of, 31, 34–35, 39,
propaganda (Communist), xi, xvi, 3, 5, 9, 22–23, 43–45, 135, 152
    Western views of, ix, 56, 58–59, 64, 65, 71, 73–74, 84–86, 105–107, 117–118, 134, 159, 172
    émigré views of, 151–152, 154–155, 161
    dissemination of, 69, 111, 171
    reception of, xviii–xx, 118, 135, 144
psychological warfare, 60–63, 72
public drunkenness. *See* alcohol

Radio Free Europe (RFE)
    analysis of interviews conducted by, xix, xx–xxi,
    audience response to, 95–96
    broadcasting practices of, xvii, 73–75
    establishment of, 72–73
    Information Items, 89
    international policy of, 73, 76–77, 106,
    interviews conducted by, xvii, xx, xxi–xxii, 88–90, 132
    methods of interpreting in Eastern Europe, xviii–xix, 90
    portrayal of Communism by, 74–77, 95, 98, 116
    portrayal of Eastern Europeans by, 75–76, 104–105
    relationship to US government, 62–63
    See also Western media
Rajk, László
    trial of, 1–7, 9–10, 12, 19–20, 22, 25
    reception of, 22
rearmament in West Germany, 12
    American government perceptions of, 132–133
    debates about, 131–132
    East European perceptions of, 12, 117, 134, 136
Rohlena, Václav, 50
Rogge, O. John, 57
Roosevelt, Eleanor, 58

saboteurs, 6, 9, 12, 16, 18, 30, 88, 102
Satellite Mentality, 83–87, 117–118, 122, 170–171
Savulescu, Traian, 43, 47–49
Szász, Béla, 19
secret speech. *See* Khrushchev, Nikita, secret speech of
secret police. *See* security services
Securitate, 66

security services, 90–97
  See also Államvédelmi Hatóság;
    Securitate; informers;
    Ministerium für Staatsicherheit;
    Státní bezpečnosti; Urząd
    Bezpieczeństwa
shortages
  and fear, xvii, 146, 166, 173
  of femininity, 155–163
  of material goods, xiv, 99, 110,
    139, 143–155
  Western politicization of, 146–147
  See also abundance under
    Communism
show trials
  antisemitism in, 27, 29–30
  of Auschnitt, Max, 17
  of Ciobanu, Vasile, 7, 14, 183n22
  function of, 1–11
  of Horáková, Milada, 14–16, 21, 26,
    93, 184n46
  of Kostov, Traïcho, 4–5, 7–9, 11,
    12, 17–18
  of Paloczi-Horvath, George, 25–26
  popular participation in,
    22–24, 26–30
  of Rajk, László, 1–7, 9–10, 12, 19–20,
    22, 25
  reactions to, 22–26
  of Slánský, Rudolf, 4–7, 9–10, 12–13,
    19, 21–22, 24–30, 184n39
  of Turner, Claude Henry, 7–8,
    10–11, 14
  usage of, 3–4
  of Vogeler, Robert, 16–17, 185n53
  Western reportage on, 20–21
Slánský, Rudolf, 5
  participation in trial of, 26–30
  trial of, 4–7, 9–10, 12–13, 19, 21–22,
    24–30, 184n39
  wife of, 25

Státní bezpečnosti (StB), 26–29, 92–94
Soviet Union
  defeat of, 134
spies
  on trial, 1, 7, 10–11, 13–14, 19,
  Western perceptions of, 70–71
  See also espionage
Stasi, see Ministerium für Staatsicherheit
Stalin, Joseph, xv, 51, 182n10
  Soviet Union under the rule of, ix, xiii
Stalinism
  in Eastern Europe, xiii–xv, 4
  Eastern European response
    to, xiv–xv
Standard Electric plant, 16
Stockholm Appeal, 50–54, 59
Stowe, Leland, 70–72, 87, 146–147, 150,
  154, 157, 174, 197n35
surveillance. See security services
Suslov, Mikhail, 31, 39, 40, 50

Taylor, A.J.P., 35–36, 38, 56, 190n24
terror in Eastern Europe, xiv–xv, 3–4, 53,
  90–91, 95, 116, 142, 174
  Eastern European perceptions of, xiv,
    34–35, 99, 102, 107, 112, 115,
    119, 166
  effects of Western media focus on,
    120, 127
  Western perceptions of, ix, 2, 61, 64,
    66, 76, 82–83, 90
  See also fear
theft. See pilfering
Tito, Josip Broz, 1, 6–9, 12
Topolski, Feliks, 36–37
torture, 20, 88–92
totalitarianism, ix, xiv, 107, 141–142,
  174–176
Truman Doctrine, ix, 57
Truman, Harry S., ix–xii, 51, 61, 77, 80
  and Andrei Zhdanov, x–xi, xvii

Truska, Karel, 68–69
Turner, Claude Henry, 7–8, 10–12, 14

Urząd Bezpieczeństwa (UB), xviii, 99, 169

Vogeler, Robert, 16–17, 185n53
Voice of America (VOA)
  analysis of interviews conducted by, xix, xx–xxi
  audience response to, 112
  broadcasting practices of, xvii, 73
  government use of, 83–84
  interview project of, xvii, xx–xxii, 83–84, 108, 123,
  listening to, xviii–xix, 111–112, 138
  methods of interpreting in Eastern Europe, xviii–xix, 138
  See also Western media

war
  doubts about, 124
  fantasies of, 117–142
  fear of, xvii, 12, 117, 126
Warsaw Pact, 140
West
  Eastern Europeans' views of, 98–101, 104, 153–155
  liberation of Communist Eastern Europe by, 117–18, 121–122
  militarization of, 117
  portrayal of by Communist media, 117
Western media
  Communist press response to, 165
  consumption of in Eastern Europe, xvii, xix, 110–111, 117, 137, 153, 176–178
  Eastern European requests made on, xix, 95–96, 138
  influence of on Eastern Europeans, 84–86, 90, 95–96, 112, 118, 137, 161, 164–165, 174, 176

  laws in Eastern Europe on, 110–111
  methods of interpreting in Eastern Europe, xvii, xviii–xx, 138
  portrayal of Eastern Europe in, ix, 75–76, 118–119
  reception of in Eastern Europe, 137, 149
women
  activism of in Eastern Europe, 32–33, 42, 50, 52, 99–100,
  activism of in US, 57–58,
  and beauty, 155–156
  Communist policy on, xiii, 145, 159–160
  and family, 157, 159–162
  married to show trial defendants, 25
  and peace movement, 32–33, 42, 50, 52, 57–58
  and work, xiii, 54–56, 145, 151, 157–161, 167–169
  See also femininity in Eastern Europe
Women's Day, 54–55
Women's International Democratic Federation (WIDF), 32, 42, 57–58
World Congress of Intellectuals, 32
  August 1948 meeting of, 33–37
World Peace Council (WPC), 32–33, 38–40, 43–50, 56–59, 131
  American work with, 57
  journal of, 51
  Western views on, 56–59
Wrocław World Congress, 34, 39–40, 43, 56

Zhdanov, Andrei
  and creation of Communist Information Agency, ix–x, xv–xvi
  and Harry S. Truman, x–xi, xvii